Philosophical Perspectives on Peace

An Anthology of Classical and Modern Sources

Edited by

Howard P. Kainz

Professor of Philosophy
Marquette University, Milwaukee

MACMILLAN
PRESS

First published 1987

Published by
THE MACMILLAN PRESS LTD
Houndmills, Basingstoke, Hampshire RG21 2XS
and London
Companies and representatives
throughout the world

Printed in Hong Kong

British Library Cataloguing in Publication Data
Philosophical perspectives on peace: an
anthology of classical and modern sources.
I. Kainz, Howard P.
327.1'72'01   B105.P4
ISBN 0–333–41606–6 (hc)
ISBN 0–333–42883–8 (pbk)

Contents

Acknowledgements

The editor and publishers wish to thank the following who have kindly given permission for the use of copyright material:

George Allen & Unwin Publishers Ltd, for 'On World Government', from *New Hopes for a Changing World*, by Bertrand Russell.

Jonathan Cape Ltd, for the excerpt from *The Fate of the Earth*, by Jonathan Schell.

Bruno Cassirer (Publishers) Ltd, for the Epistle to Alexander the Great from *Aristotle on the World State*, by S. M. Stern.

William Collins, Sons & Co. Ltd, for 'The Heart of the Problem', from *The Future of Man*, by Teilhard de Chardin; and for the excerpt from *The Book of Merlyn*, by T. H. White.

Sigmund Freud Copyrights Ltd, The Institute of Psycho-Analysis and The Hogarth Press Ltd, for the extracts from *Civilization and its Discontents* in volume 21 of *The Standard Edition of the Complete Psychological Works of Sigmund Freud*, translated and edited by James Strachey.

Harcourt Brace Jovanovich Inc., for the excerpt from *On Aggression*, by Konrad Lorenz, copyright © 1963 by D. G. Borotha-Schoeler Verlag, Vienna; English translation copyright © 1966 by Konrad Lorenz; reprinted by permission of Harcourt Brace Jovanovich Inc.

Harper & Row Publishers, for chapter XVIII (pp. 260–9) of *The Future of Man*, by Pierre Teilhard de Chardin; copyright © 1959 by Editions du Seuil; copyright © 1964 in the English translation by William Collins, Sons & Co. Ltd and Harper & Row Publishers, Inc.; reprinted by permission of Harper & Row Publishers Inc. Also, for the extract from *The Perennial Philosophy*, by Aldous Huxley; copyright © 1944, 1945, by Aldous Huxley; reprinted by permission of Harper & Row Publishers Inc. Also, for pp. 1–47 and 62–6 from *The New Federalist*, by 'Publius II' (Justice Owen J. Roberts, John F. Schmidt and Clarence K. Streit); copyright © 1946, 1947, 1948, 1949 by *Freedom and Union*; reprinted by permission of Harper & Row Publishers Inc. Also, for 'On World

Government', from *New Hopes for a Changing World*, by Bertrand Russell.

Harvard University Press, for *Eternal Peace* by Immanuel Kant; reprinted by permission of the publishers from *Inevitable Peace*, translated by Carl J. Friedrich (Cambridge, Mass.: Harvard University Press), copyright 1948 by the President and Fellows of Harvard College; copyright renewed © 1976 by Carl J. Friedrich. Also, for the extract from *A Theory of Justice*, by John Rawls; reprinted by permission of the publishers from *A Theory of Justice* by John Rawls (Cambridge, Mass.: The Belknap Press of Harvard University Press), copyright © 1971 by the President and Fellows of Harvard College.

Mrs Laura Huxley and Chatto & Windus Ltd, for the extract from *The Perennial Philosophy* by Aldous Huxley.

Alfred A. Knopf Inc., for the extract from *The Fate of the Earth*, by Jonathan Schell; copyright © 1982 by Jonathan Schell; reprinted by permission of Alfred A. Knopf Inc.

Methuen & Co. Ltd, for the extract from *On Aggression*, by Konrad Lorenz.

William Morris Agency Inc., for the extracts from *Report from Iron Mountain*, by Leonard C. Lewin; reprinted by permission of William Morris Agency on behalf of the author; copyright © 1967 by Leonard C. Lewin.

New American Library, for *A Complaint of Peace*, by Desiderius Erasmus, from *The Essential Erasmus*, translated by John P. Dolan; copyright © 1964 by John P. Dolan; reprinted by arrangement with New American Library, New York.

W. W. Norton & Co., for the extract from *Civilization and its Discontents*, by Sigmund Freud; the selection is reprinted from *Civilization and its Discontents* by Sigmund Freud, translated by James Strachey, by permission of W. W. Norton & Co. Inc.; copyright © 1961 by James Strachey.

Oxford University Press, for the extracts from *The Kingdom of God is Within You*, by Leo Tolstoy; reprinted by permission of Oxford University Press from *The Kingdom of God is Within You* by Leo Tolstoy, translated by Aylmer Maude (1936). Also, for 'Towards a Future World Order', from *A Study of History*, by Arnold Toynbee;

reprinted by permission of Oxford University Press from Arnold J. Toynbee's *A Study of History*, abridgement by D. C. Somervell (1957).

Popular Science Monthly, for 'The Moral Equivalent of War', by William James; reprinted by permission of *Popular Science Monthly*.

The Estate of John Strachey, for the extract from *The Prevention of War*, by John Strachey.

Ira Straus, Executive Director of the Association to Unite the Democracies, for the extracts from *The New Federalist*, originally published by *Freedom and Union* magazine.

The University of South Carolina Press, for the Epistle to Alexander the Great from *Aristotle on the World State* by S. M. Stern, copyright © 1968 by Samuel Stein.

The University of Texas Press, for the extract from *The Book of Merlyn*, by T. H. White, copyright © 1977 by Shaftesbury Publishing Company; reprinted by permission of the University of Texas Press.

Every effort has been made to trace all the copyright-holders, but if any have been inadvertently overlooked, the publishers will be pleased to make the necessary arrangement at the first opportunity.

I am grateful to Marquette University for some released time and designated grants which facilitated publication of this compilation; and to Bradley Wronski and Maureen Milligan for assistance in editing and proofreading the manuscript.

Introduction

In the Western world philosophical interest in, and commitment to, peace is not to be found to any great extent in the ancient and medieval eras. Exceptions would be the occasional anti-war sentiments expressed by Greeks dramatists, the fascinating but difficult-to-date fragments on world government by [?pseudo-]Aristotle, the general thrust towards cosmopolitanism of some Roman stoic philosophers, and intermittent religious pacifism among some Fathers of the Church, most notably Origen. But elaborate and detailed philosophical thinking about peace comes to the fore primarily in the last five centuries. It is probably no accident that the last five centuries have also witnessed the emergence to pre-eminence of that peculiar institution, the nation state. Not a few peace theorists have considered the nation state, and the nationalistic sentiments that come in its wake, to be the single most important cause of war and the continuation of war in modern times. But others would point to other, possibly more subtle, contributory factors.

As we consider various representaive efforts of major thinkers of the past and present to philosophize about peace, their efforts seem to divide up rather naturally into the following six categories, according to whether the relative emphasis is on (1) strongly centralized world government, (2) international federation, (3) distributive justice, (4) religious or moral revitalization, (5) the sublimation or deflection of human aggression, or (6) some paradoxes connected with military preparedness, especially in the nuclear age. The selections included here to illustrate the last category are primarily concerned with pointing out some subtle and paradoxical implications or intertwinings, a consciousness of which will be necessary if any lasting solutions are to be found to the present impasses.

1

Peace through a Highly Centralized World Government

In Arnold Toynbee's twelve-volume *Study of History*, which is concerned largely with the rise and fall of civilizations, a recurrent pattern emerges of the development of 'universal states', which appear at time of great crisis and disintegration. Judging from history, the function of these states seems to be to restore unity and order amidst chaos; and one of their characteristic features is the introduction of relatively long periods of peace to the civilized world of the time. Their peace-keeping function is often so impressive that succeeding generations of a civilization, centuries after the demise of their world state, will make feverish efforts to create 'ghost states' patterned after the original, in order to reap the benefits of peace for the world once again. In Western civilization, according to Toynbee, the Roman Empire was the 'universal state'; and the first major attempt to restore the Roman Empire was the creation of the 'Holy Roman Empire', which enjoyed its golden age in the reign of Charlemagne. Later attempts to re-create a universal state with universal peace in the West include the Napoleonic empire and Hitler's abortive inauguration of the 'Third Reich' after being solemnly presented with the regalia of Charlemagne (stolen from a Hapsburg museum) following his annexation of Austria. We should not be surprised that some theorists in the West – as the following selections demonstrate – have looked to something very much like a Western 'world state' as the solution to the endemic warfare which plagued their generations. The introduction of a Western world state would, of course, be much more complex and perilous in the nuclear age. And there is now the additional problem that the Soviet Union is vying with the West to create a world state quite different in conception from that which many in the West envisage.

1

I [?PSEUDO-]ARISTOTLE, EPISTLE TO ALEXANDER THE GREAT ON WORLD GOVERNMENT

There is some controversy as to whether this epistle as a whole is authentic. S. M. Stern, the noted medievalist and Arabist who edited, annotated and translated the Arabic text, argues for the possible validity of at least parts of the Epistle – especially the segment on the establishment of a Macedonian world empire and world peace. He shows that the arguments which have been brought against the authenticity of this segment are inconclusive and sometimes mutually contradictory. Stern goes on to argue that, even if this segment dates from the era of the Roman Empire (as some allege) rather than Aristotelian times, the document would still be significant, as one of the earliest and most detailed ecumenical visions of a world order established to inaugurate a reign of peace for future generations. Aristotle in his *Politics* is not very sympathetic to democracy as a form of government; and the Epistle also shows no overt sympathy for democracy. But one might say that the extraordinary complexities of ruling the world empire envisaged here would require a wide delegation of administrative authority, and hence a certain degree of decentralization, such as was prevalent in the Roman Empire at certain periods.

The text below is reprinted from S. M. Stern, *Aristotle on the World State* (Columbia, SC: University of South Carolina Press; and Oxford: Bruno Cassirer, 1986) pp. 3–8. Most of Stern's notes on texts, manuscripts, interpretations, and so on – items of more specialized scholarly interest – have been omitted.

It will, I think, be beneficial to your affairs and will be the cause of your lasting fame and glory, if you remove[1] the inhabitants of Persia from their places.[2] If this cannot be done with all of them, do it at least with a great number, including the ruling class, and settle them in Greece and Europe.[3] This will be acting justly towards them, since it is just according to the law of Radamanthys to do to a man as he had done.[4] The Persians have exiled many Greeks from their homes, populating with them some of their cities: such as the Milesians and the Eretrians and [the inhabitants of] other cities whose names have been handed down to us.[5] You must make it your business more especially to bring back the inhabitants of these cities;[6] but in general it will be greatly beneficial to your affairs to exile them[7] from their country. All who think about this, will easily see the reason for this. To make their common people behave well and put respect firmly into the hearts of their leaders so as to make all of them obedient to you is a difficult matter which can only be achieved over a long time and successive generations. If they find an opportunity, they will rise and find many people to assist them in this. You know what the Persians did to their different conquerors: the Lydians, the Medians, and the Babylonians, how they rose against them and defeated them.[8] Thus if you wish to behave resolutely, assure lasting good order, and be safe from trouble and strife, you must transfer all of them, or at least those possessing prestige and power. Besides, this will give you fame and repute, since in the most distant future people will ask: From where are these people, and who has settled them in this country, and how and when did this happen? It will then be said: These were once the noblemen of Asia, but when Alexander became king, he gained for the Greeks victory over them, and transferred them to this country. This will ensure you lasting fame and renown in Asia, and you will be remembered just as Attalus is remembered through having transferred the inhabitants of Phrygia from their country.[9] Even if you leave behind a glorious memory, I should wish that among the titles of your fame there should be renowned what you have done to the Persians in particular and the barbarians[10] in general.

Although[11] you have performed many renowned deeds and famous actions, you ought to crown them by your good work for the welfare of the cities. This is achieved when two things are found together: prosperity and just behaviour.[12] By the presence of both these things together, the welfare and good order of the cities are achieved. But if the two things are separated, the one causes a life of pleasure and luxury in the midst of corruption and lawlessness,[13] whereas the other causes a chaste life and virtuous behaviour in the midst of toil and hardship.[14] Therefore one who obtains the stateliness and majesty of kingship ought to seek to obtain these two things together aiming at justice.

I know that if mankind in general is destined to reach true felicity[15] within the duration of this world, there will come about that concord and order which I shall describe. Happy is he who sees the resplendence of that day when men will agree to constitute one rule[16] and one kingdom. They will cease from wars and strife,[17] and devote themselves to that which promotes their welfare and the welfare of their cities and countries. They will all enjoy safety and quiet, dividing their day into parts, part for rest and welfare of the body, part for education and attention to that noble pursuit, philosophy – studying what has been achieved and seeking what has not yet been attained. I would love to remain alive and see that age – if not all, at least part of it. If, however, my old age and the length of my past life make this impossible, I wish that my friends and brethren may see it; if they, too, will not obtain this privilege, then those who are like them and follow their ways.

TRANSLATOR'S NOTES

1.   . . . the meaning is 'to remove, to unsettle', so that Lippert is right in translating: *quod Persas (a finibus suis?) sollicites.* (I do not see why he put brackets and a question mark – perhaps because the literal rendering of his text would have been 'from their places', not 'frontiers'.). . .
2.   . . . the Fātih MS has a word meaning 'homes'.
3.   . . . 'Europe' is not a term used in Arabic, where it only occurs as the transliteration of the Greek term. Here it obviously refers to the countries neighbouring on Greece, such as Macedon and Thrace.
4.   Dr Plezia has reminded me that Radamanthys's judgement is referred to in the *Nicomachean Ethics* (V.5, 1132 b 25) . . . .
5.   Darius exiled the inhabitants of Miletus and settled them in the city of Ampe on the Tigris (Herodotus VI.20). The exiled Eretrians were settled by the same king in Anderica in Cissia where they formed a distinct community in the time of Herodotus (see VI.112). . . .
6.   This seems to mean that the Greek exiles should be returned from Persia to their homes.
7.   'Them', i.e. the Persians. In the Arabic version the transition from the repatriation of the Greeks to the exile of the Persians is unclear – the translator was obviously not quite sure of the trend of the argument. . . .
8.   Cf. Aristotle, *Politics*, iii.13 (1284 b 1 ff.): 'The king of Persia repeatedly curtailed the power of Media, Babylonia, and other parts of his realm which were made presumptuous by memories of having once had an empire themselves.' See also the sequence of the overlords of Asia in ch. 3 of the epistle: Assyrians (= Babylonians), Medes, Persians. Here there is some confusion probably due to an error in the translation: the Lydians cannot be described as former overlords, but could – and were probably in the original – described as defeated enemies. . . .
9.   . . . Greek tradition knew that the Phrygians came to Asia Minor from Thrace, see Herodotus VII.73 . . . . May we not assume that a Macedonian legend spoke of some Macedonian hero defeating the Phrygians and expelling them to Asia? Attalus would be a possible reading, and it is a good Macedonian name.
10. The Arabic word literally means 'foreigners'.
11. . . . the eleventh-century author Mubashshir quotes some passages of the epistle in a translation different from ours (which, by the way, removes any possible doubts about the Epistle having really been translated into, and not composed in, Arabic). . . .

12. 'Education', the other translation.
13. The other translation: 'If the inhabitants of the city are prosperous but not bound by education and good customs (or: laws), this leads them to evil and lawlessness.'
14. The other translation: 'If they are bound by education and the establishment of customs (laws), but live in distress, this leads them to trouble and turbulence.'
15. *Sa'ādatu jaddin* (presumably standing for εὐδαιμονία), a phrase characteristic for our translator.
16. The word *amr* is rather vague in Arabic. It can mean 'rule', but also generally 'affair' (Ibn Ezra has the variant *shay'*, which shows that the word was understood in this vague sense). It could stand for ἀρχή.
17. *Malhama* is a word which in Islamic usage has a rather well-defined meaning – political upheavals, especially in an eschatological context. I suggest it translates here στάσις, internal, civil, strife, in contrast to πόλεμος, external war.

II DANTE ALIGHIERI, *MONARCHY*, BOOK I

Dante (1265–1321) lived at a time when disunity and conflict was rife not only in his native Italy but throughout Europe. Reflecting in his more mature years on the chaos, he attributes it to the fact that nation states, which are destined to a certain relativity, make themselves into absolutes. Thus Dante interestingly anticipates many contemporary world-order theorists, who perceive the exaggeration of the claims of national sovereignty as the single greatest threat to world order and world peace. But to a medieval Italian intellectual such as Dante, looking for a counterbalance to the pretensions of nation states, the historical model that naturally suggests itself is the ancient Roman Empire. Dante shared with many of his contemporaries the vision of the restoration of that glorious past, and of the reinauguration of a Christian version of the *Pax Romana*. For practical implementation of this vision, Dante and many others looked to the elective German Holy Roman Empire, and its standard-bearer, Henry VII. Henry's untimely death dashed these hopes, but did not destroy the vision, which in its mature form comprised an admirably balanced scheme for a world government which would be looser than the highly centralized ancient Roman model, but tighter than the international near-anarchy of medieval feudalism.

After adducing in book I his philosophical and theological arguments for the necessity of a world monarchy, Dante goes on in book II to offer an apologetic for the providentiality of the Roman Empire, and in Book III to indicate some ground rules for the 'separation of Church and state' in the proposed monarchy.

The translation of book I reprinted here is that by D. Nichols (London: Weidenfeld and Nicolson, 1954; New York: Garland, 1972). The translator's shorter notes and references have been taken into the text and placed in square brackets. In a few cases their form has been adapted slightly.

i

All men whom the higher Nature [i.e. God] has imbued with a love of truth should feel impelled to work for the benefit of future generations, whom they will thereby enrich just as they themselves have been enriched by the labours of their ancestors. Let there be no doubt in the mind of the man who has benefited from the common heritage but does not trouble to contribute to the common good that he is failing sadly in his duty. For he is not 'a tree beside the running waters bearing fruit in due season' [Psalm 1:3] but rather a vicious whirlpool, forever swallowing things but never throwing them up again. Since I have often reflected much on this matter and have been afraid that I might one day be held guilty of burying my talents [Matthew 25:14ff.], I desire not simply to blossom but to bear fruit for the public good, by demonstrating truths that no one else has considered. For what fruit would a man bear if he were merely to prove once again some theorem of Euclid [in the *Elements*], or to demonstrate for the second time the nature of happiness, which Aristotle has already done [in the *Nicomachean Ethics*]? Or to undertake an apologia for old age of the sort that Cicero has produced [in *De Senectute*]? None whatever. Such a wearisome and superfluous undertaking would simply provoke disgust.

Now since the truth about temporal monarchy is the most beneficial yet most neglected of all these other beneficial but obscure truths, and yet has been neglected by all because it leads to no immediate reward,[1] I intend to draw it out of the shadows into the light. There I shall be able to examine it for the benefit of the world, and to my own glory gain the palm of so great an enterprise. This is an arduous task, and one beyond my strength, yet in addressing myself to it I am trusting not in my own talents, but in the illumination of the Giver 'who gives to all liberally and upbraids none' [James 1:5].

ii

Therefore we must first consider the meaning of 'temporal monarchy', what its essence is and what its end. The temporal monarchy that is called the Empire[2] is a single Command exercised over all persons in time, or at least in those matters which are subject to time.³ Doubts about temporal monarchy give rise to three principal questions. The first is the question whether it is necessary for the well-being of the world. The second is whether it was by right that the Roman people took upon itself the office of the Monarch. And thirdly, there is the question whether the Monarch's authority is derived directly from God or from some vicar or minister of God.

Now every truth that is not itself a first principle must be demonstrated by means of some truth that is a first principle. Therefore in any inquiry it is a prerequisite to have a full understanding of that principle which under analysis we see to guarantee the certainty of all the other propositions which are deduced from it. So the present treatise being a sort of speculative inquiry, we must begin by examining that principle which will be the basis for all our subsequent reasoning. Now it is to be noted that there are some subjects that are completely outside human control, about which we can only speculate, being unable to affect them by our actions; such are mathematics, physics and revealed truth. There are others, however, that fall within our control; not only can we speculate about them, but also we can do something about them. In these, action is not subordinate to speculation but speculation is for the sake of action, because the aim in such matters is action. Since the present subject is political⁴ – indeed, the source and principle of all just governments – and anything political lies within our power, it is obvious that the matter in hand is not primarily directed towards speculation but towards action. Again, since in practical affairs the ultimate end is the principle and cause of all that is done (the end being the original motive of the agent), it follows that the formulation of means is derived from the end in view: thus wood is shaped in one way to build a house and in another way to build a ship. Similarly if the whole process of human society⁵ has an end, then this end can serve as the principle by which to demonstrate the validity of our subsequent argument. It would be absurd to suppose that this or that society has an end without acknowledging that there is one end common to them all.

iii

Therefore let us see what is the ultimate end of human society as a whole; once that is grasped our task is more than half accomplished, as the Philosopher⁶ says in the *Nicomachean Ethics*.

In order to clarify the issue it may be noted that nature forms the thumb for one end and the whole hand for another, and the arm for yet another, whilst each of these ends is different from that to which the whole man is destined. Similarly the end towards which the individual's life is directed is different from that of the family community; the village has one end, the city another and the kingdom yet another; and last of all there is the end that the eternal God has established for the whole human race by means of nature, which is the mode of his art. It is this last-mentioned end that we are looking for and that will be the guiding principle in our inquiry.

The first point to realize is that 'God and nature never do anything in vain', for whatever is brought into existence has some purpose to serve. Yet it is not the being of any creature but its proper function that is the ultimate end of the Creator in creating, and so the proper function is not instituted for the sake of the creature but the latter is created to serve its proper function. From this it follows that there must be some particular function proper to the human species as a whole and for which the whole species in its multitudinous variety was created; this function is beyond the capacity of any one man or household or village, or even of any one city or kingdom. What this function is will become clear once the specific capacity of mankind as a whole is evident.

I say therefore that no property that is common to beings of different species represents the specific capacity of any one of them; because, since its ultimate capacity is what constitutes each species, it would follow that one being would be specifically constituted by several specifying factors – which is impossible. And so the specific capacity of man does not consist simply in *being*, since the very elements also share in being; nor does it consist in *compound being*, for this is also found in the minerals; nor in *animate being*, which the plants also enjoy; nor in the capacity to apprehend things, for this is shared by brute animals, but it consists in the capacity to apprehend by means of the *possible intellect*,[7] and it is this that sets man apart both from inferior and from superior beings. For although there are other beings endowed with intellect, their intellect is not *possible* like that of man, since such beings are completely intellectual; in them intellect and being coincide, and their very *raison d'être* is to perform intellectual operations without pause, otherwise they would not be eternal. From which it is evident that the specific capacity of mankind is an intellectual capacity or potentiality. And because that potentiality cannot wholly and at once be translated into action by one man, or by any one of the particular communities listed above, mankind has to be composed of a multitude through which this entire potentiality can be actualized. Similarly there needs to be a multitude of things which can be generated from prime matter if the entire potency of that matter is to be brought into action all the time. The alternative is for potentiality to exist separately; this is impossible. Averroes agrees with this opinion in his commentary on the *De anima*.[8]

This intellectual power of which I am speaking not only deals with universal forms or species but also extends to particulars. Hence it is commonly said that the speculative intellect becomes practical by extension,[9] and is thereby directed towards action and making things. I am referring to action as governed by the virtue of political prudence, and to the making of things as governed by art. But both are subordinate to speculation as the highest function for the sake of which the Supreme Goodness brought mankind into being.

From all this one begins to appreciate what is meant in the *Politics* by the sentence: 'Men of superior intellect naturally rule over others.' [I.2].[10]

iv

Thus it is quite clear that the task proper to mankind considered as a whole is to fulfil the total capacity of the possible intellect all the time, primarily by speculation and secondarily, as a function and extension of speculation, by action. Now since what applies to the part applies also to the whole, and since the individual man becomes perfect in wisdom and prudence through sitting in quietude,[11] so it is in the quietude or tranquillity of peace that mankind finds the best conditions for fulfilling its proper task (almost a divine task, as we learn from the statement: 'Thou hast made him a little lower than the angels' [Hebrews 2:7]). Hence it is clear that universal peace is the most excellent means of securing our happiness. This is why the message from on high to the shepherds announced neither wealth, nor pleasure, nor honour, nor long life, nor health, nor strength, nor beauty, but peace. The heavenly host, indeed, proclaims: 'Glory to God on high, and on earth peace to men of good will' [Luke 2:14]. 'Peace be with you' was also the salutation given by the Saviour of men [cf. Matthew 10:12; John 20:21], because it was fitting that the supreme Saviour should utter the supreme salutation – a custom which, as everyone knows, his disciples and Paul sought to preserve in their own greetings.

This argument shows us what is the better, indeed the very best means available to mankind for fulfilling its proper role; and also what is the most direct means of reaching that goal to which all our doings are directed – universal peace. This will serve as the basis for our subsequent argument. Such is the common ground which we declared to be essential so as to have something axiomatic to which all our proofs and demonstrations can refer.

v

Let us now return to what was said at the beginning; that there are three main problems to be solved concerning temporal monarchy, or, as it is more commonly called, the Empire. As we promised, we intend to investigate them in the order signified and on the basis of the axiom that we have established.

Thus the first question is whether temporal monarchy is necessary for the well-being of the world. Now no substantial objection either from reason or authority can be urged against it, and its truth can be demonstrated by the clearest and most cogent arguments, the first of which is derived from the authority of the Philosopher in his *Politics*. There the acknowledged authority states that when several things are directed towards a single end it is necessary for one of them to act as director or ruler and for the others to be directed or ruled. This statement is supported not only by the glorious renown of its author but also by inductive reason. Again, if we consider an individual man we see the same principle verified: since all his faculties are directed towards happiness, his intellectual faculty is the director and ruler of all the others – otherwise he cannot attain happiness. If we consider a home, the purpose of which is to train its members to live well, we see that there has to be one member who directs and rules, either the *pater familias* or the person occupying his position, for, as the Philosopher says, 'every home is ruled by the eldest'. And his function, as Homer says,[12] is to rule the others and lay down laws for them; hence the proverbial curse, 'May you have an equal in your home.' If we consider a village, whose purpose is mutual help in questions of persons and goods, it is essential for one person to be supreme over all others, whether he is appointed from outside or raised to office by the consent of the others; otherwise, not only would the community fail to provide mutual sustenance, but in some cases the community itself would be utterly destroyed through some members' scheming to take control. Similarly if we examine a city, whose purpose is to be sufficient unto itself in everything needed for the good life, we see that there must be one governing authority – and this applies not only to just but even to degenerate forms of government. If this were not so, the purpose of civil life would be frustrated and the city, as such, would cease to exist. Lastly, every kingdom (and the end of a kingdom is the same as that of a city but with a stronger bond of peace) needs to have a king to rule over and govern it; otherwise its inhabitants will not only fail to achieve their end as citizens but the kingdom itself will crumble, as is affirmed by the infallible Word: 'Every kingdom divided against itself shall be laid waste' [Matthew 12:25].

If this is true of all communities and individuals who have a goal towards which they are directed, then our previous supposition is also valid. For, if it is agreed that mankind as a whole has a goal (and this we have shown to be so), then it needs one person to govern or rule over it, and the title appropriate to this person is Monarch, or Emperor.

Thus it has been demonstrated that a Monarch or Emperor is necessary for the well-being of the world.

vi

Furthermore, the order of a part stands in the same relation to the order of the whole as the part does to the whole; therefore the order within a part has as its end the order of the whole, which brings it to perfection. Hence the goodness of the order amongst the parts does not surpass the goodness of the total order; in fact the reverse is true. Now in all things this twofold order is to be found: that is, the relation of the parts towards each other; and the relation of the parts to that unity which is not itself a part (in the same way that the parts of an army are related towards each other yet are all subordinated to their commander). Hence the relation of the parts to that unity is the superior of the two orders; and the other relation is simply a function of the superior order, not *vice versa*. Now if this pattern of relationship is found in individual

groups of human beings it must apply all the more to mankind as a
group or whole, in virtue of the previous syllogism concerning the
superior pattern of relationship. But it has been adequately proved
in the previous chapter that this pattern is in fact found in all
human groups: therefore it should also be found in the whole.

Consequently all those parts below the level of a kingdom, as
well as kingdoms themselves, must be subordinate to one ruler or
rule, that is, to the Monarch or to Monarchy.

vii

Furthermore, mankind in one sense is a whole (that is, in relation
to its component parts), but in another sense it is itself a part. It is a
whole in relation to particular kingdoms and peoples, as we have
previously shown; but in relation to the whole universe it is, of
course, a part. Therefore just as its component parts are brought to
harmony in mankind, so mankind itself has to be brought into the
harmony of its appropriate whole. The component parts of mankind are brought into harmony by a single principle (as may easily
be gathered from the preceding argument); and mankind itself is
similarly related to the whole universe, or to its principle (that is,
God, the Monarch); this harmony is achieved by one principle
only, the one Prince.

It follows that Monarchy is necessary for the well-being of the
world.

viii

And everything is at its best and most perfect when in the condition intended for it by the first cause, which is God; this is
self-evident – except to those who deny that the divine goodness
achieves supreme perfection. It is God's intention that every
created thing, in so far as its natural capacity allows, should reflect
the divine likeness. This explains why it is said: 'Let us make man
after our image and likeness' [Genesis 1:26]. Although the phrase
'after our image' cannot be applied to anything inferior to man,
'likeness' can be applied to anything whatsoever, since the whole
universe is simply a sort of shadow of the divine goodness.
Therefore the human race is at its best and most perfect when, so
far as its capacity allows, it is most like to God. But mankind is

most like to God when it enjoys the highest degree of unity, since He alone is the true ground of unity – hence it is written: 'Hear, O Israel, the Lord thy God is one' [Deuteronomy 6:4]. But mankind is most one when the whole human race is drawn together into complete unity, which can only happen when it is subordinate to one Prince, as is self-evident.

Therefore when mankind is subject to one Prince it is most like to God and this implies conformity to the divine intention, which is the condition of perfection, as was proved at the beginning of this chapter.

ix

Again, a son's condition is most perfect when the son, as far as his nature allows, reproduces the perfection of the father. Mankind is the son of the heavens, which is perfect in all its works; but man is begotten by man and the sun (according to the second book of the *Physics* [II.2]).[13] Therefore mankind's condition is most perfect when it reproduces the perfection of the heavens, so far as human nature allows. And just as the heavens are governed and directed in every movement by a single mover, which is God (as human reasoning in philosophy amply demonstrates), so, if our argument has been correct, mankind is at its best when all its movements and intentions are governed by one Prince as its sole mover and with one law for its direction.

Hence it is obvious that the world's well-being demands a Monarch or single government known as the Empire.

This is the argument that led Boethius to sigh: 'How happy you would be, O mankind, if your minds were ruled by the love that rules the heavens' [*De consolatione philosophiae* II.8].

x

And wherever there is a possibility of dispute there has to be a judgement to settle it; otherwise there would be imperfection without a remedy to heal it, which is impossible, since God and nature never fail in essentials.

It is clear that a dispute may arise between two princes, neither of whom is subject to the other, and that this may be their fault or

their subjects'; therefore a judgement between them is indispensable. However, since neither can take cognizance over the other
(neither being subject to the other – and equals do not rule over
equals), there needs to be a third person enjoying wider jurisdiction who by right rules over both of them. This person must be
either the monarch (in which case our argument is complete) or not
the monarch, in which case he himself will have an equal outside
his own jurisdiction, and it will again be necessary to have recourse to a third person. Either this process will go on to infinity
(which is impossible) or eventually it will lead us back to a first and
supreme judge whose judgement will either directly or indirectly
solve all disputes: he will be the Monarch, or Emperor.

Therefore monarchy is necessary to the world. And the Philosopher appreciated this truth when he wrote: 'Things resent being
badly ordered; but to have different rulers is bad; therefore, one
Prince' [Aristotle, *Metaphysics* XII.10].

xi

Besides, the world is best ordered when justice is at its strongest.
Hence Virgil, wishing to praise the new order that seemed to be
emerging in his day, sang: 'Now the Virgin is again returning; and
the Saturnian reign begins once more' [*Bucolics* IV.6]. By 'Virgin' he
meant Justice, which is also called Astrea; by 'Saturn's rule' he
referred to the finest ages, which are also described as 'golden'.
Justice is at its strongest only under a Monarch; therefore Monarchy or Empire is essential if the world is to attain a perfect order.

If we are to understand the minor premiss fully, it is essential to
appreciate that justice, in itself and strictly considered, is rectitude,
a rule permitting no deviation; consequently it is not subject to
shades of more or less, any more, for instance, than *whiteness*
considered in the abstract. For such forms, though realized in
particular circumstances, are simple and unchangeable in essence,
as the Master of the Six Principles rightly says.[14] In actuality,
however, these qualities vary in intensity according to the degree
in which the subjects of them are subject also to their contraries.
But where the contrary of justice is at its faintest (whether actively
or potentially), there justice is at its strongest; and then one may
truly say – as, indeed, the Philosopher does – 'Neither Lucifer nor
Hesperus is so wonderful.'[15] For then she is like Phoebe in the rosy

serenity of the dawn gazing across at her brother on the opposite horizon.

Considered in its potentiality the contrary of justice sometimes lies in the will; for even when justice is present, if the will is not entirely purified of all cupidity, justice is not present in all the splendour of its purity; because such a subject offers a certain resistance to it, however slight; hence those who try to arouse a judge's passions deserve to be censured. In regard to acts, the contrary of justice is to be found in limitations on power; for since justice is a virtue governing relations, between people, how can it operate in practice without the power of rendering to each his due? Hence the stronger the just man is in practice, the greater will be his justice.

On the basis of this exposition we reason as follows: justice is most powerful in the world when located in a subject with a perfect will and most power; such is the Monarch alone; therefore justice is at its most potent in this world when located in the Monarch alone.

This preparatory syllogism[16] is of the second figure,[17] with intrinsic negation, and takes the following form: all B is A; only C is A; therefore only C is B. That is: all B is A; nothing except C is B. The first proposition clearly holds, for the reasons already given; the other follows by reference first to the will and then to power.

To see the first clearly we must recognize, as Aristotle affirms in the fifth book of his *Nicomachean Ethics* [V.2], that the greatest obstacle to justice is cupidity. When cupidity is entirely eliminated there remains nothing opposed to justice: hence the Philosopher's maxim that 'nothing which can judged by the law should ever be left to the judge's discretion' [*Rhetoric* I.1]; and he gave this salutary warning because he feared that cupidity which all too easily distorts men's minds. But when there is nothing to be desired there can be no cupidity, because the passions cannot remain when their objects have been eliminated. But the Monarch has nothing to desire, since the ocean alone is the limit of his jurisdiction – unlike other princes, such as the Kings of Castile and Aragon, whose jurisdictions are limited by one another's frontiers. It follows that of all mortals the Monarch can be the purest incarnation of justice. Moreover, just as cupidity invariably clouds the vision of justice no matter how slightly, so charity, or rightly ordered love, illuminates and sharpens it. Therefore justice finds its strongest bastion in the place where rightly ordered love is most intense; such is the

Monarch, and so justice is at its most powerful, or at least can be, when there is a Monarch. That rightly ordered love does have this effect can be shown as follows: cupidity, scorning man's intrinsic nature, aims at other things; but charity scorns those other things, is directed towards God and man, and so towards the good of man. And since to live in peace, as we previously demonstrated, is the chief of human blessings, and since justice is the most powerful means towards it, charity gives force to justice, so that the more powerful it is the more force justice will have. That rightly ordered love should be found most of all in the Monarch is shown thus: an object is the more loved the nearer it is to the lover; but men are nearer to the Monarch than to other princes; therefore they are more greatly loved by him, or ought to be.

The first proposition becomes evident if we consider the general nature of agents and patients; the second is demonstrated by the fact that it is only as belonging to different parts that men are drawn to other princes, whereas it is through belonging to the whole that they are related to the Monarch. Again, they are brought into contact with other princes through the Monarch, and not *vice versa*. So prior and immediate tutelage over them all belongs to the Monarch, and to other princes through the Monarch, which means that their tutelage is derived from his. Again, the more universal a cause is, the more perfect a cause it is, because the subordinate cause is only such in virtue of the superior, as is shown in the *De causis*;[18] and the more perfect the cause, the more it loves its proper effect, because this love is a function of the cause as such. Since, therefore, the Monarch is of all mortals the most universal cause of human well-being (because other princes, as we have seen, are only effective in virtue of him), it follows that the good of man is most keenly desired by him.

And who but a person ignorant of the world's meaning would doubt that justice is most powerfully served by the Monarch? For if there is a Monarch then he cannot have any enemies.

The minor premiss having been proved, the conclusion is certain: that Monarchy is necessary for perfect world order.

xii

And the human race is at its best when most free.

This statement will become clear if we explain the principle of freedom, for then it will be seen that the fundamental principle of our freedom is free choice; and though many pay service to this truth with their lips, few do with their understanding. They do indeed go so far as to say that free choice is a free judgement exercised upon the will; and they speak the truth – but are far from understanding the meaning of the words. They are like our logicians who produce certain propositions mechanically, as examples in logic, such as: 'A triangle has three angles equal to two right angles.' Therefore I say that a judgement is the middle term connecting apprehension and appetite.[19] First of all, something is apprehended; then it is judged to be either good or bad; and finally the person judging either seeks or rejects it. If the judgement completely directs the appetite and is in no way deflected by it, then it is free; but if the judgement is in any way deflected or influenced by the appetite it cannot be free, because it is not independent but is dragged along captive in the wake of another. And this is why the brute beasts cannot enjoy free judgement; because their judgements always follow their appetites. It also explains how intellectual substances [i.e. angels], whose wills are immutable, and disembodied souls who depart this life in a state of grace, do not lose their free choice on account of their wills being immutable but rather enjoy it in its highest perfection.

Once this is realized, it becomes equally clear that this liberty, or this principle of all our liberty, is God's most precious gift to human nature, for by it we are made happy here as men, and happy as gods in the beyond. In which case who would not agree that mankind is at its best when it is able to make fullest use of this principle? But this plenitude of freedom it enjoys only under a Monarchy.

Hence it must be recognized that to be free means 'self-dependence, and not dependence on another', as the Philosopher maintains in the *Metaphysics* [I.2]. For whatever is dependent on another is conditioned by it even as the means is conditioned by the end it serves. But only under a Monarchy is mankind self-dependent and not dependent on another; then only are perverted forms of government rectified, such as democracies, oligarchies and tyrannies (which force mankind into slavery, as is obvious to anyone who considers the matter); their government is conducted by kings, aristocrats (known as *optimates*) and zealots for the people's freedom, because, as we have already shown, the Monarch in his supreme love for men wishes all of them to be good.

This is impossible for the perverted forms of government. Hence the Philosopher says that 'in the perverted forms a good man is a bad citizen, whereas in the true form to be a good citizen is the same as being a good man [*Politics* III.4]. And these true forms of government aim at liberty; they intend men to go on living for their own sakes. Here the citizens do not exist for the sake of the consuls, nor the people for the sake of the king; on the contrary, the king is for the sake of the people, and the consuls for the citizen. Because just as the laws are made for the sake of the body politic rather than the body politic for the laws, likewise those living under the law do not exist for the sake of the legislator but he for them (as the Philosopher asserts in the writings which he has left to us on this issue[20]). From which it is evident that although the consul or the king are lords over others in regard to means, they are themselves ministers towards others in regard to ends. And this is particularly true of the Monarch, who is to be considered the minister of everyone. Thus one can already recognize how the very purpose of law-making postulates the necessity of Monarchy.

Therefore mankind is in its best condition under a Monarch; from which it follows that monarchy is necessary for the well-being of the world.

xiii

Again, the person best suited for governing is the one who brings the best out of others; for in every action the agent (whether acting from choice or from the exigencies of its nature) seeks primarily to reproduce its own likeness. Hence every agent delights in its own action; for since everything that is desires its own being, and since the being of any agent is increased through its actions, joy is the necessary consequence, because joy always accompanies the desired object. Therefore nothing can act unless it has the quality that is to be transferred to the patient, on which account the Philosopher in the *Metaphysics* writes: 'The movement from potentiality to act takes place by means of something already in act' [IX.8]. Any attempt to act in another manner would prove vain.

And this argument refutes the error of those who believe that they can mould the lives and morals of others by speaking well and doing evil, who do not realize that it was the hands of Jacob rather than his words that proved persuasive, the former speaking truth and the latter falsehood [Genesis 27:1ff.]. Hence the Philosopher says, in the *Nicomachean Ethics*: 'In regard to passions and actions words carry less conviction than deeds' [X.1]. Similarly the voice from heaven questioned the sinner David: 'Why do you tell of my righteousness?' [Psalm 49:16] as if to say: 'Your speech is in vain so long as what you are belies your speech.'

From which it can be seen that the person wishing to bring the best out of others must himself be in the best condition. But the one in the best condition for governing is none other than the Monarch. This is demonstrated as follows: any thing is in a better and more suitable condition to acquire a particular quality or perform a particular act the less it contains of any contrary tendency. Thus persons who have never been taught anything are in a better condition for acquiring philosophical truth than those who have long been imbued with false opinions; on which Galen wisely comments: 'Such people need double the time to acquire knowledge' [*De cognoseendis curandisque animi morbis*, x]. Since the Monarch, then, can have no cause for cupidity (or, of all men, has the least cause for it, as we have already shown), and in this differs from other princes, and since cupidity alone perverts the judgement and compels justice, it follows that the Monarch is in a perfect – or at least the best possible – condition for governing, because he surpasses all others in the power of his judgement and justice. And these two qualities are those supremely fitting for the person who makes and carries out the law, as was maintained by that most holy king when he implored God to grant the things most essential for a king and his son: 'God,' he said, 'give to the king your judgement, and to the king's son your justice' [Psalm 71:1].

Therefore what was said in the minor premiss was right, that the Monarch alone is completely equipped to rule; therefore the Monarch alone is able to bring the best out of others. From which it follows that Monarchy is necessary for the perfect ordering of the world.

xiv

And it is better, wherever possible, for something to be performed by one single means rather than by several.

This is demonstrated as follows. Let *A* be the means by which a certain thing can be accomplished, and let *A* and *B* be several means by which the same thing can be accomplished. But if *A* alone is adequate for doing what *A* and *B* together can do, the introduction of *B* is unnecessary; because no consequence follows from making the assumption *B*, for the consequence desired has already been achieved by *A* alone. And since all similar assumptions are idle or superfluous, and superfluity is displeasing both to God and nature, and everything displeasing to God and nature is evil (as is self-evident), then not only is it better for something that can be accomplished by a single means to be done by that single means rather than by several, it is good in itself to use the single means and plain evil to employ several. Moreover, a thing is considered better the nearer it is to the best; and the best is found in the end envisaged; but to use a single means is to shorten the distance towards the end: therefore it is the better. That it is nearer is obvious: let *C* be the end; let it be reached by a single means *A*; let it be reached by several, *A* and *B*; clearly the distance from *A* through *B* to *C* is greater than from *A* straight to *C*.

But mankind is capable of being governed by a single supreme prince, who is the Monarch.

Of course, when we say 'mankind can be governed by one supreme prince' we do not mean to say that minute decisions concerning every township can proceed directly from him (though even municipal laws sometimes prove wanting and need supplementing from outside, as we see from the Philosopher's remarks in the fifth book of the *Ethics* [v.14], where he commends the principle of equity). For nations, kingdoms and cities have different characteristics which demand different laws for their government, law being intended as a concrete rule of life. The Scythians, for instance, live outside the seventh circle, experience extreme inequalities of day and night and endure an almost intolerably piercing frost; they require a different rule from the Garamantes who live in the equinoctial zone, where the days and nights are of equal duration and where the excessive heat makes it unbearable to wear clothes. But our meaning is that mankind should be ruled by one supreme prince and directed towards peace by a common law issuing from him and applied to those characteristics which are common to all men. This common rule, or law, should be accepted from him by particular princes, in the same way as the practical reason preparing for action accepts its major proposition from the speculative intellect and then derives from it the minor proposition appropriate to the particular case, and finally proceeds to action. It is not only possible for one movement to issue from a single source, it is necessary for it to do so in order to eliminate confusion about universal principles. Indeed this was precisely what Moses says he did in writing the Law: having called together the chiefs of the tribes of Israel he left minor judgements to them whilst reserving to himself the major decisions that affected everyone; these were then applied by the chiefs of the tribes according to the particular needs of each tribe [Exodus 18:18ff.].

Therefore it is better for mankind to be ruled by one person than by several (that is, by the Monarch who is the sole prince) and if better, then more acceptable to God; for God always wills the better. And since when only two things are being compared the better is the same as the best, then not only is rule by 'one' more acceptable to God than rule by 'several', it is the *most* acceptable. It follows that mankind is at its best when under a single ruler; and so Monarchy is essential to the well-being of the world.

xv

Again, I say that priority is attributed to 'being', 'unity' and 'goodness', in that order, according to the fifth sense of the word 'priority'. For being naturally comes before unity, and unity before goodness: the perfect being is perfect unity and the perfect unity is perfect goodness, and the further anything is removed from perfect being the further it is from being one and being good. Therefore within each kind of being the best is that which is most one, as the Philosopher maintains in the *Metaphysics*.[21] Hence unity seems to be the ground of goodness and multiplicity the ground of evil; for this reason Pythagoras in his Correlations places unity on the side of goodness and multiplicity on the side of evil, as we are told in the first book of the *Methaphysics* [I.5]. Hence we can see that to sin is to despise and abandon unity for the sake of multiplicity. The Psalmist perceived this when he said: 'They are multiplied in the fruit of corn and wine and oil' [Psalm 4:8].

It is clear, then, that every good thing is good in virtue of being one. And since concord, as such, is a good, it is obviously rooted in unity. The root of concord is discovered if we examine its definition and nature. Concord is a harmonious movement of several wills. This definition shows that the unity of will connoted by 'harmonious movement' is the root of concord or is itself concord. For just as we should describe several clods which all fell towards the same centre as concordant and say that several flames shooting out towards the same circumference were concordant (if they did so voluntarily), similarly we describe several men as being in concord when their wills are simultaneously directed towards the same formal object (which is present in their wills as the quality of gravity is present in the clods and levity in the flames). But the capacity for willing represents a potentiality and the good it apprehends is its form. This form, though one in itself, like other forms, becomes multiplied through the multiplicity of the matter on which it is impressed – just like soul and number, and other composite forms.

These premisses having been stated we can now develop the argument for the proposition we wish to maintain: all concord depends upon the unity of wills; mankind is at its best in a state of concord; for as a man is at his best in body and soul when he is in a state of concord, the same is true of a house, a city and a kingdom, and of mankind as a whole. Therefore mankind at its best depends upon unity in the wills of its members. But this is impossible unless there is one will which dominates all others and holds them in unity, for the wills of mortals, influenced by their adolescent and seductive delights, are in need of a director, as the Philosopher teaches at the end of the *Nicomachean Ethics* [X.10]. Nor can there be such a single will unless there is a prince over all, whose will guides and rules those of all others.

Now if the preceding conclusions are all true – as they are – then Monarchy is necessary for the perfect order of mankind in this world. Consequently a Monarch is essential to the well-being of the world.

xvi

The preceding arguments are confirmed by a noteworthy historical fact, that is, by the state of humanity which the Son of God either awaited or himself brought about when He was to become man for the salvation of men. For if we survey the ages and condition of men since the fall of our first parents (the false step from which all our errors have proceeded) at no time do we see universal peace throughout the world except during the perfect monarchy of the immortal Augustus. The fact that mankind at that time was resting happily in universal peace is attested by all the historians and the illustrious poets. Even the recorder of Christ's gentleness has deigned to bear witness to it [Luke 2:1[22]]. Finally Paul, also, described that blissful state as 'the fullness of time' [Galatians 4:4]. The times were indeed full, and temporal desires fulfilled because nothing that ministers to our happiness was without its minister. But what state the world has been in since that seamless garment [John 19:23][23] was rent on the nail of cupidity we may easily read – would that we could not behold it!

O humanity, in how many storms must you be tossed, how many shipwrecks must you endure, so long as you turn yourself into a many-headed beast lusting after a multiplicity of things! You are ailing in both your intellectual powers,[24] as well as in heart: you pay no heed to the unshakable principles of your higher intellect, nor illumine your lower intellect with experience, nor tune your heart to the sweetness of divine counsel when it is breathed into you through the trumpet of the Holy Spirit: 'Behold how good and pleasant it is for brethren to dwell together in unity' [Psalm 132:1].

TRANSLATOR'S NOTES

1. As in many other passages of the *Monarchy* the overtones here are unmistakable. Dante is referring to those Papal and Imperial publicists who defended the Papacy and the Empire out of a desire for promotion.
2. Here Dante seems to be distinguishing between *Monarchia* (a philosophical concept: the rule of one person) and *Imperium* (a historical institution in which the rule of one person is a given fact).
3. As opposed to eternal concerns.
4. 'Politics' here is used in a much broader sense than is customary in the twentieth century. It includes all the activities for the orderly government of human society.
5. For the meaning of *universalis civilitas humani generis* cf. A. P. D'Entrèves, *Dante as a Political Thinker* (Oxford, 1952), pp. 47–8.
6. The Philosopher is Aristotle, who acquired this title in the Middle Ages because it was commonly held that he had come as close to ultimate truth as was possible for any human being unaided by divine Revelation. The passage of the *Nicomachean Ethics* is Book I.8.
7. The meaning of *possible intellect* is best seen by contrasting it with the

intellects of the angels, who are the beings referred to in the next sentence. For whereas an angelic intellect is perpetually acting to the fullest extent of its powers, individual human beings do not necessarily achieve this intellectual plenitude. Hence the human being's is a *possible* intellect.

8. Averroes (1126–98) was an Arabic philosopher whose commentaries on Aristotle greatly influenced medieval thinkers. Since Averroes' doctrine of the possible intellect involves denial of individual immortality, Dante, by quoting him here, is laying himself open to the charge of heresy. Indeed, it was this very passage which brought the wrath of Vernani upon him. How far Vernani's accusations were justified is well discussed by E. Gilson in *Dante the Philosopher* (London, 1948), pp. 168–71.

9. For although the speculative intellect deals with universals and the practical intellect with particulars they are both intellectual.

10. The fact that Dante quotes Aristotle's *Politics* does not prove that he had read the work; his quotations may very well be derived, at second hand, from St Thomas.

11. It is a commonplace of scholastic thought that some degree of leisure is essential if a man is to acquire wisdom (cf. Ecclesiasticus 38:25; Aristotle's *Physics*, VIII.20).

12. This quotation from Homer's *Odyssey* (IX) comes from Aristotle's *Politics*, I.2, which is also the source for the preceding quotation about the home being ruled by the eldest. Dante, of course, did not know Homer in the original.

13. The curious view of human reproduction which Dante uses as the basis for the curious argument of this chapter should astonish us less now that anthropologists have taught us how long it has taken man to discover the secrets of reproduction.

14. The Master of the Six Principles, Gilbert de la Porrée, Bishop of Poitiers (1070–1154), was given this title on account of his work, *De Sex Principiis*. The forms that are intrinsically absolute, not themselves subject to degree (e.g. rectitude and whiteness), may yet be more or less present in different subjects.

15. Dante takes this saying of Aristotle's from St Thomas Aquinas, *Summa Theologia*, II.ii, Q. 58, art. xii.

16. Preparatory in the sense that its conclusion is meant to serve as the premiss for the main syllogism.

17. In Aristotelian logic syllogisms fall into one of three shapes, or figures; it is the position of the middle or common term which determines whether it is a syllogism of the first, second or third figure. Thus Dante's syllogism here is of the second figure because the '*A*' occurs as a predicate in both the major and the minor premiss.

   The 'intrinsic negation' is due to the use of the negating, or exclusive, term 'only' in 'only *C*'.

18. An anonymous work greatly esteemed by medieval thinkers. Translated from Arabic into Latin by Gerard of Cremona in the twelfth century, it was attributed for a long time to Aristotle.

19. *Appetitus* does not bear the restricted meaning usually given nowa-

days to the English word 'appetite'; it is directed not essentially towards things of the senses but towards those of the mind and spirit.

20. Not a direct quotation from the *Politics*, this principle is a commonplace amongst medieval writers upon politics.
21. Dante's whole discussion of unity is inspired by the tenth book of Aristotle's *Metaphysics*.
22. Though this verse of Scripture does not specifically mention peace, it was assumed by commentators that Augustus could not have issued a universal edict if there had not been universal peace (cf. Dante's Letter VII.3).
23. The seamless garment is taken to symbolize the unity of the Empire, which was rent by the Donation of Constantine. . . .
24. The higher or speculative intellect, and the lower or practical intellect.

III BERTRAND RUSSELL, 'ON WORLD GOVERNMENT'

The English philosopher and logician Bertrand Russell (1872–1970) was a pacifist in his earlier years, but abandoned pacifism at the outbreak of the Second World War to take what he considered to be a more realistic anti-war position. Although he rather consistently opposed American militarism in his later years, it is interesting to note that the world government advocated in the following essay, reprinted from *New Hopes for a Changing World* (New York: Harper and Row, 1952) pp. 699–703, could conceivably have the United States at its helm.

For technical reasons it becomes advantageous that social units should increase in size as technique becomes more elaborate. Marx made the world familiar with this thesis in economics, though even there it has applications which he did not think of. Commerce, so far as it still exists, has tended to become an affair of trade between nations, in which the part of merchants is taken by governments. The economic links between an industrial and an agricultural country, for example between Britain and Argentina, are important; and the fact that both countries are sovereign states makes trade between them a prickly matter, tending to cause hatred between governments and peoples. This, of course, is absurd. A butcher needs bread and a baker needs meat. There is, therefore, every reason why the butcher and the baker should love one another, since each is useful to the other. But if the butcher is one sovereign state and the baker is another, if the number of loaves that the butcher can exchange for his joints depends upon his skill with the revolver, it is possible that the baker may cease to regard him with ardent affection. This is precisely the situation in international trade at the present day; and if it did not occur we should say that mankind could not be capable of anything so ridiculous. Economic interdependence is very much greater than at any former time, but owing partly to the fact that our economic system has developed from one of private profit, and partly to separate national sovereignties, interdependence, instead of producing friendliness, tends to be a cause of hostility. As economics everywhere has come to be more and more intimately connected with the state, it has become more and more subordinate to politics. Marx held that politics is determined by economics, but that was because he was still under the influence of eighteenth-century rationalism, and imagined that what people most desire is to grow rich. Experience since his time has shown that there is something which people desire even more strongly, and that is to keep others poor. This is a matter in which military power necessarily plays a great part as soon as trade has come to be mainly between nations rather than between individuals. That is why politics has more and more come to predominate over economics.

The advantages of increasing the size of a social unit are nowhere so obvious as in war. In fact, war has been the main cause of the growth of units from families to tribes, from tribes to nations, and from nations to alliances of nations. But it is beginning to dawn upon some people that although large units are a great help towards victory, there is something which is even better than victory, and that is avoidance of war. In the past, war was often a profitable enterprise. The Seven Years War certainly brought the English a good return on the capital expended, and the profitableness of earlier wars to the victors is even more evident. But modern war is an altogether different matter. This is due in the main to two causes: one, that weapons have become enormously expensive; and the other, that the social groups concerned in modern wars are very large. It is a mistake to think that modern war is more destructive of life than the simpler wars of former times. The actual casualties in the past were often quite as high a percentage of the forces engaged as they are now; and apart from casualties in battle, the deaths from disease were usually enormous. Over and over again in ancient and medieval history, you find whole armies practically exterminated by the plague. The atom bomb is, of course, more spectacular, but the actual mortality rate among combatant populations, even where the atom bomb is employed, is not as great as in many former wars. The population of Japan increased by about 5 millions during the Second World War, whereas it is estimated that during the Thirty Years War the population of Germany was halved. Broadly speaking, it is not in general the case that as weapons become technically more efficient, the mortality in war is increased.

There is, however, in the use of the atom bomb and the hydrogen bomb a new danger, a danger which is not only new in kind but greater in degree than any that has existed in previous wars. We do not quite know what may be the effects of letting loose great floods of radioactivity. There are those – among them Einstein – who think that the result may be the extinction of all life on our planet. Short of that, it may easily happen that large fertile regions become infertile and uninhabitable, and that the populations of considerable areas are wiped out. I do not say that this will happen if atomic energy is employed in war; no one knows yet whether it will happen or not. But there is a risk that it may happen, and if it does repentance will come too late.

There is an oscillation in warfare between the strength of the attack and the strength of the defence. The happy ages are those in which the defence is strong; the unhappy, those in which the attack has the advantage. There is always a danger in our scientific age that at some moment the attack may acquire a really disastrous advantage. Bacteriological warfare, for example, may exterminate the enemy, but would be very likely to exterminate at the same time those who had inaugurated it. On the whole, increase of scientific skill makes war more dangerous, even if at any given moment it does not make it more deadly.

Apart from mortality, there are other respects in which modern war is worse than most wars of former times. Owing to the increased productivity of labour, it is possible to set aside a greater part of the population for the business of mutual slaughter, and the dislocation of daily life is greater in a modern world war than in most of the wars of former times. Fear of atomic bombs has made it irrational for populations to live in great cities. Americans, who have room to expand, are seriously contemplating spreading the population of New York over a large area. In England no such possibilities exist, short of large-scale emigration. In the pleasant and comfortable wars of the eighteenth and nineteenth centuries, it was chiefly the combatants who suffered; now the suffering falls increasingly upon civilians. I am an old man, and I can remember a time when it was not thought quite the thing to make war on women and children; but that happy age is past.

For all these reasons, war is a greater menace now than it was formerly. The prevention of war has become necessary if civilized life is to continue, perhaps if any kind of life is to continue. This matter is so imperative that we must not shrink from new forms of political thought or from the realization of new problems which could formerly be ignored, if not with impunity, at any rate without ultimate disaster.

War may be avoided by makeshifts and expendients and subtle diplomacy for a time, but precariously; and so long as our present political system continues, it must be taken as nearly certain that great wars will occur from time to time. This will inevitably happen so long as there are different sovereign states, each with its own armed forces, and each the unfettered judge of its own rights in any dispute. There is only one way in which the world can be made safe from war, and that is the creation of a single worldwide authority, possessing a monopoly of all the more serious weapons.

If a world government is to prevent serious wars, there are certain minimum powers that it must possess. First and foremost, it must have a monopoly of all the major weapons of war, and adequate armed forces for their employment. Whatever steps may be necessary must be taken to ensure that the armed forces will in all circumstances be loyal to the central government. The world government should proclaim certain rules for the employment of its armed forces. The most important of these should be that, in any dispute between two states, each must submit to the decision of the world government. Any employment of force by any state against any other shall constitute it a public enemy, and shall bring punishment by the armed forces of the world government. These are the essential powers if the preservation of peace is to be possible. Given these, others will follow. There will be need of bodies to perform legislative and judicial functions. These will develop naturally if the military conditions are fulfilled; the difficult and vital point is the placing of irresistible force in the hands of the central authority.

The central government may be democratic or totalitarian; it may owe its origin to consent or to conquest; it may be the national government of a state which has achieved world conquest, or it may be an authority in which each state, or alternatively, each human being, has equal rights. For my part I believe that, if it is constituted, it will be on a basis of consent in some regions and conquest in others. In a world war between two groups of nations, it may be that the victorious group will disarm the defeated group and proceed to govern the world by means of unifying institutions developed during the war. Gradually the defeated nations could be admitted to partnership as war hostility cooled. I do not believe that the human race has sufficient statesmanship or capacity for mutual forbearance to establish a world government on a basis of consent alone. That is why I think that an element of force will be needed in its establishment and in its preservation through the early years of its existence.

But although force may be necessary at first in some parts of the world, there will be no stability and no possibility of a liberal and democratic system unless certain great causes of conflict cease to be operative. I am not thinking of the day-to-day conflicts that at present characterize the cold war, nor of the see-saw of power politics. What I am thinking of are matters in which, as things stand, there is a genuine clash between the interests of one part of the world and the interests of another. I am thinking of matters regarded as so important that each side would sooner fight then yield. For instance: shall South East Asia continue to be over-crowded, or shall Australia and South America cease to be white men's countries? Such really difficult causes of conflict centre round three problems: population, race, and creed.

I have already spoken of the population problem, but a few words must be added about its political aspects. Until it is solved it will be impossible to bring the poorer parts of the world to anything like the same level of prosperity as is now enjoyed by the richer parts, and until there is a certain economic equalization throughout the world, there will be causes of envy and hatred such as will make any world government dependent upon continual exercise of force by the stronger nations. Such a state of affairs will be unstable and dangerous and harsh. It will be impossible to feel that the world is in a satisfactory state until there is a certain degree of equality, and a certain acquiescence everywhere in the power of the world government, and this will not be possible until the poorer nations of the world have become educated, modernized in their technique, and more or less stationary in population. This, you may think, is a distant prospect, but it need not be so. Vital statistics in the West during the last half-century have shown what is possible, and certainly hardly anybody in the West would have thought anything of the kind possible in the year 1800.

The conclusion to which we are driven by the facts that we have been considering is that, while great wars cannot be avoided until there is a world government, a world government cannot be stable until every important country has a nearly stationary population. As this is very far from being the case at present, our conclusion may seem depressing. But there is another side to it which is by no means depressing. In former days most children died in infancy, mortality in adult life was very high, and in every country the great majority of the population endured abject poverty. Now certain nations have succeeded in preserving the lives of the overwhelming majority of infants, in enormously lowering the adult death rate, and in nearly eliminating abject poverty. All this would have been impossible but for the fall in the birth rate. Other nations, where disease and abject poverty are still the rule, could achieve the same level of well-being by adopting the same methods. There is therefore a new hope for mankind. The hope cannot be realized unless the causes of present evils are understood. But it is the hope that needs to be emphasized. Modern man is master of his fate. What he suffers, he suffers because he is stupid or wicked, not because it is nature's decree. Happiness is his if he will adopt the means that lie ready to his hands.

IV   JAMES STRACHEY, 'TWO POSSIBILITIES' (*extract*)

The English politician and theorist James Strachey (1901–63) wrote his last book, *On the Prevention of War* (1962), at a time when only the United States and the Soviet Union were *bona fide* nuclear powers, when the attempts of these two super-powers to forge a nuclear-test-ban treaty were proving unsuccessful, and when Britain and France were just beginning to make moves to join the 'nuclear club'. Strachey conjectures that a nuclear-test-ban treaty between the United States and the USSR would offer the two super-powers the auspicious opportunity to enter into a hegemony over the rest of the world – and thus bring about a political and economic stability that might never again be possible should the proliferation of nuclear armaments gain momentum. As an alternative he envisages for the 1970s or 1980s a hegemony among the five or six nuclear powers that he expects to have emerged by that time. If his proposal seems radical or unrealistic, it nevertheless raises the question of how, short of such a hegemony, an effective nuclear-test-ban treaty could be *practically* implemented *for the world*.

Strachey's 'first possibility' – a US–USSR hegemony – has been revived more recently by Richard Falk, who in his book *A Study of World Futures* (New York: Macmillan, 1975) pp. 206–9, reluctantly recommends as one viable model of world order a US–Soviet 'condominium', based on certain specific police powers which may be needed to prevent nuclear proliferation among terrorist groups and, in general, to decelerate the strategic-armament build-up. Like Strachey, Falk sees such an eventuality as at best a pragmatic necessity for preventing mishaps while the nations of the world seek to establish a more stable framework for world order.

The text below is reprinted from *On the Prevention of War* (London: Macmillan; and New York: St Martin's Press, 1962) pp. 288–99. Square brackets are editorial.

The problem of the maintenance of peace for an indefinite period is clearly extremely difficult, even if it is not, as many men of affairs suppose, so remote of solution as to be not worth talking about.

True, the thing has been done before, over fairly long periods and fairly wide areas, but only by the unification of a 'known world' by means of a knock-out tournament; and that method is no longer available. The Communist solution by way of universal revolution is also closed to us, not only because it would be, perhaps, as violent as wars of conquest themselves, but also because much recent evidence goes to show that it is an illusion to suppose that post-revolutionary nation states are particularly likely to unite voluntarily. And finally the solution of the men of peace, by way of the United Nations and general and complete disarmament, is, partly, vitiated by the illusion that there can be, in our time at any rate, a powerless world.

What remains? There remains at any rate the conceptual possibility that two or more of the super-powers might pool their authority, for the one purpose of preventing the outbreak of full-scale nuclear war. Such a pooling of power might take place either in the fairly immediate future between the two existing super-powers, America and Russia (their respective allies consenting or 'influenced' to consent). Or it could take place one or two decades from now between a group of, say, half a dozen nuclear super-powers which may have come into existence by then. . . .

. . . All that is necessary is that we should consider two possibilities for the unification of nuclear power: (i) as between two rival super-powers and (ii) as between a number.

American–Russian predominance?

Let us in the first place then examine the possibility of America and Russia taking joint action to stabilize and perpetuate their present nuclear predominance, and in so doing discovering that they have a joint interest in the prevention of nuclear war.

At first sight the possibility of any such a getting-together of America and Russia, even for this strictly limited purpose, is too remote to be worth discussing. Their stark mutual hostility, based upon what each supposes the other to be like, much exceeds even the normal degree of mutual hostility between rival nation states. It stands like a brick wall in the way. It is hard to say which would prove the more intractable obstacle, the violent, largely instinctive American repugnance for communist Russia and all she stands for, or the rigidly thought-out, doctrinaire, repugnance of the communists for capitalist America and all she stands for. In much of recent American practice, and in communist theory and practice, each government has almost invariably and throughout the world supported those national and social forces which the other has opposed, and opposed those forces which the other has supported. How could they possibly combine their wills for even the most strictly limited purpose? If, then, the subject is worth discussing, as I evidently believe that it is, it must be because strong and pervasive forces can be descried which, given time, will tend to overcome this present impasse of extreme mutual hostility. I believe that it is not difficult to identify these forces.

The indispensable minimum

First, however, we must be clear about the nature and extent of the task. If nuclear war could only be prevented by a close alliance, or *a fortiori*, by some sort of federation, between America and Russia, the world's situation might indeed be judged to be hopeless.

Fortunately far less than this is needed, at any rate, initially. What is indispensable is some form of workable, effective agreement between American and Russia (while they maintain their nuclear predominance):

(a) to prevent any other state acquiring or using nuclear arms;
(b) to abstain from resorting to their use between themselves.

If they could do that they could pursue their national rivalries as heretofore without destroying themselves, and us. Let us see if there is any method by which this limited goal might be reached . . . .

Mr Herman Kahn, who is often, though wholly unjustly, accused of being a nuclear warmonger rather than a pacifist idealist, has actually proposed that the Russian and American Governments should sign a one-clause treaty binding themselves never to use their nuclear weapons except for the coercion of any state which itself used such weapons. This is indeed the essence of the matter. Nevertheless, the signing of such a treaty might mean little in itself: it would only be significant if it gave formal approval to a world policy which the two super-powers were visually pursuing. Moreover there is, surely, a much more practicable and politically acceptable method of approach to this goal. And that is, I repeat, the successful conclusion of a test-ban treaty.

. . . The conclusion of a test ban treaty [is] at once a far more difficult and a far more important thing than is usually realized. For such a treaty would either quickly break down or would commit the American and Russian governments to a policy of denying nuclear weapons to all other countries in the world. . . . Once the governments of the two super-powers were embarked upon such a policy as that (acting no doubt through the United Nations) they would find themselves collaborating in one of the most important of all international purposes, namely the prevention of the spread of nuclear weapons.

Moreover this purpose is in effect identical with the concentration of ultimate power in the hands of the two existing super-powers. It is not, in my view, impossible to envisage the American and Russian governments, influenced by the developing social forces enumerated below and, in spite of their intense mutual hostility and suspicion, engaging in a policy so naturally attractive to their own self-regard and interests. For the two 'top dogs' in any situation, even if they fear each other, may yet combine to prevent any of the other dogs from challenging their joint hegemony. But of course that would only take them part of the way. As well as effectively forbidding everyone else from making nuclear war they would have to show effectively, and by their actions, that they would in no circumstance make nuclear war upon each other. That is a goal still more difficult of attainment, and one towards which an effective test-ban treaty would be only a short step. Such a treaty might be completely successful in preventing the spread of the nuclear arms race to the rest of the world, while making only a small contribution to abating the arms race between Russia and America. For those very considerations which would, probably, make it safe enough to sign such a treaty, even with only partially effective inspection provisions, depend for their validity . . . upon the fact that the further perfection of the nuclear warheads themselves is not now the main theme of the arms race. What really matters is the perfection and rendering invulnerable of the means of delivery. Therefore, the nuclear arms race might, in principle, continue almost unabated between America and Russia even when they had signed a test-ban treaty.

Nevertheless, the conclusion of such a treaty would be a step, at least, towards a truce even between the super-powers themselves. As they learned to co-operate in suppressing the nuclear capabilities of everyone else, they would almost certainly learn a certain toleration for each other. No doubt their world rivalry would continue for many years; it could be fought out by economic, political, and even, if needs be, by local wars fought by allies and by conventional forces – as has happened already. But the mere fact that a *common purpose*, namely the prevention of anyone else from waging nuclear war, had been recognized would surely have a considerable mitigating effect. It is extraordinary to realize that such an epoch-making event as the conclusion of a test-ban treaty came far nearer, at any rate, to consummation than any other recent proposal in the field of disarmament. That is what gives it its quite exceptional importance. A test-ban treaty is at one and the same time by far the most important and by far the most practicable disarmament proposal before the world today.

What sort of a peace?

Two objections may at once be raised against the better prospects of survival which a test-ban treaty would open up before the world. Even if, it may be objected, a test-ban treaty might prove the 'growth point' out of which a joint American–Russian world hegemony for the prevention of nuclear war developed, would a world peace so achieved prove either stable or just? The answer is, of course not. What planet do such objectors suppose that they inhabit? This is the earth; if they want perfectly stable and perfectly just solutions to the problem of achieving a long-term peace in the nuclear age they had better try Mars or Venus. They are not likely to find them on earth. What can be said is that the conclusion of a test ban treaty would lead the American and Russian governments towards the indefinite maintenance of a joint world nuclear hegemony; and this would be a far more stable state of things than either a multi-nuclear world or than the present 'delicate balance of terror'. . . .

. . . But the real reason why unfortunately the stabilization of a joint American–Russian nuclear hegemony seems doubtful is the time factor. Those positive forces driving the world towards some sort of unity, in order to escape destruction, will hardly have had time to make a decisive impact, before the American–Russian hegemony has evaporated. For these forces, though very powerful, are slow moving.

The nuclear world of the 1970s

We must therefore face the alternative hypothesis that by, say, the 1970s or 1980s the Russian and American nuclear predominance has slipped, or is slipping, away: that half-a-dozen or so nuclear super-powers occupy the centre of the world stage, and that effective and cheap nuclear capacity threatens to spread to many smaller, poorer and less responsible nation-states . . . .

The dangers of such a world situation need no emphasis. (Unless the idea of such a world frightens the reader, this is not the book for him.) Clearly the creation of a unique centre of nuclear power would in such conditions be a more complex business. . . . *Given the will* – and by the 1970s, for reasons to be stated, such a will really may have come into existence – there will still be a way by which a single centre of world nuclear authority might be evolved.

A 'concert of the world'

Here too, after all, we are not without historical precedents and analogies. Just as there have been 'periods of contending states', in which the maintenance of a balance of power has been the only way to keep, for a while, a precarious peace; and just as there have been knock-out tournaments which have been fought to a finish, so also there have been periods in which peace has been maintained, though not indefinitely, by 'a concert of powers'. The 'concert of Europe' in the nineteenth century is the obvious example. . . . But we must remember that such a concert of nuclear super-powers would inevitably have to contain, as well as America and Russia, Communist China . . . .

Perhaps such a 'concert', or committee, of nuclear super-powers would begin to assert its authority in the same way that America and Russia thought at least of beginning to assert theirs in the early 1960s, namely by seeking to prevent anyone else from acquiring nuclear capacity. And perhaps they would actually try to do it by a test-ban treaty or a 'cut-off' in nuclear production or both. No doubt the conclusion of such a treaty between five or six roughly equal nuclear powers would be in itself more difficult even than the conclusion of such a treaty between the two super-powers of the sixties (and Britain) proved to be. On the other hand the second part of the requirement for long-term survival might actually be easier to achieve by six or more such powers than by two. For a treaty (written or established by usage, and no doubt in either case operated through the United Nations) between five or six super-powers must contain at least two provisions. First that the contracting parties bind themselves to prevent any further nation states from acquiring nuclear capacity. Second that they would set upon, with all their nuclear forces, and so extinguish, anyone of themselves who, for any cause whatsoever and however just that cause might be held to be, resorted to the use of nuclear weapons.

Once again all claims that peace so procured would necessarily be stable or just must be repudiated. These speculations are not travel-bookings for Utopia; they are attempts to descry a gleam of light which might guide us towards the possibility of survival in the nuclear age. . . .

The nature of world power

At this point in the argument it is indispensable to spell out the conception of world power as it is used in these pages. Otherwise it may be said that when it comes to the point all that is being suggested is some sort of functional world authority engaged in enforcing a test-ban treaty, or a nuclear cut-off, relying upon the authority of either the two existing super-powers or of a concert of five or six future super-powers. This *is* indeed what is suggested in the first instance; but only as the growth point out of which a real, political, world authority may develop. And this not merely because without a real, political, authority the prevention of nuclear war could not be accomplished but also because there can be, in the supreme, nuclear, sphere at any rate, no such thing, in the long run, as a limited functional authority.

The truth is that there can be, *in principle*, no limitation upon power. If, that is to say, America and Russia, or five or six super-powers jointly, were able, and did in fact, prevent the rest of the world from acquiring nuclear capability then they would be able, in theory at least, to prevent it from doing anything else either. There is no way, no paper constitution, no safeguard, by means of which, if once nuclear authority is being exercised over the world, that authority can be circumscribed. Power, much more than peace, is *in principle* indivisible. Nevertheless, this alarming conclusion would be much mitigated *in practice* by the size and complexity of the world. In practice our super-powers would be hard put to it indeed to do more than enforce that one indispensable commandment of our epoch – 'thou shalt not make nuclear war'. They would *have* to leave a great deal of freedom to the local governments of the world. We may rely on this not because we should trust their good intentions, but because those local governments would be so many, so different and, we may be sure, so 'difficult'.

Moreover, initially of course America and Russia, or the concert of five or six super-powers, would have differing and conflicting purposes, so that the rest of the world could, and no doubt would, retain a great deal of freedom by playing off one against another, as indeed they do now. But this sort of freedom would be highly dangerous, since it would inevitably tend towards the break-up of the emergent world authority. The fact is that either the super-powers would have to resist those divisive pressures and by so doing grow into a firmer and firmer authority, or the world would break down again into its present state of nature.

2
Peace through International Federation

Before considering international federative proposals, we should be cognizant of an important distinction to be made between a 'confederation' and a 'federation'. In contemporary parlance, a confederation is a much looser sort of union than a federation. In *The Federalist Papers* (numbers 16, 18, 19 and 39), James Madison and Alexander Hamilton point out the tendencies to anarchy and civil war in various political confederations, including the thirteen American colonies organized under the Articles of Confederation. However, Madison and Hamilton sometimes used the term 'federation' synonymously with 'confederation', and in general they spoke about a compromise between 'national' and 'federal' government in order to convey what we now mean by the single term 'federation'. In line with the above terminological distinction, the peace plans of Rousseau and Kant which follow would be best characterized as 'confederative', although the term 'federal' may be used by them, while the proposals of Publius II and Toynbee envision an international 'federation' in the stricter sense of the word, i.e. a compromise between the sovereignty of individual member nations and the sovereignty of an international executive authority. For example, the United Nations Organization at present is at most an international confederation. In order for it to become an international federation, a legislative representative of the citizens of member nations (not just composed of representatives sent by the governments of the individual nations), a judiciary with power to levy sanctions and a central executive power with much greater authority than the present 'Security Council' would have to be incorporated into the United Nations.

I   JEAN-JACQUES ROUSSEAU, *A PROJECT OF PERPETUAL PEACE*

This essay, published in 1761, is actually an edited, updated, revised, and drastically abridged version of a treatise published in 1713 by the Abbé de Saint-Pierre (1658–1743). Rousseau (1712–78) appends a short explanatory introduction to his version and a critical evaluation (the 'Judgement', not reprinted below). Saint-Pierre was passionately committed to the possibility of a 'confederation' among the warring absolute monarchs of Europe which would resolve differences by arbitration through a central diet or congress, and thus alleviate future wars. Saint-Pierre's proposal captured the imagination of many eighteenth-century thinkers, although its wider dissemination and acceptance was impeded by Saint-Pierre's cumbersome and tedious writing-style and remarks which in the mid eighteenth century were obscure or outdated. Rousseau thought Saint-Pierre should get a wider hearing, and so, with the permission of Saint-Pierre's representatives, set himself to the task of presenting the essence of the treatise in more palatable form. Rousseau himself, however, is forced to conclude in his 'Judgement of Perpetual Peace', following the essay, that Saint-Pierre is too optimistic about the reasonableness of men involved in international political associations, and in particular about the willingness of absolute monarchs to accept positions of mere equality *vis-à-vis* one another. A relativizing confederation of absolutist governments would exceed the tolerances of human nature.

The translation reprinted below, in slightly abridged form, is that by Edith M. Nuttall (London: Richard Cobden-Sanderson, 1927). Some of the translator's notes have been omitted. The footnotes are Rousseau's. Square brackets are editorial.

As no grander, finer, or more useful project has ever occupied the human mind than that of a perpetual and universal peace between all the peoples of Europe, so no author has better deserved the attention of the public than he who proposes means for putting this project into execution. It is indeed difficult to believe that such a scheme as this can leave any man of feeling and virtue untouched by enthusiasm; and I incline to think that the illusions of a truly human heart, whose zeal takes all things as possible, are to be preferred to that sour and repellent reason whose indifference to the public good is always the chief obstacle to every endeavour to promote it.

I do not doubt that many readers will forearm themselves with incredulity, in order to resist the pleasure of yielding to conviction, and I pity them for so sadly mistaking obstinacy for wisdom. But I hope that every generous soul will share the delight with which I take up my pen on a subject of such concern to mankind. I see, as in a vision, men living together in unity and good will. I conjure up a sweet and peaceful society of brothers, living in eternal concord, all guided by the same principles, all happy in a common happiness, and as my imagination realizes a picture so touching, an image of the unattained, I enjoy a momentary taste of true happiness.

I could not help writing these opening words in response to the feelings which filled my heart. Now let us try to reason coolly. Being determined to assert nothing that I cannot prove, I have the right to ask the reader in his turn to deny nothing he cannot refute; for it is not the logicians I fear so much, as those who, though refusing to accept my proofs, are unwilling to formulate their objections thereto.

No long reflection on the means of perfecting any government is needed to bring into view the embarrassments and hindrances which spring less from its internal constitution than from its foreign relations; so that the greater part of that attention which ought to be given to administration must needs be devoted to defence, and more care spent to enable it to resist other powers than to perfect its own institutions. If the social order were, as is pretended, the work of reason rather than of the passions, should we have been so long in seeing that either too much or too little has been done for our happiness; that, as we are each of us in the civil state with our fellow citizens, and in the state of nature with the rest of the world, we have prevented private feuds only to fan the flames of public wars which are a thousand times more terrible; in short mankind, by gathering itself into groups, has become its own enemy?[1]

If there is any means of getting rid of these dangerous contradictions, it can be only by a confederative form of government, which, uniting nations by bonds similar to those which unite individuals, submits them all equally to the authority of the laws. Such a government, moreover, appears to be preferable to all others in that it comprehends at one and the same time the advantage of both large and small states, that it becomes formidable abroad by reason of its power, that its laws are rigorously enforced, and that it is the only possible way of restraining equally subjects, rulers and foreigners.

Although in some respects this method may seem new (and as a matter of fact it has really been understood by the moderns only), yet the ancients were not unacquainted with it. The Greeks had their amphictyonic councils, the Etruscans their lucumones, the Latins their feriae and the Gauls their city leagues, whilst the last expiring sighs of Greece were glorified in the Achaean League. But none of these confederations approached in wisdom that of the Germanic Body, the Swiss League and the States-General.[2] And if such institutions as these are still so few in number, and so far from the perfection which we feel they might attain, it is because the best schemes never work out exactly as they were supposed, and because, in politics as in morals, the growth of our knowledge reveals only the vast extent of our woes.

In addition to these public confederations, others less apparent but none the less real, may be tacitly formed by some union of interests, by the acceptance of a common policy, by conformity of customs, or by other circumstances which create a common bond between nations otherwise separate. Thus it is that all the European powers form among themselves a sort of system which unites them by the same religion, the same international law, by customs, literature, commerce, and by a kind of balance, a necessary consequence of all this which, without anyone's studying actually to preserve it, would nevertheless not be quite so easy to disturb as many believe.

This society of the nations of Europe has not always existed, and the particular causes that gave it birth serve still to maintain it. Before the Roman conquests the peoples of this part of the world, being all barbarians and unknown to one another, had nothing in common save the quality of being men, a quality which, disgraced as it was by slavery, scarcely differed in essence from the state of the brute. Accordingly the Greeks, in the pride of their philosophy, actually divided the human kind into two species, one of which (their own, to wit) was made to rule, and the other, which comprised the rest of the world, solely to serve. From this it followed that a Gaul or Iberian was of no more account to a Greek than a Kaffir or an American Indian is to us; and the barbarous tribes themselves were as much divided from one another as they all were from the Greeks.

When, however, this people, a sovereign race by nature, had submitted to their slaves the Romans, and half of the known hemisphere had accepted the same yoke, there came to be formed a political and civil union between all the members of a single empire. This union was drawn closer by the principle, either a very wise or a very foolish one, of bestowing on the conquered all the rights of the conquerors, and above all by the famous decree of Claudius[3] which incorporated all the subjects of Rome into the Roman citizenship.

To the political bond which thus united all the members in one body were joined its civil institutions and laws, which gave a new strength to these ties by determining in an equitable manner, clearly and precisely, or at least as far as possible in so vast an empire, the duties and reciprocal rights of prince and subjects, and of citizen to citizen. The Theodosian Code,[4] and afterwards the law-books of Justinian were a new bond of justice and reason, opportunely substituted for that of the imperial power, when it was being visibly relaxed. This accrual of strength considerably delayed the dissolution of the Empire, and for a long time preserved to it a sort of jurisdiction over the very barbarians who were laying it waste.

A third bond, stronger than those already mentioned, was that of religion; and undeniably it is above all to Christianity that Europe still owes today the kind of society which has been perpetuated among its members. So much so, that the only one of them who has not adopted the opinions of the others in this matter has always remained a stranger among them. Christianity, so despised at its birth, served in the end as a refuge for its detractors. After having persecuted it so cruelly and so vainly the Roman Empire found in it resources which its own strength could no longer provide. Christian missions were of more avail than pagan victories. Rome sent out its bishops to repair the failures of its generals; its priests triumphed when its soldiers were beaten. Thus it was that the Franks, the Goths, the Burgundians, the Lombards, the Avars, and a thousand others finally recognized the authority of the Empire after they had conquered it, and made at least a show of accepting, along with the Gospel law, the law of the prince who had made it known to them.

Such was the respect that was still paid to this great dying power that up to the last moment its destroyers gloried in its titles, and one saw the same conquerors who had humbled it become officials of the Empire. The greatest kings accepted, nay even intrigued for, the patrician honours, the office of prefect and of consul, and like a lion which fawns upon the man it could devour, these terrible conquerors were to be seen rendering homage to the imperial throne which they had the power to overthrow.

This is how the Church and the Empire formed a social bond for various types of peoples who, without any real community of interests or of laws or of allegiance, had one of maxims and opinions, whose influence still remained when its basis had been destroyed. The ancient phantom of the Roman Empire continued to form a kind of liaison between the members who had composed it; and since Rome's dominion survived in another form after the destruction of the Empire, this double tie* left a more closely knit society amongst the nations of Europe, where the heart of the two powers had lain, than ever existed in other parts of the world, where the different people, too scattered to get into communication, had besides no focus of reunion.

Add to this that Europe has special advantages over the other continents. It is more equally populated, more evenly fertile, and more compact in all its parts. The continual blending of interests, which the ties of blood and the business of commerce, of the arts and of colonization have formed between sovereigns; the large number of rivers the variety of whose courses make all communications easy; the restlessness of the inhabitants ceaselessly moving about and frequently travelling beyond their own frontiers; the invention of printing and general taste for letters, which has given them a common stock of studies and knowledge; and finally the large number and small size of the states, combined with the craving for luxury and the diversities of climate, make every part of Europe necessary to every other. All these causes combined, form out of Europe no mere fanciful collection of peoples with only a name in common as in Asia and Africa, but a real society which has its religion, its manners, its customs and even its laws, from which none of the people who compose it can withdraw without at once causing trouble.

To see on the other hand the perpetual dissensions, the brigandage, the usurpations, the rebellions, the wars, the murders which daily distress this venerable abode of sages, this resplendent sanctuary of science and art, and to think of our fine talk and then of our horrible actions, so much humanity in principle, so much cruelty in deed, a religion so gentle and an intolerance so blood-

---

* Respect for the Roman Empire has so fully survived its power, that many legal authorities have questioned whether the Emperor of Germany was not the natural sovereign of the world; and Bartholus[5] has gone so far as to treat as a heretic anyone who dared to doubt it. The canonical books are full of similar decisions on the temporal authority of the Roman Church.

thirsty, a political system so wise on paper, so harsh in practice, rulers so benevolent and peoples so miserable, governments so moderate and wars so cruel, one hardly knows how to make these strange contradictions agree; and this pretended brotherhood of the nations of Europe seems nothing but a term of derision to express ironically their mutual animosity.

Nevertheless in this, things only follow their natural course; every society without laws or rulers, every union formed or maintained by chance, necessarily must degenerate into quarrels and dissensions at the first change of circumstances. The ancient union of the nations of Europe has complicated their interests and rights in a thousand ways; they touch one another at so many points that the least movement of one is sure to give a shock to the others; the disaster of a rupture is in proportion to the closeness of their relations, and their frequent quarrels are almost as cruel as civil wars.

Let us agree, then, that in relation to one another the European powers are properly speaking in a state of war, and that all the partial treaties between particular powers represent passing truces rather than true peace, either because these treaties have generally no other guarantee than that of the contracting parties, or because the rights of the two parties are never thoroughly settled, and that these unextinguished rights, or, it may be, the claims of the powers who recognize no superior, will infallibly become sources of new wars, as soon as a change of circumstances gives new strength to the claimants.

Moreover, as the public law of Europe has not been established or sanctioned by concerted action, and as it has no general principles, and varies constantly according to times and circumstances, it abounds in contradictory rules which can be reconciled only by the right of the stronger; so that reason without an assured guide, in matters of doubt being always biased towards personal considerations, war would still be inevitable, even when everyone wished to be just. All one can do with the best intentions is to decide questions of this sort by an appeal to arms or to abate the controversy by temporary treaties, but soon when occasion revives these disputes, other facts enter in which modify them; everything becomes confused and complicated; one no longer sees to the bottom of things; usurpation passes for law, and weakness for wrong; and amidst this disorder everyone finds that without his knowing it the ground beneath him has shifted, insensibly indeed yet so profoundly that if one could get back to solid and original rights there would be few sovereigns in Europe who would not have to surrender everything they possess.

Another source of war, to us less visible but no less real, is that things do not change their form in changing their nature, that states in fact hereditary remain elective in appearance, that there are parliaments or national estates in monarchies and hereditary heads of republics, that a power actually dependent on another still preserves an appearance of liberty, that all the peoples ruled by the same power are not governed by the same laws, that the order of succession is different in the different states of the same sovereign, and lastly that every government always tends to change without there being any possibility of preventing this process. These, then, are the general and particular causes which unite us in order to destroy us, and make us write our fine theories of brotherly love with hands always stained with human blood.

Once the sources of the evil are recognized, they indicate their own remedy, if any such exists. Everyone sees that all societies are moulded by common interests; that all divisions spring from opposing interests; that a thousand accidental occurrences can change and modify both these factors, once society is called into being; therefore there must be necessarily be some power with sanctions to regulate and organize the movements of its members, in order to give to common interests and mutual engagements that degree of solidity which they could not assume by themselves.

It would be a great mistake to hope for this state of lawlessness ever to change in the natural course of things and without artificial aid. The European system possesses just enough cohesion to allow perpetual disturbances to take place without risking its complete overthrow, and, though our woes may not increase, still less can they come to an end, because any far-reaching revolution is henceforth impossible.

In proof of this, let us begin with a summary glance at the present state of Europe. The lie of the mountains, seas and rivers, which provide the boundaries of the nations who inhabit it, seems to have decided the number and size of those nations; and we may say that the political organization of this part of the world is, to a certain extent, the work of nature.

In short let us not imagine that this boasted balance of power has been achieved by anyone, or that anyone has done aught with intent to maintain it; it certainly exists, and those who do not feel themselves strong enough to break it down conceal their private ends under the pretext of supporting it. But whether one is conscious of it or not, this balance exists, and can well maintain itself without outside interference. If it should be broken for a moment on one side it would soon re-establish itself on another; so that, if the princes who were accused of aspiring to universal monarchy did really aspire to it, they showed therein more ambition than wit. For how can we give a moment's consideration to this project without seeing its absurdity? How not feel that there is no single potentate in Europe so much mightier than the others as ever to be able to become their master? All the conquerors who have ever caused vast upheavals have invariably appeared with unexpectedly great forces or with foreign troops used to some distinctive discipline, as against peoples who were defenceless, divided, or untrained to war. But where should a European prince find these unexpected forces with which to overwhelm the other states, as long as the the most powerful of them represents only a small fraction of the whole, and all the rest are alert and on their guard against him? Will he have more troops than all the rest together? He cannot, or if he has he will only be ruined the sooner by it; or else his troops will be of worse quality because of their greater number. Will his men be better trained for war? He will then have fewer of them in proportion. Moreover, discipline is more or less on a par everywhere, or in a short time will have become so. Will he have more money? The sources of money are universal, and money never yet won great victories. Will he make a sudden invasion? Famine or fortresses would stop him at every step. Will he endeavor to win inch by inch? He gives his enemies the means of uniting to resist him. It will, therefore, not be long before time, money and men fail him. Will he divide the other powers in order to use some to conquer the rest? The traditions of Europe make such a policy a vain one, and the most stupid of princes would not fall into that trap. Finally, as none of them can command a monopoly of resources, the resistance in the long run is a match for the attack, and time soon makes good the violent accidents of fortune, if not for each particular prince, at least for the general balance of power.

Let us now suppose that two or three powerful rulers make an alliance to subdue the rest. These three potentates together, whoever they may be, will not make up the half of Europe. Then the other half will certainly be united against them, and they will have to conquer a force stronger than themselves. I may add that their aims are too much opposed, and that too great a jealousy exists between them ever to permit of their forming such a project. I may add further that if they should have formed it, and put it into execution, even fairly successfully, their very successes would have the effect of sowing seeds of discord among the conquering allies, because it would be impossible for the spoils to be so equally divided that each would be satisfied with his own share, and the least fortunate would soon set himself to oppose the progress of the others, who, for a like reason, would not be long about quarrelling among themselves. I doubt whether since the beginning of the world there have ever been seen three, or even two great powers uniting to subdue certain others, without falling out over their respective contributions or over the division of the spoils or later, by their own misunderstandings, giving new sources of strength to their victims. Thus whatever supposition we may invent, it is improbable that either prince or league would be able in the future to make any important or permanent change in the state of our affairs. . . .

But if the present system is founded on a rock it is on that account all the more exposed to storms, for there flows between the European powers a tide of action and reaction which, without upsetting them altogether, keeps them in a constant state of unrest, and their efforts are always vain and always recurring, like the waves of the sea which incessantly disturb its surface without ever changing its level, so that nations are constantly afflicted without any visible advantage to their rulers. . . .

If I have insisted on the equal distribution of force which is the result in Europe of the present constitution, it was in order to deduce a conclusion of importance to the project for establishing a general league; for, to form a solid and durable confederation, all its members must be placed in such a mutual state of dependence that not one of them alone may be in a position to resist all of the others, and that minor associations which would have the power to injure the general body may meet with sufficient hindrances to prevent their formation, without which the confederation would be vain, and each would be really independent under an apparent subjection. But if these obstacles are such as I have just described, now that all the powers are entirely free to form leagues amongst themselves and to make offensive alliances, it can be surmised what they will become when there is a great armed league always ready to prevent those who undertake to destroy or resist it. This is enough to show that such an association would not consist in useless deliberations which each could defy with impunity, but that an efficient power would spring from it, capable of forcing ambitious nations to keep within the limits of the general treaty.

The above survey leads inevitably to three conclusions. The first is, that with the exception of the Turk, there exists among the peoples of Europe a social relation, imperfect, but closer than the loose and general bonds of humanity; the second is, that the imperfection of this society makes the condition of those who compose it worse than if there were no society at all amongst them. The third is, that these primitive ties which render this society harmful, at the same time render it easy to perfect; so that all its members might discover their happiness in that which at present causes their misery, and change the state of war which exists amongst them into a perpetual peace.

Let us now see in what way this great work, begun by chance, can be brought to perfection by reason, and how the free and voluntary fellowship which unites the European states, by assuming the strength and stability of a true political body, can be changed into a real confederation. It is beyond doubt that such a settlement by giving to this association the perfection it lacks will destroy the abuse of it, increase its advantages, and force all parties to co-operate for the common good. But for this it is necessary that the confederation should be so general that no considerable power would refuse to join it; that it should have a judicial tribunal with power to establish laws and regulations binding on all its members; that it should have an enforcing and coercive power to constrain each state to submit to the common counsels, whether for action or for abstention. Finally, that it should be firm and enduring, so that its members should be prevented from detaching themselves from it at will the moment they think they see their own particular interest running contrary to the general interest. These are the sure signs by which the institution will be recognized as a wise, useful, and permanent one. The next point is to extend our supposition so as to find out by analysis what effects ought to result from it, what means are best adapted to establish it, and what reasonable hope we can have of putting it into execution.

From time to time there are held amongst us, under the name of congresses, general diets whither representatives of all the states of Europe solemnly go only to return as they went; where they assemble together to say nothing; where all public matters are handled pettily; where there are full debates on such questions as whether the table shall be round or square, whether the hall shall have more or fewer doors, whether such a plenipotentiary shall have his face or his back to the window, whether another shall walk two inches more or less in paying a call, and a thousand other questions of equal importance, which have been uselessly discussed for three centuries, and which are assuredly worthy to occupy the politicians of our own.

Possibly the members of one of the assemblies may some day be endowed with common sense; it is even not impossible that they may be sincerely interested in the public good, and for reasons which will appear later it is even conceivable that, after having smoothed away a good many difficulties, they may receive orders from their respective sovereigns to sign the treaty of the general confederation, which I suppose to be summarily contained in the five following articles.

By the first, the contracting sovereigns shall establish amongst themselves a perpetual and irrevocable alliance, and name plenipotentiaries to hold in some fixed place a permanent diet or congress, where the differences of contracting parties would be regulated and settled by way of arbitration or judicial decisions.

By the second shall be specified the number of sovereigns whose plenipotentiaries are to have a voice in the assembly, those who are to be invited to agree to the treaty, the order, the time, and the manner in which the presidency shall pass from one to the other for equal terms, and finally the relative quota of the contributions to the common expenses and the manner of raising them.

By the third, the confederation shall guarantee to its members the possession and government of all the states each of them controls at the moment, as well as the succession, elective or hereditary, according to whichever is established by the fundamental laws of each country; and in order to put an end once and for all to all the disputes which are constantly reviving, it shall be agreed to take present possession and the latest treaties as the basis of the mutual rights of the contracting powers, at the same time renouncing for ever and reciprocally all anterior pretensions, with the exception of future contested successions and other rights which may fall due, and which shall all be decided by the ruling of the diet, no member being permitted under any pretext whatsoever to take the law into his own hands, or take up arms against his fellow members.

By the fourth the cases shall be specified in which any ally guilty of infringing the treaty is to be put under the ban of Europe and proclaimed a common enemy – that is to say, if he refuse to carry out the decisions of the great alliance, if he make preparations for war, if he negotiate treaties contrary to the terms of the confederation, and if he take up arms to resist it or to attack any one of the allies.

I shall be agreed also by the same article that the states shall arm and act together offensively and conjointly, and at the common expense against any state under the ban of Europe, until it shall have laid down its arms, carried out the sentences and rulings of the congress, repaired the wrongs, refunded the costs, and even given compensation for any warlike preparations it may have made contrary to the treaty.

Lastly, by the fifth article, the plenipotentiaries of the European federal body shall always have the power, on the instructions of their courts, to frame in the diet by a majority of votes, provisionally (and by a three-quarter majority five years afterwards, finally), the regulations which they shall judge to be important in order to secure all possible advantages to the European Republic and each one of its members; but it shall never be possible to change any of these five fundamental articles except with the unanimous consent of all the members of the confederation.

These five articles thus abridged and couched in general rules are, I am aware, subject to a thousand small difficulties, of which several would need long explanations; but small difficulties can be removed easily at need, and they do not matter very much in such an important enterprise as this. When it becomes a question of the details of the policy of the Congress, a thousand obstacles will be found, and ten thousand means of overcoming them. Here it is a question of examining whether in the nature of things the enterprise is possible or not. We should be lost in an ocean of trivial details if we had to foresee and answer them all. Whilst keeping to unquestionable principles we must not try to please all minds, nor solve all objections, nor say how everything will be done; it is enough to show it can be done.

What are the questions that must be put to enable us to form a correct judgement upon this system? Two only; for it is an insult I will not offer the reader to prove to him that in general a state of peace is to be preferred to a state of war.

The first question is whether the proposed confederation would attain its end with certainty and be sufficient to give to Europe a solid and enduring peace; the second, whether it is to the interest of the rulers to establish this confederation and to purchase a stable peace at this price.

When its general and particular utility has been thus demonstrated, one no longer sees in the nature of things what cause could prevent the successful working of an institution which only depends on the will of those interested.

In order to discuss the first article let us apply what I have said of the general system of Europe and of the common action which limits each power very nearly to its own frontiers and does not permit it entirely to crush others out of existence. To make my meaning clearer on this point I subjoin here a list of the nineteen powers which may be said to compose the European Republic, so that were each one to have an equal voice there would be nineteen votes at the congress: the Emperor of the Romans, the Emperor of Russia, the King of France, the King of Spain, the King of England, the States-General, the King of Denmark, the King of Sweden, the King of Poland, the King of Portugal, the Papal States, the King of Prussia, the Elector of Bavaria and his associates, the Elector Palatine and his associates, the Swiss Republic and its associates, the Ecclesiastical Electors with their associates, the Venetian Republic, the King of Naples, the King of Sardinia.

Several less important sovereigns, such as the Republic of Genoa, the dukes of Modena and Parma, and others omitted in this list would be joined to the less powerful in the form of an association, and would hold in common with them a right of suffrage similar to the *votum curiatum* of the counts of the Empire. It is useless to give a more precise enumeration here, because, until the project is carried out, events may at any moment happen which would necessitate remaking the list, but would change none of the ground-work of the system.

We have only to glance at this list to be convinced that it is not possible for any of the powers which compose it to be in a position to oppose all the others united together in one body, nor for any partial league to be formed capable of holding its own against the great confederation.

For how would this league be made? Would it be drawn up between the most powerful? We have shown that it could never last, and it is easy now to see also that it is incompatible with the special policy of each great power, and with the interests inseparable from its constitution. Would it then be between one great state and several little ones? But the other great states, united to the confederation, would soon crush the league, and obviously the great alliance being always united and armed would find it easy by virtue of the fourth article to forestall and suppress from the outset every separate and seditious alliance which should tend to disturb the general peace and order. Let us see what happens in the German states, in spite of the abuses in their organization and the extreme inequality of their members. Is there a single one even among the strongest of them who would dare to incur the ban of the Empire by openly offending against its constitution, at least unless he had good reasons for believing that there was no fear that the Empire would take strong action against him?

Thus I maintain it to be demonstrated that the European diet once established need fear no revolt, and that although some abuses might creep in they could never go so far as to defeat the object of the institution. It remains to be seen whether that object would be fulfilled satisfactorily by our federal institution.

As to that, let us consider the motives which make princes take up arms. These motives are either to make conquests or to defend themselves against an invader, or to weaken a too-powerful neighbour, or to maintain their own rights when assailed, or to end a quarrel which has not been settled amicably, or lastly to fulfil the engagements of a treaty. There is neither cause of nor pretext for war that you cannot place under one of these six heads. But it is evident that none of these six motives can exist in the new state of things that I contemplate.

First, conquests will have to be renounced from the impossibility of making them, considering that everyone is sure to be stopped on the way by greater forces than those he is able to marshal; thus, whilst risking the loss of everything, it is beyond his power to gain anything. An ambitious prince who wishes to increase his possessions in Europe does two things: he begins by strengthening himself with good alliances, then he tries to take his enemy unawares. But private alliances would be of no use against the stronger alliance already in existence; and as no prince will any longer have any pretext for arming, he cannot do so without its being noticed, prevented, and punished by an ever-armed confederation.

The same reason which deprives each prince of any hope of conquests deprives him at the same time of any fear of being attacked; and not only are his estates (guaranteed to him by all Europe) assured to him just as are the private possessions of the citizens in a civilized country, but they are even more so than were he their own sole defender, in proportion as the whole of Europe is stronger than he is alone.

He no longer has any reason for wishing to weaken a neighbour from whom he has no longer anything to fear, and having no hope of success in such an enterprise, he is under no temptation to attempt it.

As regards maintaining their rights, it must first be said that innumerable obscure quibbles and intricate claims will be completely swept away by the third article of the confederation, which settles definitely all the reciprocal rights of the allied sovereigns upon the basis of present possession. Thus all possible demands and claims will become clear for the future, and will be adjudged in the diet as they arise. Add to this, that if my rights are attacked, I must defend them by the same means. Now they cannot be attacked by arms without incurring the ban of the diet; so it is not by arms that I must needs defend them. The same thing can be said of the injuries, wrongs, and reparations, and of all the different unforeseen disputes which might arise between two sovereigns; the same power which has to defend their rights, has to redress their grievances.

As to the last article the solution is obvious. You can see that having no aggressor to fear there is no need for a defensive treaty, and as no such treaty can be firmer or surer than that of the great confederation, any other would be useless, unlawful, and consequently void and worthless.

It is impossible therefore for the confederation once established to leave any seeds of war amongst its members, or for its object of perpetual peace not to be perfectly realized by the proposed scheme if it were carried out.

It remains for us now to examine the other question, which concerns the advantage of the contracting parties; for one feels how vain it would be to give the public interest precedence over the private. To prove that peace is generally preferable to war means nothing to whosoever thinks he has reasons for preferring war to peace, and to show him how to establish a lasting peace is only to incite him to oppose it.

In fact, they will say, you take away from sovereigns the right of doing justice to themselves, that is to say the precious right of being unjust when they please. You take away from them the power of aggrandizing themselves at the expense of their neighbours. You make them renounce antiquated claims which owe their value to their obscurity, because they expand them as their fortune warrants; this display of power and terror with which they like to frighten the world, and that pride of conquest from which they derive their renown; in a word, you force them to be just and peaceable. What will be the compensations for so many cruel deprivations?

I should not be so bold as to reply with the Abbé de Saint-Pierre that the true glory of princes consists in securing the public good and the happiness of their people; that all their interests should be subordinated to their reputation, and that the reputation to be gained among the wise is measured by the good they do to men; that the enterprise of establishing perpetual peace, being the greatest undertaking that has ever been conceived, is the most capable of covering its author with immortal glory; that this same enterprise, being on the one hand the most useful to peoples, is on the other the most honourable to sovereigns; and above all it is the only one unsoiled with blood, rapine, tears, and curses. And that finally the surest means of distinguishing oneself amongst the crowd of kings is to work for the public welfare. Let us leave to the speechifiers those discourses which in the cabinets of ministers have covered their author and his project with ridicule, but do not let us, like them, treat his reasons with contempt, and, whatever virtues kings may possess, let us confine ourselves to their interests.

All the powers of Europe have rights or claims one against the other. These rights are not of such a nature that they can ever be perfectly cleared up, because there is no common invariable rule by which to judge them, and they are often based on ambiguous or uncertain facts. The disputes they cause could never be ended without fear of their returning, as much for the want of a competent arbitrator as because each prince, as occasion occurs, will not scruple to repudiate those concessions forced from him in treaties by greater potentates than himself, or as a result of unsuccessful wars. It is, then, an error to think only of our own claims on others, and to forget those of others upon us, when there is no more justice or advantage on either side in the methods they use for enforcing these mutual claims. Directly everything depends on chance, present possession becomes of such value that prudence will run no risk of losing it for any future gain, even if the chances are even; and everyone condemns a well-to-do man who, in the hope of doubling his wealth, dares to risk it on a single throw. But we have shown that in schemes of aggrandizement each one, even in the present system, must find a resistance superior in strength to his own effort; whence it follows that the stronger having no reason to gamble, nor the weaker any hope of profit, it would be an advantage for all to renounce what they covet, in order to keep what they already possess.

Let us consider the waste of men, of money, of forces of all kinds, and the exhaustion into which the most successful war throws any state, and compare these injuries with the advantages it gains from it. We shall find that it often loses when it thinks it gains, and the victor, always weaker than before the war, has only the consolation of seeing the vanquished more enfeebled than himself. Again that advantage is less real than apparent, because the superiority, which he may have acquired over his adversary, he has at the same time lost in regard to neutral powers who, without changing their own condition, are relatively strengthened through his enfeeblement.

If all kings do not yet recognize the folly of conquests, it seems at least as if the wiser ones are beginning to understand that conquests sometimes cost more than they are worth. Without going into a thousand distinctions in this matter, which would carry us too far afield, we may say broadly that a prince, who, in order to push forward his frontiers, loses as many of his old subjects as he gains new ones, only weakens himself by this aggrandizement, because with a larger area to defend he has no more men to defend it with. Now it is well known that as the result of the way wars are waged to-day the loss of life is least on the battlefield. It is there that the loss is most evident and visible, but at the same time the state suffers much graver and more irreparable loss than that of the men who die, by reason of those men who will never be born, by the increase of taxation, by the interruption of commerce, by deserted countrysides and abandoned agriculture. This evil, unperceived at first, makes itself cruelly felt later on, and it is then that a country is astonished to find itself so weak as the result of having made itself so powerful.

What makes conquest still less attractive is that we know now by what means power can be doubled and trebled, not only without extending territory but sometimes through restricting it, as the Emperor Hadrian[6] very wisely did. We know that men alone make the strength of kings, and it results from what I have just said that of two states which support the same number of inhabitants the one which occupies the least extent of territory is really the most powerful. It is then by good laws, by a wise policy, by broad economic views that a judicious sovereign is sure of adding to his strength without any risk. The real conquests he makes over his neighbours are the public improvements he institutes in his domains, and all the additional subjects born to him are worth so many more enemies slain.

It must not be objected here that I prove too much, in that if things were as I represent them, everyone having a genuine interest in not going to war, and private interests being at one with the common interest to maintain peace, this peace would establish itself of itself and last for ever without any confederation. This would be extremely bad reasoning in the present state of things; for although it would be better for all to be always at peace, the common lack of security in this respect brings it about that each one, not being able to be sure of avoiding war, tries at least to begin it to his own advantage when opportunity favours him, and to forestall a neighbour who would not hesitate to forestall him in the opposite circumstances, so that many wars, even offensive ones, are unjust precautions to safeguard one's own possessions rather than means of seizing what belongs to others. However salutary in general the principles of public welfare may be, it is certain if one considers nothing but the object that he has in view in politics, and often even in morals, these principles become harmful to him who persists in practising them towards everyone when no one will practise them towards him.

I have nothing to say about armaments because without a solid basis either of fear or of hope, this outward show is a child's game, and kings should not play with dolls. I say nothing either about the glory of conquerors, because, if there were monsters who were distressed solely because they had no one to massacre, it is no use reasoning with them, but the means of exercising their murderous fury should be taken away from them. The guarantee of the third article having anticipated all sound reasons for war, there could be no motive for kindling war against our neighbours which would not equally apply to their attacking us; and it is a great gain to be rid of a risk where each one is alone against all.

As to the dependence which each one will be under to the common tribunal, it is very clear that it will diminish none of the rights of sovereignty, but on the contrary will strengthen them, and will make them more assured by article three, which guarantees to each one not only his territory against all foreign invasion, but also his authority against all rebellion by his subjects. The princes accordingly will be none the less absolute, and their crowns will be all the more secure, so that in submitting their disputes to the judgement of the diet as among equals, and renouncing the dangerous power of seizing the possessions of others they only make sure of their true rights and give up those which do not belong to them. Moreover there is a great deal of difference between being dependent on one's neighbours or only on a body of which one is a member, and of which each one is the head in his turn, for in this last case his liberty is only ensured by the guarantees that are given to him. It would be alienated in the hands of a master, but is confirmed in the hands of associates. This is proved by the example of the Germanic states, for although the sovereignty of its members may be weakened in many respects by its constitution, and so they are in a less favourable position than the states of the European body would be, there is nevertheless not a single one of them, however jealous it may be of its own authority, who would wish, when it could, to assure itself an absolute independence by detaching itself from the Empire.

Mark further that as the German states have a permanent head, the authority of this head must necessarily and unceasingly tend to become arbitrary, which could not happen in the same way under the European diet, where the presidency would rotate without regard to disparity of power.

To all these considerations another is added more potent still to persons as eager for money as princes always are. I mean the advantage of having much more of it; for great wealth would accrue to their people and to themselves from a continual peace, from the enormous saving effected by the reduction of the military establishment with a multitude of fortresses and an enormous quantity of troops, which swallow up their revenues and become daily a heavier charge on their people and themselves. I know it would not be well for all sovereigns to disband all their troops and not to have any standing public force to stifle an unexpected rising or repulse a sudden invasion.* I know too that a contingent will have to be furnished for the confederation, both for the defence of the frontiers of Europe and for the upkeep of the confederative army which is intended to uphold when necessary the decrees of the diet. But when all these expenses have been met and the extraordinary expenses of war have been suppressed for ever, there would still remain more than half of the ordinary military expenditure to distribute between the relief of the subject and the coffers of the prince; so that the people would pay much less, whilst the prince, being much richer, would be in a position to encourage commerce, agriculture and the arts, and to found useful institutions which would further increase the wealth of his people as well as his own, and the state would be in a much more perfect state of safety than it could obtain by means of its armies and all that machinery of war which is incessantly exhausting it in the midst of peace.

It may be said perhaps that the frontier countries of Europe would then be in a more disadvantageous position and might have all the same to sustain wars with the Turks, the Corsairs of Africa, or with the Tartars.

To that I reply: (1)   That these countries are in the very same position today, and consequently it should not be quoted as a positive disadvantage to them, but only as one advantage the less, and an inevitable inconvenience to which their situation exposes them. (2) That, delivered from all anxiety on the European side, they would be in a much better position to resist outsiders. (3) That the suppression of all the fortresses of the interior of Europe and the cost of keeping them up would make it possible for the confederation to establish a large number on the frontiers without expense to the confederates. (4) That these fortresses, constructed, kept up, and garrisoned at the common expense, would be so many pledges and means of economy for the frontier powers whose territories they would defend. (5) That the troops of the confederation, distributed on the borders of Europe, would always be ready to repulse the aggressor. (6) That finally a body as

---

* Other objections present themselves; but as the author of the *Project* has not brought them forward, I have postponed them until my criticisms [the 'Judgement': see headnote].

formidable as the European Republic would take away from foreign countries the desire to attack any of its members, as the Germanic body, infinitely less powerful, is still enough so to make itself respected by its neighbours and usefully to protect all those princes who belong to it.

Again, it might be said that, if Europeans had no more wars among themselves, the art of war would fall gradually into oblivion, that the troops would lose their courage and their discipline, that there would be no more generals or soldiers, and that Europe would lie at the mercy of the first comer.

My reply is that one of two things would happen: either Europe's neighbours would attack and make war on her, or they would be afraid of the confederation and leave her in peace.

In the first case here are chances for cultivating military talent and genius and for training and forming the troops. The armies of the confederation would be in this respect the school of Europe. They would go to the frontier to learn about war; peace would reign in the heart of Europe; and by this means the advantages of both would be combined. Does anyone think that it is always necessary to be fighting at home to become warlike? Are Frenchmen less brave because the provinces of Touraine and Anjou do not make war on one another?

In the second case it is true that there would be no more training for war, but there would be no need. Why be trained for fighting if there is no one to fight? Which is the better, to cultivate a noxious art or to render it unnecessary? If a secret prescription for the enjoyment of perpetual health were available would there be any sense in rejecting it on the ground that it would deprive doctors of opportunities for gaining experience? This parallel helps us to see which of the two arts is the more beneficial in itself, and which best deserves to be kept up.

Let them not threaten us with sudden invasion; we know very well Europe has none to fear, and that this 'first comer' will never come. The days have gone by when irruptions of barbarians seemed to fall from the clouds. Ever since we have been able to cast an inquiring eye over the surface of the earth nothing can reach us which cannot be foreseen at a great distance. There is no power in the world which is now in a state to threaten the whole of Europe, and if one should ever arise, either there would be time to prepare, or at least we should be in a better state to resist it being united in one body, than if it were necessary suddenly to end longstanding quarrels and reunite in haste.

We have just seen that all the pretended inconveniences of the confederative state, when well weighed, come to nothing. We now ask if anyone in the world would dare to say as much of those inconveniences which result from the present method of settling differences between prince and prince by the right of the strongest, that is to say of the state of uncivilization and war which the absolute and mutual independence of all the sovereigns, in the imperfect society which reigns amongst them in Europe, necessarily engenders. That the reader may be in a better position to weigh these inconveniences I am going to sum them up in a few words which I shall leave him to investigate.

1. No rights assured but those of the strongest.
2. Continual and inevitable changes in the relations between the nations, which prevent anyone of them from retaining in its hands the power that it enjoys.
3. No perfect security so long as neighbours are not subdued or annihilated.
4. The general impossibility of reducing them to helplessness, seeing that while one enemy is being subjugated others appear on the scene.
5. Immense precautions and expense in always being in a state of defence.
6. Lack of power of defence during minorities [of royal heirs-apparent?] and rebellions, for when the state is divided who can support one of the parties against the other?
7. Unreliability of mutual pledges.
8. No hope of justice from others without immense expenses and losses which do not always obtain it, and for which the matter in dispute when gained seldom compensates.
9. The inevitable risking of one's territories and sometimes of one's life in pursuit of one's rights.
10. The necessity in spite of one's self of taking part in the quarrels of one's neighbours and of making war when one least desires it.
11. The interruption of commerce and the public revenues at the moment when they are most needful.

12. The continual danger from a powerful neighbour if one is weak, and from a coalition if one is strong.
13. Finally, the uselessness of wisdom where fortune holds sway; the continual distress of nations; enfeeblement of the state both in successes and reverses; complete impossibility of ever establishing a good government, counting on one's own possessions or making either one's self or others happy.

Let us also recapitulate the advantages of European arbitration for the princes of the confederation.

1. A complete assurance that their present and future quarrels will always be terminated without war; an assurance incomparably more useful to them than that of never having lawsuits would be to an individual.
2. Matters of dispute eliminated or reduced to a very small compass by the cancellation of all bygone claims which will compensate the nation for what they give up and confirm them in what they possess.
3. Entire and perpetual security of the person of the prince and of his family and of his territories and of the order of succession fixed by the laws of each country, both against the presumption of unjust and ambitious pretenders and against the revolts of rebel subjects.
4. Perfect certainty of the execution of all reciprocal engagements between prince and prince by the guarantee of the European Commonwealth.
5. Perfect and perpetual liberty and security of trade, both between state and state and for each state in distant lands.
6. Total and perpetual suppression of their extraordinary military expenditure by land and by sea in time of war, and considerable diminution of their ordinary expenditure in time of peace.
7. A marked progress in agriculture and population, in the wealth of the state, and in the revenues of the prince.
8. An opportunity for the promotion of all the institutions which can increase the glory and authority of the sovereign, the public resources, and the happiness of the people.

I leave as I have already said to the judgement of my readers the examination of all these articles, and the comparison of the state of peace which results from the confederation, with the state of war which results from the unsettled constitution of Europe.

If we have reasoned logically in the statement of this project, it has been demonstrated, first, that the establishment of perpetual peace wholly depends on the consent of sovereigns, and raises no other difficulty than their resistance to it; secondly, that this establishment would be useful to them in every way, and that even for the princes there is no comparison between the disadvantages and the advantages; in the third place, that it is reasonable to suppose that their wishes accord with their interests; and lastly that this institution once formed on the proposed plan, would be solid and durable, and would perfectly fulfil its object.

Certainly it does not follow that the sovereigns would adopt this project (who can answer for other people's intelligence?) but only that they would adopt it if they consulted their true interests; for the reader must observe that we have not supposed men to be such as they ought to be – good, generous, disinterested, and loving public good from motives of human sympathy – but such as they are, unjust, greedy, and preferring their own interests to everything else. The only thing we assume on their behalf is enough intelligence to see what is useful to themselves, and enough courage to achieve their own happiness. If, in spite of all this, this project is not carried into execution, it is not because it is chimerical, it is because men are crazy and because to be sane in the midst of madmen is a sort of folly.

TRANSLATOR'S NOTES

1. Rousseau means, of course, that the half-way stage between a state of nature and a unified world government has led to wars between nations even worse than the duels and private wars which national governments had suppressed.
2. Amphictyonic leagues existed in Greece from time immemorial. They were associations of neighbouring tribes or cities, made by Hellenes for the purpose of mutual intercourse and for the protection of a common temple or sanctuary. There were many such leagues of which the Delphic was the most important. The members registered a vow as recorded by Aechines (*The False Legation*, II.115): 'We will not destroy any city of the Amphictyons, nor cut off the supply of running water, either in war or peace, and if any member break this oath, we will make war upon him and destroy his cities, and if any member plunder the property of the god, or be privy to any such design, or make any plan to that effect, we will punish him with hand

and foot and voice and all our power.' A terrible curse was affixed to
the oath.

It will be seen that the germ of such organizations as the League of
Nations is to be found in the Amphictyonic Leagues.

The lucumo was a leader, apparently of a priestly character, among
the Etruscans. Each city had a lucumo and the power of the king,
who was elected for life, was inferior to that of the lucumo. Livy
(IV.23) mentions an Etrurian league. He records that the Veii and
Falisci, two members of the league, sent envoys to all the twelve
cities, asking them to convene a conference of the whole of Etruria at
the temple of Voltumna.

Rousseau seems to have confused the lucumones (leaders) with the
Concilium.

See Macaulay, 'Horatius':

> And plainly and more plainly
> Now might the burghers know,
> By port and vest, by horse and crest,
> Each warlike Lucumo.

The Latin League existed from very early times, under the traditional leadership of Alba, the most ancient of the Latin cantons.
There were thirty cities in the League. Mommsen [*The History of
Rome*, 1907, I, 50]: 'The rendezvous of this union was . . . the "Latin
festival" (*feriae Latinae*), at which, on the "Mount of Alba" (*Mons
Albanus, Monte Cavo*), upon a day annually appointed by the chief
magistrate for the purpose, an ox was offered in sacrifice by the
assembled Latin stock to the "Latin God" (*Jupiter Latinaris*).' The
Latin League, however, seems to have been almost entirely a military
league, without exercising any humanizing influence, such as those
practised by the amphictyonic.

See again Macaulay, 'The Battle of Lake Regillus':

> How the Lake Regillus
> Bubbled with crimson foam,
> What time the Thirty Cities
> Came forth to war on Rome.

In fact, the Gauls had not much federal organization, although
they made attempts to league their cantons together when attacked
by Caesar. This want of unity led to their rapid conquest. As Tacitus
says in the *Agricola*, 'While the individual groups fight, the whole are
conquered' (*Dum singuli pugnant, universi vincuntur*).

The Achaean League is here correctly described by Rousseau.
'Early in the third century BC, the League struggled unsuccessfully
against Antigonus Gonatas.' Grote says [*The History of Greece*, 1906,
XII, 301]: 'The Achaean league . . . developed itself afterwards as a
renovated sprout from the ruined tree of Grecian liberty, though
never attaining to anything better than a feeble and punny life, nor
capable of sustaining itself without foreign aid.'

As regards the German, Swiss, and French assemblies, they are so closely interwoven with the national life that a study of their history is equivalent to a study of the history of the respective countries.

3. The Emperor Claudius, in a speech which has been preserved, brought forward a motion in the Senate for admitting Gaulish chiefs to senatorial rank.

4. Theodosius II (d. 450 AD) was less celebrated than his grandfather, Theodosius the Great. But he is memorable for having published the Codex Theodosianus in 438, which is a collection of imperial contributions to guide the action of public officials. This is one of our main sources of information about the government of the Empire in the fifth century.

   Justinian's memorable *Corpus Juris* was given the effect of law in 534 AD. Gibbon says (*Decline and Fall of the Roman Empire*, ch. 44): 'The vain titles of the victories of Justinian are crumbled into dust; but the name of the legislator is inscribed on a fair and everlasting monument. Under his reign, and by his care, the civil jurisprudence was digested in the immortal works of the *Code*, the *Pandects*, and the *Institutes*: the public reason of the Romans has been silently or studiously transfused into the domestic institutions of Europe; and the laws of Justinian still command the respect or obedience of independent nations.'

5. Bartholus (1314–1357) was one of the most esteemed of Italian civil jurists. He lectured at Perugia, which he raised to great eminence among law schools. He won much fame by his *Commentaries on the Code of Justinian.*

6. 'The resignation of all the eastern conquests of Trajan was the first measure of his reign. He restored to the Parthians the election of an independent sovereign; withdrew the Roman garrisons from the provinces of Armenia, Mesopotamia, and Assyria; and in compliance with the precepts of Augustus, once more established the Euphrates as the frontier of the empire' (Gibbon, *Decline*, ch. 1).

II IMMANUEL KANT, *ETERNAL PEACE*

The German philosopher Immanuel Kant (1724–1804) was strongly influenced by the political philosophy of Jean-Jacques Rousseau. He possibly took Rousseau's *Project of Perpetual Peace* (see preceding section) even more seriously than Rousseau took the *Project* himself. At any rate, the present essay, published in 1795, seems both to take the Saint-Pierre plan for a European peace council as a starting-point, and to go beyond that peace plan. Kant's proposal differs sharply from that presented by Rousseau, not only in so far as it applies only to democratically oriented nations ('republics'), but also in so far as it works out an institutionalized peacekeeping agency in much more elaborate detail. President Wilson's League of Nations and its successor, the United Nations, are close in concept to the 'union of nations' proposed by Kant. Kant's 'secret article' (concerning an advisory role for philosophers in government) probably has no more chance for being accepted than did Plato's proposal of a 'philosopher king' millennia before. However, some of his other proposals seem to be particularly relevant to the contemporary international situation: for instance, the proposal regarding the limitation of the national debt, in view of the function of budget deficits (even deficits produced by defence spending) in generating the conditions for war.

It is noteworthy that, as this book is going to press, President Mitterand of France and Chancellor Kohl of West Germany are spearheading a movement to create an European federation. If this federation were established and became a 'United States of Europe', it would be a fulfilment of the concept of union propounded by Kant in the present essay, and also possibly a step in the direction of the larger goal – a world federation – adumbrated by Kant, but spelled out more concretely in the twentieth century (see sections III and IV of this chapter).

The translation of Kant's essay reprinted below is that by Carl Friedrich in his *Inevitable Peace* (Cambridge, Mass.: Harvard University Press, 1948), to which it forms the Appendix. The text is reprinted here minus Kant's own appendix. Kant's notes are labelled 'a', 'b', etc., to distinguish them from Friedrich's (numbered '1', '2', etc.). Friedrich's interpolations in Kant's notes and text appear in square brackets. Both sets of notes are placed at the end of the section.

'To Eternal Peace'

Whether the above satirical inscription, once put by a certain Dutch innkeeper on his signboard on which a graveyard was painted, holds of men in general, or particularly of the heads of states who are never sated with war, or perhaps only of those philosophers who are dreaming that sweet dream of peace, may remain undecided. However, in presenting his ideas, the author of the present essay makes one condition. The practical statesman should not, in case of a controversy with the political theorist, suspect that any danger to the state lurks behind the opinions which such a theorist ventures honestly and openly to express. Consistency demands this of the practical statesman, for he assumes a haughty air and looks down upon the theorist with great self-satisfaction as a mere theorizer whose impractical ideas can bring no danger to the state, since the state must be founded on principles derived from experience. The worldly-wise statesman may therefore, without giving himself great concern, allow the theorizer to throw his eleven bowling-balls all at once. By this 'saving clause' the author of this essay knows himself protected in the best manner possible against all malicious interpretation.

First Section, which contains the preliminary articles of an eternal peace between states.

1 *No treaty of peace shall be held to be such, which is made with the secret reservation of the material for a future war.*

For, in that event, it would be a mere truce, a postponement of hostilities, not *peace*. Peace means the end of all hostilities, and to attach to it the adjective 'eternal' is a pleonasm which at once arouses suspicion. The pre-existing reasons for a future war, including those not at the time known even to the contracting parties, are all of them obliterated by a genuine treaty of peace; no search of documents, no matter how acute, shall resurrect them from the archives. It is Jesuitical casuistry to make a mental reservation that there might be old claims to be brought forward in the future, of which neither party at the time cares to make mention, because both are too much exhausted to continue the war, but which they intend to assert at the first favourable opportunity. Such a procedure, when looked at in its true character, must be considered beneath the dignity of rulers; and so must the willingness to attempt such legal claims be held unworthy of a minister of state.

But, if enlightened notions of political wisdom assume the true honour of the state to consist in the continual increase of power by any and every means, such a judgement will, of course, evidently seem academic and pedantic.

2 *No state having an independent existence, whether it be small or great, may be acquired by another state, through inheritance, exchange, purchase, or gift.*

A state is not a possession (*patrimonium*) like the soil on which it has a seat. It is a society of men, which no one but they themselves is called upon to command or to dispose of. Since, like a tree, such a state has its own roots, to incorporate it as a graft into another state is to take away its existence as a moral person and to make of it a thing. This contradicts the idea of the original contract, without which no right over a people can even be conceived. Everybody knows into what danger, even in the most recent times, the supposed right of thus acquiring states has brought Europe. Other parts of the world have never known such a practice. But in Europe states can even marry each other. On the one hand, this is a new kind of industry, a way of making oneself predominant through family connections without any special effort; on the other, it is a way of extending territorial possessions. The letting out of troops of one state to another against an enemy not common to the two is in the same class. The subjects are thus used and consumed like things to be handled at will.

3   *Standing armies shall gradually disappear.*

Standing armies incessantly threaten other states with war by their readiness to be prepared for war. States are thus stimulated to outdo one another in number of armed men without limit. Through the expense thus occasioned peace finally becomes more burdensome than a brief war. These armies are thus the cause of wars of aggression, undertaken in order that this burden may be thrown off. In addition to this, the hiring of men to kill and be killed, an employment of them as mere machines and tools in the hands of another (the states), cannot be reconciled with the rights of humanity as represented in our own person. The case is entirely different where the citizens of a state voluntarily[1] drill themselves and their fatherland against attacks from without. It would be exactly the same with the accumulation of a war fund if the difficulty of ascertaining the amount of the fund accumulated did not work a counter effect. Looked upon by other states as a threat of war, a big fund would lead to their anticipating such a war by making an attack themselves, because of the three powers – the power of the army, the power of alliance, and the power of money – the last might well be considered the most reliable instrument of war.

4   *No debts shall be contracted in connection with the foreign affairs of the state.*

The obtaining of money, either from without or from within the state, for purposes of internal development – the improvement of highways, the establishment of new settlements, the storing of surplus for years of crop failure, etc. – need create no suspicion. Foreign debts may be contracted for this purpose. But, as an instrument of the struggle between the powers, a credit system of debts endlessly growing though always safe against immediate demand (the demand for payment not being made by all the creditors at the same time) – such a system, the ingenious invention of a trading people in this century, constitutes a dangerous money power. It is a resource for carrying on war which surpasses the resources of all other states taken together. It can only be exhausted through a possible deficit of the taxes, which may be long kept off through the increase in commerce brought about by the stimulating influence of the loans on industry and trade. The facility thus afforded of making war, coupled with the apparently innate inclination thereto of those possessing power, is a great obstacle in the way of eternal peace. Such loans, therefore, must be forbidden by a preliminary article – all the more because the finally unavoidable bankruptcy of such a state must involve many other states without their responsibility in the disaster, thus inflicting upon them a public injury. Consequently, other states are at least justified in entering into an alliance against such a state and its pretensions.

5   *No state shall interfere by force in the constitution and government of another state.*

For what could justify it in taking such action? Could perhaps some offence do it which that state gives to the subjects of another? Such a state ought rather to serve as a warning, because of the example of the evils which a people brings upon itself by its lawlessness. In general, the bad example given by one free person to another (as a *scandalum acceptum*) is no violation of the latter's rights. The case would be different if a state because of internal dissension should be split into two parts, each of which, while constituting a separate state, should lay claim to the whole. An outside state, if it should render assistance to one of these, could not be charged with interfering in the constitution of another state, as that state would then be in a condition of anarchy. But as long as this inner strife was not decided, the interference of outside powers would be a trespass on the rights of an independent people struggling only with its own inner weakness. This interference would be an actual offence which would so far tend to render the autonomy of all states insecure.

6   *No state at war with another shall permit such acts of warfare as must make mutual confidence impossible in time of future peace: such as the employment of assassins, of poisoners, the violation of articles of surrender, the instigation of treason in the state against which it is making war, etc.*

These are dishonourable stratagems. Some sort of confidence in an enemy's frame of mind must remain even in time of war, for otherwise no peace could be concluded, and the conflict would become a war of extermination. For after all, war is only the regrettable instrument of asserting one's right by force in the primitive state of nature where there exists no court to decide in accordance with law. In this state neither party can be declared an unjust enemy, for this presupposes a court decision. The outcome of the fight, as in the case of a so-called 'judgement of God', decides on whose side the right is. Between states no war of punishment can be conceived, because between them there is no relation of superior and subordinate.

From this it follows that a war of extermination, in which destruction may come to both parties at the same time, and thus to all rights too, would allow eternal peace only upon the graveyard of the whole human race. Such a war, therefore, as well as the use of the means which might be employed in it, is wholly forbidden.

But that the methods of war mentioned above inevitably lead to such a result is clear from the fact that such hellish arts, which are in themselves degrading, when once brought into use do not continue long within the limits of war but are continued in time of peace, and thus the purpose of the peace is completely frustrated. A good example is furnished by the employment of spies, in which only the dishonourableness of others (which unfortunately cannot be exterminated) is taken advantage of.

Although all the laws above laid down would objectively – that is, in the intention of the powers – be negative laws (*leges prohibitivae*), yet some of them are strict laws, which are valid without consideration of the circumstances. They insist that the abuse complained of be abolished at once. Such are our rules number 1, 5, and 6. The others, namely rules number 2, 3, and 4, though not meant to be permitting exception from the 'rule of law', yet allow for a good deal of subjective discretion in respect to the application of the rules. They permit delay in execution without their purpose being lost sight of. The purpose, however, does not admit of delay till doomsday – 'to the Greek Calends', as Augustus was wont to say. The restitution, for example, to certain states of the freedom of which they have been deprived, contrary to our second article, must not be indefinitely put off. The delay is not meant to prevent restitution, but to avoid undue haste which might be contrary to the intrinsic purpose. For the prohibition laid down by the article relates only to the mode of acquisition, which is not to be allowed to continue, but it does not relate to the present state of possessions. This present state, though not providing the needed just title, yet was held to be legitimate at the time of the supposed acquisition, according to the then current public opinion.

Second section, which contains the definitive articles for eternal peace among states

The state of peace among men who live alongside each other is no state of nature (*status naturalis*). [The latter] is a state of war which constantly threatens even if it is not actually in progress. Therefore the state of peace must be *founded*; for the mere omission of the threat of war is no security of peace, and consequently a neighbour may treat his neighbour as an enemy unless he has guaranteed such security to him, which can only happen within a state of law.[a]

FIRST DEFINITIVE ARTICLE OF THE ETERNAL PEACE. *The civil constitution in each state should be republican.*

A republican constitution is a constitution which is founded upon three principles. First, the principle of the *freedom* of all members of a society as men. Second, the principle of the *dependence* of all upon a single common legislation as subjects, and third, the principle of the *equality* of all as *citizens*. This is the only constitution which is derived from the idea of an original contract upon which all rightful legislation of a nation must be based.

This republican constitution is therefore, as far as law is concerned, the one which underlies every kind of civil constitution, and the question which we are now facing is, whether this is also the only one which can lead to eternal peace.

The answer is that the republican constitution does offer the prospect of the desired purpose, that is to say, eternal peace, and the reason is as follows: If, as is necessarily the case under the constitution, the consent of the citizens is required in order to decide whether there should be war or not, nothing is more natural than that those who would have to decide to undergo all the deprivations of war will very much hesitate to start such an evil game. For the deprivations are many, such as fighting oneself, paying for the cost of the war out of one's own possessions, and repairing the devastation which it costs, and to top all the evils there remains a burden of debts which embitters the peace and can never be paid off on account of approaching new wars. By contrast, under a constitution where the subject is not a citizen and which is therefore not republican, it is the easiest thing in the world to start a war. The head of the state is not a fellow citizen but owner of the state, who loses none of his banquets, hunting-parties, pleasure castles, festivities, etc. Hence he will resolve upon war as a kind of amusement on very insignificant grounds and will leave the justification to his diplomats, who are always ready to lend it an air of propriety.

It is important not to confuse the republican constitution with the democratic one as is commonly done. The following may be noted. The forms of a state (*civitas*) may be classified according to the difference of the persons who possess the highest authority, or they may be classified according to the method by which the people are governed by their rulers, who ever they may be. The first method is properly called the form of rulership (*forma imperii*).[2] Only three such forms are conceivable; for either *one*, or a *few* associated with each other, or all who together constitute civil society possess the power to rule (*autocracy, aristocracy,* and *democracy* – the power of princes, of the nobility, and of the people).

The second method is the form of government (*forma regiminis*) and relates to the way in which the state employs its sovereign power – the constitution, which is an act of the general will by which a mass becomes a nation. The form of government in this case is either *republican* or *despotic*. Republicanism means the constitutional principle according to which the executive power (the government [*Regierung*]) is separated from the legislative power. *Despotism* exists when the state arbitrarily executes the laws which it has itself made; in other words, where the public will is treated by the prince as if it were his private will.

Among the three forms of state (or rulership), that of *democracy* is necessarily a *despotism* in the specific meaning of the word, because it establishes an executive power where all may decide regarding one and hence against one who does not agree, so that all are nevertheless not all – a situation which implies a contradiction of the general will with itself and with freedom. For all forms of government which are not *representative* are essentially *without form*, because the legislative cannot at the same time and in the same person be the executor of the legislative will; just as the general proposition in logical reasoning cannot at the same time be the specific judgement which falls under the general rule.[3] The other two forms of rulership [*Staatsverfassung*] are defective also in so far as they give a chance to this (despotic) form of government. But it is at least possible that they provide a method of governing which is in accord with the *spirit* of a representative system. Frederick II *said* at least that he was merely the highest servant of the state – while the democratic system makes this impossible, because all want to be ruler.

It is therefore possible to say that the smallest number of truly representative rulers approximates most closely to the possibility of a republicanism and may be expected to reach it eventually by gradual reforms. Such an evolution is harder in an aristocracy than in a monarchy, while in a democracy it is impossible to achieve this kind of constitution – which is the only constitution perfectly in accord with law and right [*Recht*] – except through a revolution.[b]

The people are very much more concerned with the form of government in this sense than with the form of rulership [*Staatsform*], although a good deal depends upon the latter's adequacy to realize the former's end. But if the form of government is to be appropriate to the idea of law and right, it requires the representative system. For only in this system is a republican form of government possible. Without it the form of government is despotic and violent, whatever the constitution may be.

None of the ancient, so-called republics knew this representative system, and hence they were bound to dissolve into despotism, which is the more bearable under the rule of a single man.

SECOND DEFINITIVE ARTICLE OF THE ETERNAL PEACE. *The law of nations (Völkerrecht) should be based upon a* federalism *of free states.*

Nations may be considered like individual men which hurt each other in the state of nature, when they are not subject to laws, by their very propinquity. Therefore each, for the sake of security, may demand and should demand of the other to enter with him into a constitution similar to the civil one where the right of each may be secured. This would be a *union of nations* [*Völkerbund*] which would not necessarily have to be a *state of nations* [*Völkerstaat*]. A

state of nations contains a contradiction, for every state involves
the relation of a superior (legislature) to a subordinate (the subject
people), and many nations would, in a single state, constitute only
one nation, which is contradictory since we are here considering
the right of nations toward each other as long as they constitute
different states and are not joined together into one.

We look with deep aversion upon the way primitive peoples are
attached to their lawless liberty – a liberty which enables them to
fight incessantly rather than subject themselves to the restraint of
the law to be established by themselves; in short, to prefer wild
freedom to a reasonable one. We look upon such an attitude as
raw, uncivilized, and an animalic degradation of humanity. Therefore, one should think, civilized peoples (each united in a state)
would hasten to get away from such a depraved state as soon as
possible. Instead, each *state* insists upon seeing the essence of its
majesty (for popular majesty is a paradox) in this, that it is not
subject to any external coercion. The lustre of its ruler consists in
this, that many thousands are at his disposal to be sacrificed for a
cause which is of no concern to them, while he himself is not
exposed to any danger. Thus a Bulgarian Prince answered the
Emperor who good naturedly wanted to settle their quarrel by a
duel: 'A smith who has prongs won't get the hot iron out of the fire
with his bare hands.' The difference between the European savages and those in America is primarily this, that while some of the
latter eat their enemies, the former know how better to employ
their defeated foe than to feast on them – the Europeans rather
increase the number of subjects, that is the number of tools for
more extended wars.

In view of the evil nature of man, which can be observed clearly
in the free relation between nations (while in a civil and legal state
it is covered by governmental coercion), it is surprising that the
word *law* [*Recht*] has not been entirely banned from the politics of
war as pedantic, and that no state has been bold enough to declare
itself publicly as of this opinion. For people in *justifying* an aggressive war still cite HUGO GROTIUS, PUFENDORF, VATTEL and others
(all of them miserable consolers). This is done, although their code
of norms, whether stated philosophically or juristically, does not
have the least *legal* force; nor can it have such force, since states as
such are not subject to a common external coercion. There is not a
single case known in which a state has been persuaded by argu-

ments reinforced by the testimony of such weighty men to desist from its aggressive design.

This homage which every state renders the concept of law (at least in words) seems to prove that there exists in man a greater moral quality (although at present a dormant one), to try and master the evil element in him (which he cannot deny), and to hope for this in others. Otherwise the words *law* and *right* would never occur to states which intend to fight with each other, unless it were for the purpose of mocking them, like the Gallic prince who declared: 'It is the advantage which nature has given the stronger over the weaker that the latter ought to obey the former.'

In short, the manner in which states seek their rights can never be a suit before a court, but only war. However, war and its successful conclusion, *victory*, does not decide what is law and what right. A *peace treaty* puts an end to a particular war, but not to the state of war which consists in finding ever new pretexts for starting a new one. Nor can this be declared strictly unjust because in this condition each is the judge in his own cause. Yet it cannot be maintained that states under the law of nations are subject to the same rule that is valid for individual men in the lawless state of nature: 'that they ought to leave this state'. For states have internally a legal constitution and hence [their citizens] have outgrown the coercion of others who might desire to put them under a broadened legal constitution conceived in terms of their own legal norms. Nevertheless, reason speaking from the throne of the highest legislative power condemns war as a method of finding what is right. Reason makes [the achievement of] the state of peace a direct duty, and such a state of peace cannot be established or maintained without a treaty of the nations among themselves. Therefore there must exist a union of a particular kind which we may call the *pacific union* (*foedus pacificum*) which would be distinguished from a *peace treaty* (*pactum pacis*) by the fact that the latter tries to end merely *one* war, while the former tries to end *all* wars for ever. This union is not directed toward the securing of some additional power of the state, but merely toward maintaining and making secure the *freedom* of each state by and for itself and at the same time of the other states thus allied with each other. And yet, these states will not subject themselves (as do men in the state of nature) to laws and to the enforcement of such laws.

It can be demonstrated that this idea of *federalization* possesses objective reality, that it can be realized by a gradual extension to all states, leading to eternal peace. For if good fortune brings it to pass that a powerful and enlightened people develops a republican form of government which by nature is inclined toward peace, then such a republic will provide the central core for the federal union of other states. For.they can join this republic and can thus make secure among themselves the state of peace according to the idea of a law of nations, and can gradually extend themselves by additional connections of this sort.

It is possible to imagine that a people says: 'There shall be no war amongst us; for we want to form a state, i.e., to establish for ourselves a highest legislative, executive, and juridical power which peacefully settles our conflicts.' But if this state says: 'There shall be no war between myself and other states, although I do not recognize a highest legislative authority which secures my right for me and for which I secure its right', it is not easy to comprehend upon what ground I should place my confidence in my right, unless it be a substitute [*Surrogat*] for the civil social contracts, namely, a free federation. Reason must necessarily connect such a federation with the concept of a law of nations, if authority is to be conceived in such terms.

On the other hand, a concept of the law of nations as a right *to make* war is meaningless; for it is supposed to be a right to determine what is right not according to external laws limiting the freedom of each individual, but by force and according to one-sided maxims. Unless we are ready to accept this meaning: that it serves people who have such views quite right if they exhaust each other and thus find eternal peace in the wide grave which covers all the atrocities of violence together with its perpetrators. For states in their relation to each other there cannot, according to reason, be any other way to get away from the lawless state which contains nothing but war than to give up (just like individual men) their wild and lawless freedom, to accept public and enforceable laws, and thus to form a constantly growing world *state of all nations* (*civitas gentium*) which finally would comprise all nations. But states do not want this, as not in keeping with their idea of a law of nations, and thus they reject in fact what is true in theory. Therefore, unless all is to be lost, the positive idea of a *world republic* must be replaced by the negative substitute of a *union* of nations which maintains itself, prevents wars, and steadily expands. Only such a union may under existing conditions stem the tide of the law-evading, bellicose propensities in man, but unfortunately subject to the constant danger of their eruption (*furor impius intus – fremit horridus ore cruento*. VIRGIL).

THIRD DEFINITIVE ARTICLE OF THE ETERNAL PEACE. *The cosmopolitan or world law shall be limited to conditions of a universal hospitality.*

We are speaking in this as well as in the other articles not of philanthropy, but of *law*. Therefore *hospitality* (good neighbourliness) means the right of a foreigner not to be treated with hostility when he arrives upon the soil of another. The native may reject the foreigner if it can be done without his perishing, but as long as he stays peaceful, he must not treat him hostilely. It is not the right of becoming a permanent guest [*Gastrecht*] which the foreigner may request, for a special beneficial treaty would be required to make him a fellow inhabitant [*Hausgenosse*] for a certain period. But it is the right to visit [*Besuchsrecht*] which belongs to all men – the right belonging to all men to offer their society on account of the common possession of the surface of the earth. Since it is a globe, they cannot disperse infinitely, but must tolerate each other. No man has a greater fundamental right to occupy a particular spot than any other.

Uninhabitable parts of the earth's surface, the oceans and deserts, divide this community. But *ship* or *camel* (the ship of the desert) enable men to approach each other across these no-man's regions, and thus to use the right of the common *surface* which belongs to all men together, as a basis of possible intercourse. The inhospitable ways of coastal regions, such as the Barbary Coast, where they rob ships in adjoining seas or make stranded seamen into slaves, is contrary to natural law, as are the similarly inhospitable ways of the deserts and their Bedouins who look upon the approach (of a foreigner) as giving them a right to plunder him. But the right of hospitality, the right, that is, of foreign guests, does not extend further than to the conditions which enable them to attempt the developing of intercourse with the old inhabitants.

In this way, remote parts of the world can enter into relationships which eventually become public and legal and thereby may bring mankind ever nearer to an eventual world constitution.

If one compares with this requirement the *inhospitable* conduct of the civilized, especially of the trading, nations of our continent, the injustice which they display in their *visits* to foreign countries and peoples goes terribly far. They simply identify visiting with *conquest*. America, the lands of the Negroes, the Spice Islands, the Cape of South Africa, etc., were countries that belonged to nobody, for the inhabitants counted for nothing. In East India (Hindustan) they brought in foreign mercenaries, under the pretence of merely establishing trading-ports. These mercenary troops brought suppression of the natives, inciting the several states of India to extended wars against each other. They brought famine, sedition, treason and the rest of the evils which weigh down mankind.

China[4] and Japan, who had made an attempt to get along with such guests, have wisely allowed only contact, but not settlement – and Japan has further wisely restricted this privilege to the Dutch only, whom they exclude, like prisoners, from community with the natives. The worst (or viewed from the standpoint of a moral judge the best) is that the European nations are not even able to enjoy this violence. All these trading-companies are on the point of an approaching collapse; the sugar islands, which are the seat of the most cruel and systematic slavery, do not produce a yield – except in the form of raising recruits for navies; thus they in turn serve the conduct of war – wars of powers which make much ado about their piety and who want themselves to be considered among the morally elect, while in fact they consume [the fruits of] injustice like water.

The narrower or wider community of all nations on earth has in fact progressed so far that a violation of law and right in one place is felt in *all* others. Hence the idea of a cosmopolitan or world law is not a fantastic and utopian way of looking at law, but a necessary completion of the unwritten code of constitutional and international law to make it a public law of mankind. Only under this condition can we flatter ourselves that we are continually approaching eternal peace.

First addition. On the guarantee of eternal peace

No one less than the great artist *nature* (*natura daedala rerum*) offers such a *guarantee*. Nature's mechanical course evidently reveals a teleology: to produce harmony from the very disharmony of men even against their will. If this teleology and the laws that effect it is believed to be like an unknown cause compelling us, it is called *fate.* But if it is considered in the light of its usefulness for the evolution of the world, it will be called *providence* – a cause which, responding to a deep wisdom, is directed toward a higher goal, the objective final end [*Endzweck*] of mankind which predetermines this evolution.[5] We do not really *observe* this providence in the artifices of nature, nor can we *deduce* it from them. But we can and must *add this thought* (as in all relations of the form of things to ends in general), in order to form any kind of conception of its possibility. We do this in analogy to human artifices.[6] The relation and integration of these factors into the end (the moral one) which reason directly prescribes is very sublime in *theory*, but is axiomatic and well-founded in practice, e.g. in regard to the concept of a duty toward eternal peace which that mechanism promotes.

When one is dealing as at present with theory (and not with religion), the use of the word *'nature'* is more appropriate in view of the limits of human reason which must stay within the limits of possible experience as far as the relation of effects to their causes is concerned. It is also *more modest* than the expression *'providence'*, especially a providence understandable to us; for by talking of providence we are arrogantly putting the wings of Icarus on our shoulders as if to get closer to the secret of its unfathomable purpose.

But before we ascertain more specifically how the guarantee is worked out, it is necessary to explore the situation which nature has created for those who are actors upon its great stage, and which in the last analysis necessitates its guarantee of peace. Only after that can we see how nature provides this guarantee.

Nature's provisional arrangement consists in the following: (1) she has seen to it that human beings can live in all the regions where they are settled; (2) she has by war driven them everywhere, even into the most inhospitable regions, in order to populate them; (3) she has forced them by war to enter into more or less legal relationships. It is marvellous to notice that in the cold wastes of the Arctic Sea some mosses grow which the *Reindeer* scratches out of the snow thus being enabled to serve as food or as a draft animal for the Samoyeds. Such ends become even more apparent when one discovers that furred animals on the shores of the Arctic Sea, walruses and whales provide food through their meat and heat through their fat for the inhabitants. But nature's care causes the greatest admiration when we find that drift wood, the origin of which is not well known, is carried to these regions, since without this material the inhabitants could neither build boats and weapons, nor huts in which to dwell. In that situation they seem to be sufficiently occupied with war against the animals to live peacefully with each other.

But it was probably war which *drove* the inhabitants to these places. The first *instrument of warfare* among all the animals which man during the time of populating the earth learned to tame and to domesticate was the *horse*; for the elephant belongs to a later time, when established states made greater luxury possible. The same is true of the culture of certain kinds of grasses, now called *grain*, the original form of which we no longer know, as well as of multiplying and refining of fruit trees by transplanting and grafting – in Europe perhaps only two species, the wild apples and wild pears. Such achievements could take place only in established states with fixed property in real estate. Before this men had progressed from the lawless freedom of *hunting*,[c] fishing and sheep-herding to cultivating the land. After that *salt* and *iron* were discovered, perhaps the first articles of trade between nations which were in demand everywhere, through which they were first brought into a *peaceful relationship* with each other. This in turn brought them into understanding, community, and peaceful relations with the more remote nations.

Nature, by providing that men *can* live everywhere on earth, has at the same time despotically wanted that they *should* live everywhere, even against their inclination. This 'should' does not presuppose a duty which obliged them to do it by a moral law. Instead, nature chose war to bring this about.

We observe peoples which by their common language reveal their common ancestry, such as the *Samoyeds* on the Arctic Sea and a people of similar language, about two hundred miles away, in the Altaic Mountains. Between those two a Mongolian, horse-riding and hence belligerent, tribe have wedged themselves in, driving one part of these people far away, and the rest into the most inhospitable regions of ice and snow, where they surely would not have gone by choice.

In the same manner the Finns in the northernmost part of Europe, called the Lapps, were separated from the Hungarians to whom they are related in their language by intruding Gothic and Sarmatian tribes. And what could have driven the Eskimos in the North, and the Pescheras in the South of America as far as it did, except war which nature uses everywhere as a means for populating the earth? War itself does not require a special motivation, since it appears to be grafted upon human nature. It is even considered something noble for which man is inspired by the love of honour, without selfish motives. This martial courage is judged by American savages, and European ones in feudal times, to be of great intrinsic value not only *when* there is a *war* (which is equitable), but also so *that* there may be war. Consequently war is started merely to show martial courage, and war itself invested with an inner *dignity*. Even philosophers will praise war as ennobling mankind, forgetting the Greek who said: 'War is bad in that it begets more evil people than it kills.' [So] much about what nature does in pursuit of its own purpose in regard to mankind as a species of animal.

Now we face the question which concerns the essential point in accomplishing eternal peace: what does nature do in relation to the end which man's reason imposes as a duty, in order to favour thus his *moral intent*? In other words: how does nature guarantee that what man ought to do according to the laws of freedom, but does not do, will be made secure regardless of this freedom by a compulsion of nature which forces him to do it? The question presents itself in all three relations: *constitutional* law, *international* law, and cosmopolitan or world law. – And if I say of nature: she wants this or that to take place, it does not mean that she imposes a *duty* to do it – for that only the non-compulsory practical reason can do – but it means that nature itself does it, whether we want it or not (*fata volentem ducunt, nolentem trahunt*).

1. If internal conflicts did not compel a people to submit itself to the compulsion of public laws, external wars would do it. According to the previously mentioned arrangement of nature, a people discovers a neighbouring people who are pushing it, against which it must form itself into a *state* in order to be prepared as a *power* against its enemy. Now the *republican* constitution is the only one which is fully adequate to the right of man, but it is also the hardest to establish, and even harder to maintain. Therefore many insist that it would have to be a state of angels, because men with their selfish propensities are incapable of so sublime a constitution. But now nature comes to the aid of this revered, but practically ineffectual general will which is founded in reason. It does this by the selfish propensities themselves, so that it is only necessary to

organize the state well (which is indeed within the ability of man), and to direct these forces against each other in such wise that one balances the other in its devastating effect, or even suspends it. Consequently the result for reason is as if both selfish forces were non-existent. Thus man, although not a morally good man, is compelled to be a good citizen. The problem of establishing a state is solvable even for a people of devils, if only they have intelligence, though this may sound harsh. The problem may be stated thus: 'To organize a group of rational beings who demand general laws for their survival, but of whom each inclines toward exempting himself, and to establish their constitution in such a way that, in spite of the fact that their private attitudes are opposed, these private attitudes mutually impede each other in such a manner that the public behaviour [of the rational beings] is the same as if they did not have such evil attitudes.' Such a problem *must* be solvable. For it is not the moral perfection of mankind, but merely the mechanism of nature, which this task seeks to know how to use in order to arrange the conflict of unpacific attitudes in a given people in such a way that they impel each other to submit themselves to compulsory laws and thus bring about the state of peace in which such laws are enforced. It is possible to observe this in the actually existing, although imperfectly organized states. They approach in external conduct closely to what the idea of law prescribes, although an inner morality is certainly not the cause of it (just as we should not expect a good constitution from such morality, but rather from such a constitution the good moral development of a people). These existing states show that the mechanism of [human] nature, with its selfish propensities which naturally counteract each other, can be employed by reason as a means. Thus reason's real purpose may be realized, namely, to provide a field for the operation of legal rules whereby to make secure internal and external peace, as far as the state is concerned. – In short, we can say that nature *wants* irresistibly that law achieve superior force. If one neglects to do this, it will be accomplished anyhow, albeit with much inconvenience. 'If you bend the stick too much, it breaks; and he who wants too much, wants nothing' (Bouterwek).

2. The idea of a law of nations presupposes the separate existence of many states which are independent of each other. Such a situation constitutes in and by itself a state of war, unless a

federative union of these states prevents the outbreak of hostilities. Yet such a situation is from the standpoint of reason better than the complete merging of all these states in one of them which over-powers them and is thereby in turn transformed into a universal monarchy. This is so, because the laws lose more and more of their effectiveness as the government increases in size, and the resulting soulless despotism is plunged into anarchy after having extermi-nated all the germs of good [in man]. Still, it is the desire of every state (or of its ruler) to enter into a permanent state of peace by ruling if possible the entire world. But *nature* has decreed differ-ently. – Nature employs two means to keep peoples from being mixed and to differentiate them, the difference of *language* and of *religion*.[d] These differences occasion the inclination toward mutual hatred and the excuse for war; yet at the same time they lead, as culture increases and men gradually come closer together, toward a greater agreement on principles for peace and understanding. Such peace and understanding is not brought about and made secure by the weakening of all other forces (as it would be under the aforementioned despotism and its graveyard of freedom), but by balancing these forces in a lively competition.

3. Just as nature wisely separates the nations which the will of each state would like to unite under its sway either by cunning or by force, and even in keeping with the reasoning of the law of nations, so also nature unites nations which the concept of a cosmopolitan or world law would not have protected from vio-lence and war, and it does this by mutual self-interest. It is the *spirit of commerce* which cannot coexist with war, and which sooner or later takes hold of every nation. For, since the money power is perhaps the most reliable among all the powers subordinate to the state's power, states find themselves impelled (though hardly by moral compulsion) to promote the noble peace and to try to avert war by mediation whenever it threatens to break out anywhere in the world. It is as if states were constantly leagued for this pur-pose; for great leagues *for* the purpose of making war can only come about very rarely and can succeed even more rarely. – In this way nature guarantees lasting peace by the mechanism of human inclinations; however the certainty [that this will come to pass] is not sufficient to *predict* such a future (theoretically). But for practi-cal purposes the certainty suffices and makes it one's duty to work toward this (not simply chimerical) state.

Second Addition. A secret article concerning eternal peace

A secret article in negotiations pertaining to *public* law is a contradiction objectively, i.e. as regards its substance or content; subjectively, however, i.e. as regards the quality of the person which formulates the article, secrecy may occur when such a person hesitates to declare himself publicly as the author thereof.

The sole article of this kind [in the treaty on eternal peace] is contained in the following sentence: *the maxims of the philosophers concerning the conditions of the possibility of public peace shall be consulted by the states which are ready to go to war.* Perhaps it would seem like belittling the legislative authority of a state to which one should attribute the greatest wisdom to suggest that it should seek instruction regarding the principles of its conduct from its *subjects* (the philosophers); nevertheless this is highly advisable. Hence the state will *solicit* the latter *silently* (by making it a secret) which means that it will *let them talk* freely and publicly about the general maxims of the conduct of war and the establishment of peace (for they will do it of their own accord, if only they are not forbidden to do so). The agreement of the states among themselves regarding this point does not require any special stipulation but is founded upon an obligation posited by general morality legislating for human reason. This does not mean that the state must concede that the principles of the philosopher have priority over the rulings of the jurist (the representative of governmental power); it only means that the philosopher be *given a hearing.* The jurist who has made the *scales* of law and right his symbol, as well as the *sword* of justice, commonly employs the sword not only to ward off all outside influence from the scales, but also to put it into one of the scales if it will not go down (*vae victis*). A jurist who is not at the same time a philosopher (morally speaking) has the greatest temptation to do this, because it is only his job to apply existing laws, and not to inquire whether these laws need improvement. In fact he counts this lower order of his faculty [in the university] to be the higher, simply because it is the concomitant of power (as is also the case of the other two faculties) – The philosophical faculty occupies a low place when confronted by all this power. Thus, for example, it is said of philosophy that she is the *handmaiden* of theology (and something like that is said regarding the other two). It is not very clear however 'whether she carries the torch in front of her gracious lady or the train of her dress behind'.

It is not to be expected that kings philosophize or that philosophers become kings, nor is it to be desired, because the possession of power corrupts the free judgement of reason inevitably. But kings or self-governing nations will not allow the class of philosophers to disappear or to become silent, but will let them speak publicly, because this is indispensable for both in order to clarify their business. And since this class of people are by their very nature incapable of forming gangs or clubs they need not be suspected of carrying on *propaganda*.

AUTHOR'S NOTES

a. It is often assumed that one is not permitted to proceed with hostility against anyone unless he has already actively hurt him, and this is indeed very true if both live in a civic state under law, for by entering into this state one man proffers the necessary security to another through the superior authority which has power over both. – But man (or the nation) in a mere state of nature deprives me of this security and hurts me by this very state, simply by being near me, even though not actively (*facto*). He hurts me by the lawlessness of his state (*statu iniusto*) by which I am constantly threatened, and therefore I can compel him either to enter into a communal state under law with me or to leave my vicinity. – Hence the postulate which underlies all the following articles is this: all men who can mutually affect each other should belong under a joint civic constitution.

There are three kinds of constitution under law as far as concerns the persons who belong under it: (1) the constitution according to the law of national citizenship of all men belonging to a nation (*ius civitatis*); (2) the constitution according to international law regulating the relation of states with each other (*ius gentium*); (3) the constitution according to the law of world citizenship which prevails in so far as men and states standing in a relationship of mutual influence may be viewed as citizens of a universal state of all mankind (*ius cosmopoliticum*).

This classification is not arbitrary but necessary in relation to the idea of eternal peace. For if even one [state] were in a relation of physical influence upon another and yet in a state of nature, the state of war would be connected with it, and to be relieved of this state is our very purpose.

b. Mallet du Pan claims in his profound sounding, yet hollow and empty language that after many years' experience he had come to accept the truth of Pope's well-known saying: 'O'er forms of government let fools contest;/that which is best administered is best.' If that is to mean that the best-led government is the best led, then, to use a phrase of Swift, he has cracked a nut which rewarded him with a worm. If it is to mean that the best-led government is the best form of government, i.e. constitution, then it is very false; examples of good governing do not prove anything about the form of government. Who has governed better than a *Titus* or a *Marcus Aurelius*? Yet the one was succeeded by a *Domitian*, the other by a *Commodus*. This would have been impossible under a good constitution, since their incapacity to govern was known soon enough.

c. Among all the ways of living the hunting life is unquestionably most at variance with a civilized constitution: because the families which are separated from each other soon become alien, and soon thereafter, dispersed in extended forests, hostile to each other, since each requires much room for its feeding and clothing. The Mosaic law forbidding the eating of blood, Genesis 9:4–6 appears to have been originally nothing else but an attempt to forbid people to live as hunters; because in this life there often occur situations where meat must be eaten raw, and hence to forbid the eating of blood means forbidding a hunting life. This law, several times re-enacted, was later, with a quite different purpose, imposed by the Jewish Christians as a condition upon the newly acccepted heathen Christians.

d. *Difference of religion*: a strange expression! as if one were to speak of different *morals*. There may be different *kinds of faith* which are historical and which hence belong to history and not to religion and are part of the means in the field of learning. Likewise there may be different *religious books* (Zendavesta, Vedam, Koran, etc.). But there can only be one *religion* valid for all men and for all times. Those other matters are nothing but a vehicle of religion, accidental and different according to the difference of time and place.

TRANSLATOR'S NOTES

1. Presumably, the word *freiwillig* here refers to the citizens acting as a whole, and through a majority, not the individuals separately.
2. Kant here uses the term *Form der Beherrschung*, which is rulership – but further on down he shifts to *Staatsform* and *Staatsverfassung*; the essential point, however, is the distinction between form of rulership and form of government.
3. It seems to be clear from Kant's analogy that the 'cannot' of this sentence has a strictly logical connotation – i.e. All men have two legs; *A* is a man; therefore *A* has two legs.
4. I am omitting a lengthy and obsolete footnote on the origin of the word China, in spite of its interest in showing Kant's keen personal delight in concrete historical detail.
5. In a lengthy footnote at this point, Kant discusses the concept of *providence* as something necessary to explain the basic 'form' of events in their totality. He rejects the idea as illogical, when applied to specific events, but allows it as a general founding, governing, and directing providence. The discussion follows the treatment in the *Critique of Practical Reason*.
6. When the end shapes the means and tools.

III PUBLIUS II, *THE NEW FEDERALIST*, CHAPTERS 1–12, 16

Alexander Hamilton, James Madison and John Jay wrote the original *Federalist* under the collective pseudonym 'Publius' in order to argue the case for federal union at a time when there was much opposition to the idea of federation among the thirteen American colonies. Almost two centuries later, in the aftermath of the Second World War, Justice Owen J. Roberts (1875–1955), in collaboration with John F. Schmidt and Clarence K. Streit, under the aegis of the Atlantic Union Committee, joined forces to write *The New Federalist*, under the pseudonym 'Publius II', in order to argue the case for an international federal union of democratic countries, as a means of security and stability for the world. They applied to the modern international situation many of the basic principles enunciated by Publius I and bolstered the logic of their arguments with a persuasive appeal to the historic and undeniable success of the United States in forging and sustaining the union of so many disparate 'local states'. But the opposition to the formation of any kind of true international federation was, at the time of the publication of *The New Federalist* – and still is – even more formidable than the sort of opposition encountered by Publius I. Unperturbed by this opposition, however, the three pioneers in the national federalist movement even proceeded to elaborate in detail in the latter half of *The New Federalist* the constitutional articulation and procedural machinery of the proposed international federation. Chapter 16, on the executive, from the latter half, should be of especial interest, and is reprinted below following the more general remarks of Chapters 1–12, from the first half.

The text is reprinted from Publius II, *The New Federalist* (New York, Harper, 1950). Chapters 1–11, 16 are printed in full; of chapter 12 only the beginning is printed here. The initials at the end of each chapter indicate authorship of the chapter ('O. J. R.' = Roberts; 'J. F. S.' = Schmidt; 'C. K. S.' = Streit). Square brackets are editorial. A few references given as footnotes have been placed in parentheses and taken into the text.

1 On our purpose

The people of the Atlantic community had already invented the political machinery for peaceful, free government before they began inventing the mechanical machines that are making the world one. These political inventions, which freed other creative energies in man, preceded the community's rise to prosperity and power.

Many forget this. Some do worse: for example, the purveyors of isms that make government officials rich and keep the people poor, who cannot tolerate that private citizens should be wealthier than the chief of state, or that the poorest citizen should feel free to criticize the head of the government. They gain power by deluding the people into believing that only 'have' nations can afford the luxury of individual freedom. They keep power by persuading the people that to become rich and powerful enough to be free, they must begin by sacrificing what freedom they have to some benevolent planner-potentate.

The fact is that the 'have' nations were once poorer than their neighbours in almost everything but individual freedom. They gained their wealth and power by safeguarding and developing this freedom, not by sacrificing it. Political revolution among the people of the North Atlantic opened the way for their industrial revolution, and for all the world's.

Only to the English was England the greatest power on earth in the long period when its people were making one of the basic political inventions on which freedom rests – representative government. Without this invention democracy could operate, as Aristotle said, only within the area that a man's voice could reach.

Few were so poor as to envy the Pilgrims when they entered a wintry wilderness with a compact whose opening words proclaimed the principle that we the people are the creators of free government. The envoys of the thirteen states were vainly begging loans from the courts of Europe in 1787, when Americans worked out in their Constitution another great invention – federal union. It solved the hitherto insoluble problem of applying the principles of free representative government between the people of sovereign states. It preserved the advantages to liberty in both local and central government. It achieved the miracle of uniting big and little states to their mutual satisfaction, and made a democratic republic effective and enduring.

As for the French, one need only review the nomenclature of free government to remember our debt to them. Congress comes from their *Congrès*, Parliament from *Parlement*, judge and jury from *juge* and *jurer*. Constitution, union, federal, federation, nation, president, premier, legislature – all these words are drawn without change from the French language.

True, the English and Americans gave new or freer meaning to these terms while autocracy treated the French as dogs. But it was this *canaille* who, adding fraternity to the liberty of the English and equality of the Americans, then asserted the principle of *Libertè, Egalitè, Fraternitè* against all Europe's wealth and power.

Thanks primarily to the English, American and French revolutions there now exists not only a number of free representative governments but also a number of free federal unions. And thanks to the scientific and mechanical development that these political advances have fostered, all the nations of the world are nearer to each other, in travel and in missile time, than were the thirteen states when they formed the first federal union.

The task of our generation is to extend to a larger area the basic federal union principles that have already stood the test of time, rather than invent new machinery. This is no easy task.

The thirteen colonies stood out separately from London like spokes without a rim, but they did have a hub. Their governments were quite independent of each other, but in 1787 none was even two hundred years old, and none had ever made war on another.

To unite in federal union by free agreement merely two nations of the same language that have warred against each other, even a century ago, is clearly a formidable undertaking. It is easy only when compared to the task of federating forty, fifty or sixty old established nations that have never been united even by a common hub, and whose people have tried to kill each other recently, and time and again. Yet freedom and peace depend on our succeeding now in this task of extending between at least some nations the principles of federal union, of beginning at least the nucleus of a world republic. To this problem we address ourselves.

We shall leave it to others to demonstrate the necessity and utility of making this next step in federal union. We propose to elucidate briefly the basic principles of federal union, and distinguish between the primary and the secondary in them. We mean to bring out the essential differences between a federal union and a bloc, alliance, league or confederation on the one hand, and a nation or empire on the other, and show why federal union works where the others fail. We propose to deal also with such practical and tightly interrelated problems of international federation as where and how to begin – with what peoples as founders, with what federal powers, with what type of federal structure.

To quote *The Federalist*, from which we draw much more than inspiration, our arguments 'will be offered in a spirit which will not disgrace the cause of truth'. We shall keep this to heart, too:

> So numerous, indeed, and so powerful are the causes, which serve to give a false bias to the judgment, that we, upon many occasions, see wise and good men on the wrong as well as on the

right side of questions of the first magnitude to society. This circumstance, if duly attended to, would furnish a lesson of moderation to those who are ever so much persuaded of their being right in any controversy. And a further reason for caution in this respect might be drawn from the reflection that we are not always sure that those who advocate the truth are influenced by purer principles than their antagonists.

Our problem 'speaks its own importance'. And the role of the Atlantic community in it now is as decisive as the one America had when Hamilton opened *The Federalist* with these words:

> It seems to have been reserved to the people of this country by their conduct and example to decide the important question whether societies of men are really capable or not of establishing good government from reflection and choice, or whether they are forever destined to depend, for their political constitutions, on accident and force. If there is any truth in the remark, the crisis at which we are arrived may with propriety be regarded as the era in which that decision is to be made; and a wrong election of the part we shall act may in this view deserve to be considered as the general misfortune of mankind.

(C. K. S.)

2   Basic federal principle

Winston Churchill won, in June 1940, the distinction of being the first head of a great-power government – Britain – to propose a union with another power – France. Recently, in a speech at Zurich, he proposed a European union whose main pillars would be France and Germany, with Britain apparently a benevolent outsider.

Mr Churchill said repeatedly that what he was proposing was 'a United States of Europe'. He identified it the more with the United States of America and a true federal system by also calling it a 'union'.

But then Mr Churchill used 'regional structure' and 'European grouping' to describe what he proposed. Still more indicative of the apparent confusion in his mind of blocs and leagues with the federal system and the United States was this statement: 'The

League of Nations did not fail because of its principles or conceptions. It failed because these principles were deserted by those states who had brought it into being.'

This is one of error's hardy perennials. If the League's principles were sound, then it would follow that the proposed United States of Europe might as well be built on them as on federal principles. If it is true that Geneva's principles could have worked among all the nations of the world, who had never united on anything, they would surely also work in the United States of America if the people of its forty-eight states – who have lived together all their lives, speak the same language, have the same political concepts and many other common bonds – were to replace their federal Constitution tomorrow with the League Covenant. But would Mr Churchill follow his thought through to this, its logical conclusion?[1]

The confusion that Mr Churchill's use of terms typifies is so widespread and dangerous that the essential difference between a federal union and a league, alliance or bloc needs to be highlighted. The latter differ from federal union as black from white. The easiest way to distinguish between the two is through their basic units. There are only two such units that can be used in organizing international society: an existing political body, the nation, taken as a whole, or the human beings who compose it, taken as individuals.

The way that takes the nation as the sovereign unit treats it as if it were itself a person, with the government its head and the citizens mere cells in its body. To start on this basis is to end by giving each nation, regardless of the size of its population, one vote, to be cast by its government – the citizen having little more to say about it than a cell in his toe has to say about his own decisions.

You end, too, (1) by subordinating the freedom of the citizen to the freedom or sovereignty of the nation, whose maintenance thus becomes the supreme purpose of your international organization; (2) by finding that the smallest possible conflict that your organization can face is a conflict between armed nations, with the weakest possible violator of its rules an armed nation.

You do not get a government, a union, a federation, a federal republic, or anything remotely resembling the United States of America. You get instead an entente, a 'fraternal association', an alliance, a coalition, a bloc, a grouping, a league such as the Wilsonian one or the United Nations. You get a system that has been tried time and again, but has always failed to keep the peace within its jurisdiction or secure human freedom and prosperity.

Consider what inevitably follows when you take individual man, instead, for the unit of your international society.

All the laws of the government you form operate on the citizen directly. That means that you have reduced the conflicts in your international society to conflicts in which individual persons, rather than any body they may represent, are the essential responsible elements. It gives as time-tested a guarantee that it can keep the peace among the people of its member nations as the United States gives that it can keep the peace among the people of the forty-eight states.

True, there is still the possibility of civil wars. But whereas the United States has suffered one civil war in 161 years, it has eliminated entirely the kind of war between two member states which brought down the Geneva League in the Japan–China, Italy–Ethiopia series, and which has been the curse of every system that took the state as unit. Its civil war decided once for all that the basic difference between a federal union and a league is the one we are stressing here: that its unit is the citizen, not the state.

If you start with the citizen for unit, you get a government not only *of* but *by* the people. For you are led to give each citizen one vote in the international government, just as in the national government. You apportion representation in its legislature basically according to population, with the representatives elected by the people themselves, divided in districts, instead of appointed by their government's executive. You get the possibility of the divisions within each nation being healthily reflected along party lines in the international legislature, instead of the false picture of national unity which each nation by its single vote presents in the United Nations, or any other system based on the state as unit.

Finally, if you take the citizen as your unit, the equality this implies, if nothing else, leads you to make government not only of and by but *for* the people. Its central aim must be to preserve the freedom, sovereignty and security of its supreme unit, the citizen. Like each democratic national government in a federated union, its government must be subordinated to the people. Its powers, too, must be strictly limited in the interests of the people, and it, too, must be designed to secure the Rights of Man as individual sovereigns, rather than the rights of nations as sovereigns.

The difference in unit is, of course, not the only difference between a federal union and a league, alliance, or bloc. But it is the basic one, and all the other differences can be traced back to it.

(C.K.S.)

3 Sovereignty

A confusion, like that between the terms 'union' and 'league', grows out of the use of the term *sovereignty* when we speak of co-operation on a plane above the national level. The word sovereign has an appealing sound. When you and I call our nation sovereign, we seem to swell up and take on a superior dignity. That is gratifying, no doubt. But we ought to analyse what we say. We ought to try to see just what we mean when we claim sovereignty as the essence of statehood.

The use of the term to mark the quality of a state has no basis in history. In the common speech of the past, a sovereign is a monarch. He makes and enforces the rules for men's conduct in his kingdom. By a derivative use of the word, we sometimes call a nation a sovereign. Britain once held mastery of the seas and we spoke of her as queen or sovereign of the seas.

But in our day we mean no such thing when we speak of a nation as sovereign. We mean that a nation has independent power; that no man or nation may make a rule for its conduct. This use of the term came naturally from the quality of the person who asserts sovereignty over his subjects. Since we assume his power is absolute, we must concede that no king of any other nation can rule his acts. Kings then, by virtue of their sovereignty, cannot be subject to a higher law; they can act jointly only by agreement; and their agreements are not to be enforced by any superior power.

On the other hand, democratic states are the fruit of a creed that denies to any man or group of men the right to rule the conduct of others. They spring from the belief that all men are equal in political status.

Men express this belief by the phrases, 'sovereignty resides in the people'; 'every citizen is a sovereign'; 'government must rest on the consent of the governed'. So in a democracy we have no sovereign who is independent of the citizens. Through our chosen agents, we collectively act as a government. This is 'government of the people, by the people, for the people'.

No government of this sort has existed to regulate the common interests of the men of different nations because we have carried over into the relations of nations the concept of absolute monarchy. Though we are a democracy, we have arrogated to ourselves collectively as a nation the independence of an absolute monarch. As no subject of the king and no subject of any other king can control the royal will, so, we say, no other nation can limit our national will.

Here emerges the error we note in present-day talk about uniting nations for prevention of war. Men say we can attain joint national action only if each nation will surrender some of its sovereignty. But how can a nation surrender part of its sovereignty? If every state is sovereign it can recall or ignore its plighted word at will. Take our own case. Our agents in the Congress may alter or annul their ratification of the United Nations Charter at any time. So it is with each UN member. If a state is truly sovereign, it cannot effectively surrender its essential nature. The ideas of sovereignty and irrevocable surrender of the right to act contrary to a treaty or contract contradict each other.

Also, if we are right that sovereignty in our political scheme rests in the citizen alone, the United States as an entity cannot give up a part of its sovereignty. This, because it has none to give; the people have all of it. For the sake of internal order and national security, they exercise it through their own agents – the members of Congress. But those agents have no power they can confer on others. They must employ the powers given them. They cannot redelegate those powers.

In the light of these facts let us examine the structure of the United Nations. We can appreciate the obstacle the delegates at San Francisco faced. They were bound by the tradition of state sovereignty. They had an impossible task. That was to tie together the peoples of separate states, yet to keep intact the sovereignty of the states to which those people belonged. What was the result? A league – a multi-party treaty – that all member states ratified. Thus we have an alliance of sovereign states, not a union of people.

But what difference does that make? All the difference between anarchy and government. No agency formed by sovereign states can make rules – laws – for those states or for their citizens. In contrast, a government made up of the agents of the citizens themselves can make rules that bind its citizens and can provide the means to enforce the rules.

If democracies are to be united for action in behalf of the citizens of all of them as one group, the act of union must be the act of the citizens of all. As we have seen, a democratic government has no sovereignty to give up. Only its members can delegate their sovereign power to their chosen agent. Such delegation is not a surrender of anything. It is an exercise of the sovereignty, the power, that rests in the individual. It is confined to the agent to be used as the citizens direct.

How then are we to have order in the international field? How can we secure the reign of one law over all the people of several nations? Only if they, the people, freely endow an agency of their own with the function of making the rules and the power to enforce the rules. These, as we have seen, are uses of the sovereignty that abides in men, not in the state.

Can the citizens of an autocracy and those of a democracy jointly create such an agency? No one has yet shown how they can. For an autocrat speaks and acts, not as agent for his people, but as their ruler. He is sovereign and independent. He can make a treaty, though his subjects do not want it. He can cancel or disregard that treaty, though his subjects wish to keep it. If on their behalf he commits their interests to a legislative system, he can, of his own will, revoke the committal.

Contrast the case of a democracy. The people may irrevocably agree that they shall be bound by the rules made by their own agency – the government they erect.

National sovereignty is the enemy of international law. Its affirmation is the negation of law above the national level. The people must abandon the false doctrine of national sovereignty if they are to unite in a world government of law. They must assert and exercise the sovereignty vested in each of them as human beings. So, and only so, can men of many nations form an enduring union of laws superior to their own national laws, for the protection and regulation of the interests they, as human beings, have in common.

(O. J. R)

4 Neither league nor nation

The confusion on what a federal union is develops from opposite sides. Many, we have seen, assume that a federal union is, for all practical purposes, the same as an alliance, coalition or league, such as the United Nations. They treat the proposal for a union of democracies as a project for a 'bloc of democracies'.

At the other extreme, many [wrongly] assume that a federal union is a centralized national government, and as wrongly assail or defend it on this ground.

A federal union partakes enough of both extremes to make the confusion about it understandable. But it is neither one nor the other. It occupies the position in between these extremes, and differs from both. It is formed by the common-sense process of discarding the faults in either extreme, and combining the good into something new, different, and far better.

We have brought out the basic difference between a federal union and an alliance, bloc or league. The supreme or sovereign unit in a union, it was stressed, is the individual citizen, whereas in all other forms of interstate organization the unit is a body politic, a state or nation. A federal union operates directly on the citizen. It also operates up from him through representatives he elects, and for the sake of his individual liberty. It takes, in short, the same unit as the nation does, and operates in all these ways as does any nation. Moreover, as regards the outside world, it has all, or nearly all, the attributes of sovereignty that any nation has.

Small wonder, then, that it is often assimilated with nations, and that many hastily see in it a utopian or nightmarish superstate that seeks to wipe out all national differences on home rule. Even so intelligent a statesman as Senator Taft has expressed fear that federal union would simply mean a new high in the dangers he sees in 'big government'.

The United States is a federal union, but its own citizens and officials have sunk into the habit of calling it, instead, a 'nation'. They refer to the federal government as the 'national government' as any Frenchman might refer to his own state. Americans, indeed, have drifted so far toward the nomenclature of the Old World that they now usually think of labour organization when they see the word 'union', a word that to Lincoln meant only the United States. Andrew Jackson made famous the toast, 'Our Federal Union, it must be preserved.' One wonders what he would think if he knew how few Americans have preserved this term which truly describes the United States.

In thinking of their federal union as if it were a mere nation,

Americans have done much to confuse themselves and everyone, to the great loss of freedom and peace.

It may surprise many of them to learn that the Founding Fathers deliberately rejected 'national' as a description of the government they established. The Virginia Plan which was submittted to the Federal Convention on 29 May 1787 did call for a 'National Legislature', a 'National Executive', a 'National Judiciary'. But you will not find that adjective in the Constitution the Convention adopted. On 20 June, Madison records, the Convention unanimously decided to 'drop the word *national*, and retain the proper title, "the United States".'

The great debate in the Convention was over the question: Should the United States become a nation with an all-powerful central government and the states reduced to mere subdivisions, as the Virginia Plan proposed, or should it, as the New Jersey Plan urged, remain a league of states? After hot argument that almost wrecked the Convention, the answer was to make the United States neither nation nor league. Its founders compromised between these two and created something never known before, and that later came to be called a federal union,[2] to mark its distinctive character.

We have already seen some ways in which it resembles a centralized nation or state. Wherein does it differ? Chiefly in this: It is composed of states or nations which retain their original sovereign attributes in all respects except those that their citizens have expressly delegated in the constitution to the union. The status of a state in the union is far stronger than that of the county in the state, or any subdivision in a non-federal nation.

Legally, the state remains as supreme in the fields it retains as the union becomes in the fields given it. True, the federal Constitution provides that 'This Constitution and the Laws of the United States which shall be made in Pursuance thereof . . . shall be the Supreme Law of the Land; and the Judges in every State shall be bound thereby, any Thing in the Constitution or Laws of any State to the Contrary notwithstanding.' But the same Constitution in its Tenth Amendment sweepingly provides that 'the powers not delegated to the United States by the Constitution, nor prohibited by it to the States, are reserved to the States respectively, or to the people'.

In the American union, no state government can enter the field reserved to the federal government, nor can the latter enter that reserved to every state. This concept of government is far removed from that of the totalitarian nation.

The federal-union system seeks to secure liberty for the individual by dividing the powers of government between the union on the one hand, and the states on the other. The result is to make neither of them a complete nation in the usual European sense, to allow the citizen to play one of them against the other, and to divide his loyalty between them.

The people of several states unite to form a federal union only when the lack of a strong central government threatens their liberties and lives. It is therefore natural that federalists should now stress the dangers to freedom and peace in national sovereignty, and the advantages to be gained in these respects from union. But the rights or sovereignty that the state or nation retains in entering a federal union are just as important to its guarantee of liberty as are the union's rights or sovereignty. Federal union comes not to destroy national sovereignty entirely, but to preserve it wherever it truly makes for individual freedom. As *Union Now* explained: 'Union does not mean eliminating all national rights. It means eliminating them only where elimination clearly serves the individuals concerned, and maintaining them in all other respects — not simply where maintenance clearly serves . . . individual interest, but . . . in all doubtful cases.'

(C. K. S.)

5 Federal union's basic balance

It cannot be stressed too much that the rights that federal union leaves to the member state are as important to it as those that it gives the union. Both spring from its second basic principle. Its first principle makes its supreme or operating unit never a nation, state or other body politic, but always the same unit that is used in every state, namely, individual man. The citizen is its sovereign.

Federal union's second principle is to keep state and union government independent of each other but dependent on the citizen, who delegates part of his sovereignty to his representatives in both. This principle divides the rights of government between them so as to secure the citizen's freedom not only by wise delegation of each right but by checking union and state against each other. Recognizing the tendency of all power to become excessive, federal union dynamically balances the union with its states to free the citizen from both overcentralization and over-decentralization, from both tyranny and anarchy.

The American people acquired the hard way the genius for liberty through balance that has allowed them to grow so individually free and unitedly powerful, while facing time and again potential deadlocks between Congress and the Executive, and between the Senate and House.

They began by rebelling against the overcentralization of the British colonial system, when London imposed taxes on the colonies without their even being represented in its parliament. From this species of tyranny they swung to the other extreme. The thirteen colonies declared themselves independent not only of the British Crown but of one another. Their Articles of Confederation asserted the sovereignty of each state, as the United Nations Charter does. They replaced Parliament with a Congress in which each state government was equally represented, but they gave it no power to tax any of them, or execute any of its decisions in them. The result of this excessive decentralization was to expose individual liberty in each state to the dangers of weakness and anarchy. With no central government to restrain the state governments, boundary and trade disputes developed among them. Soon even such democratic states as Rhode Island were asserting more and more power over the citizens. They had avoided tyranny in the Confederacy only to be threatened with excessive government in each state.

This experience with both extremes led them to work out the golden mean that federal union represents. Two plans faced each other in the Convention of 1787, we noted. The Virginia Plan aimed to change the confederacy into a 'national' government. The New Jersey Plan aimed to keep it a league of states. The delegates, after bitter debate, compromised the two conceptions into something new, federal union's division of the attributes of sovereignty between local and central government.

One of this system's significant distinguishing characteristics is embodied in its oath of loyalty. Many patriotic oaths put prejudice above common sense, make reason bow to the accident of birth, subordinate free principle to person or place. The American oath does the opposite.

The idea that the citizen should fight for the territory of the states was deliberately omitted from the Constitution. It was knocked out in the Convention by this argument of George Read of Delaware: 'Mr Read [Madison noted 11 June 1787] disliked the idea of guaranteeing territory. It abetted the idea of distinct States which would be a perpetual source of discord. There can be no cure for this evil but in doing away with States altogether and uniting them all into one great Society.'

The first statute that Congress passed under the Federal Constitution – law No. 1 of the USA, approved 1 June 1789 by President Washington – made this the American oath: 'I, A. B., do solemnly swear or affirm (as the case may be) that I will support the Constitution of the United States.' The present wording binds Americans to 'support and defend the Constitution of the United States against all enemies, foreign and domestic'.

The American, then, is sworn to defend only a set of principles – those of federal union, which the Constitution embodies – and not a land, ruler, race, religion, nation, class or even people. Land and people do enter the picture, of course. But how secondary they are, and how important is the federal-union principle of balance was demonstrated clearly in the Civil War.

Americans then fought Americans for four years on American soil with foes as noble as Lincoln and Lee each believing himself loyal to his oath. Both sides agreed that freedom lay in the principle of balance between the rights of the union and of the states, between the freedom and equality of men and the freedom and equality of their states. But the Southern Americans held that the Constitution struck this balance in favour of the states; the Northerners held it gave the edge to the union. Both died to maintain the federal principle as they saw it against Americans who became their enemies by seeking to upset it.

They all died loyal to federal union in the deepest sense, to determine more clearly what its principles really were. Lincoln did not distinguish between them when he spoke of the 'brave men, living and dead, who fought here'.

The fact that Americans once proved ready to give the last full measure of devotion to prevent disunion has preserved freedom in the United States from the dangers of absolute state sovereignty that have wrecked every league. But the fact that other Americans proved just as ready to die to maintain what they deemed to be the just rights of the states, remains a powerful protection to all the

American people against freedom's other foe – overcentralization.
That foe is the one that now threatens freedom not only in the
United States but in every nation. But the remedy lies not in
greater local sovereignty. Machines have made the free peoples of
the world now as interdependent in fact as the thirteen free states
were once. In the spiral of man's progress, such states as the
United States, Britain and France now stand where Virginia, Pennsylvania and Massachusetts stood, not in 1861 but in 1787, when
government was gaining more and more power in most of the
thirteen states. Freedom then was threatened because the community of the free was divided among sovereign states with no
union government to balance them. That is the situation today,
only on a large scale. Freedom then was saved by federal union of
the free coming in to right the balance. And so the free need to
make a greater union now.

(C. K. S.)

6 Federal union's division of power

A federal union, as we have seen, establishes government between
nations on the same unit, the individual citizen (which each national government uses), and then it divides powers between the
union and the national governments. But how does it divide them?

All existing federal unions, such as the United States, Canada,
Switzerland, etc., divide these powers in such a way as to create:
(1) union citizenship, (2) union diplomatic and defence force, (3)
union customs-free economy, (4) union currency and (5) union
postal and communications system.

In other words, they transfer from the governments of the
member states to the government of the union the sole or supreme
power in five fields. They give it these broad rights:

1. To grant citizenship and passports.
2. To represent them as a body politic in all diplomatic and military
   relations with the outside world, in peace and in war; and
   therefore to maintain their strongest armed force.
3. To create a free market within the union and regulate its interstate and foreign trade.
4. To coin and issue money, fix other measures.

5. To operate the postal service and to regulate or operate all other interstate communication services.

As for the rights left to the state governments, some federal unions, notably the United States, provide that all rights that are not specifically given to the union are retained by the states or the people. Canada reverses this and stipulates that all powers not specifically left to the provincial government are given to Ottawa.

All existing federal unions grant to both the union and the state governments the same power to enforce their laws directly on the citizen, and to tax him directly. These two shared powers, and the five that are transferred from the states to the union have proved to be the minimum needed for a federal government to operate successfully.

There seems little need, for present purposes, to go into all the powers retained by the states. The danger at the start, in any union that is freely made, is not that the state governments will lose too much power, but that they will remain too strong for the union to be effectively balanced.

The problem facing the world is one of getting peoples who have long been habituated to living independently, to consent to form a federal union. The centrifugal forces in such a project are already so powerful that they can be depended on to prevent any excessive centralization. One can be sure that no free people will enter any federal union that does not guarantee them the right to govern independently all their home affairs, in their own language, according to their own customs, and in their own way – whether by republic or kingdom, presidential, cabinet or other form of government, free enterprise or socialism.

Among free peoples there is another factor in the division of power that is of the highest importance: The rights or powers reserved to the individual citizen. This factor is most important because the supreme purpose for which they reserve certain powers to the union and other powers to the states is to secure the citizen's life, liberty and happiness.

It is not enough, therefore, that a free federal constitution should stipulate that the union government has no power to act in certain fields reserved to the states, and that the states have no power to act in other fields reserved to the union. It should also provide that neither the union nor the state have any power to operate in still other fields that are reserved to the citizen – to pass any law, for example, depriving him of his freedom of speech or of association. Or it should provide that certain rights be left to the citizen, just as others are assigned by him either to the union or to the state governments. These provisions are usually known as the Bill of Rights. They should form part of the constitution both of the union and of the states in it.

Free peoples, when forming a federal union, cannot keep too clearly in mind the importance of the citizen's rights. His life, liberty and happiness are secured not merely by having certain rights specifically guaranteed, or reserved to him, but by the division of power between the union and the state governments. This division, in itself, serves his freedom. It permits him to check one agency with the other, and leaves them both incomplete and dependent on him.

The way this division is executed affects him even more. In determining which powers to give each, free peoples should apply this test: *Which will best serve individual freedom, in the broadest sense – to give this particular power to the union government, or to the state government, or both, or to neither?*

If we apply this test, we research the answer already embodied, as we have seen, in the oldest and most successful federal unions. This is not surprising, for these unions were formed voluntarily for freedom's sake by such liberty-loving peoples as the American and the Swiss. The former, indeed, invented the federal-union system expressly as a means of securing 'the blessings of liberty'.

It is well to note that the division of power which makes a union effective enough to stand the test of time also meets the test of individual freedom. Clearly, not only efficiency but liberty requires that both the union and the state governments shall independently enjoy the right to tax the individual and enforce on him the laws they pass. If either the union or the state cannot directly support itself or enforce its will in its own field, but must depend on the agency of the other, there results anarchy or tyranny, either of which destroys liberty.

As for the powers that neither the union nor the states should have – the rights reserved to the citizen – clearly a union of the free should have no power in any field where the nations forming it had none. Put more positively, its Bill of Rights should include every right that was previously guaranteed the citizen in all the founder nations. As for those rights which only a majority of the founders guaranteed, the union might extend these to the others.

Certainly it would have to assure them wherever they already existed. Liberty would also require it to let each nation in it give still greater rights to its own citizens. That again would follow the successful US example. There such rights as woman suffrage began in one state and spread to others until they extended through the union.

There remain the five powers that all federal unions have transferred from the member states to the federal government. These transfers of power also clearly make for individual freedom.

                                                                    (C. K. S.)

7   Where union brings freedom

The people who constitute a federal union need to have some criterion for establishing the division of power that characterizes this system. This division, we have seen, is not simply between the rights of the people and the rights of the government. It means also a division of the rights of government between two agencies that stem *directly and independently* from the people: the new union legislature, executive and judiciary; and the existing legislature, executive and judiciary, of the states or nations whose people enter the union.

When free people form a federal union, they seek thereby to secure both their peace and freedom. But since every free people will renounce peace to secure their individual liberties and will not renounce these rights to secure peace, it is clear that their *supreme* purpose in forming government is not – as many assume – to prevent war but to preserve and promote human liberty.

Their final criterion in dividing power in a federal union must therefore be: *Which will serve our individual freedom best, to give to the union or leave to the nation the right to govern us in this particular field?*

Wherever the free have federated – whether in the United States, Switzerland, Canada, Australia – we have seen, they have always so divided power as to create (1) union citizenship, (2) union diplomatic and defence force, (3) union customs-free economy, (4) union currency and (5) union postal, communications, measures and patent system. With minor exceptions, they have left all other fields of government to the states, cantons or provinces.

Jefferson boiled the division down to one between the domestic and the foreign activities of the states in the union, the latter being transferred to the union and the former left undisturbed. His division is an illuminating one, particularly for the many who forget that the US Constitution began not as a national or domestic government but as a foreign policy, a way of handling the relations of each of the thirteen states with each other and the rest of the world. For present purposes, however, it will be clearer to apply our test of freedom to each of the five fields we have listed in the above paragraph.

Manifestly, since the supreme unit in a federal union is the citizen and not his state or nation, the citizens of each member state or nation must also be equally citizens of the union. This obviously gives each person whose state enters a federal union an enormous gain in individual freedom, provided, of course, that the people of the other states in the union practice liberty, too.

The gain in individual freedom effected by transferring the other four fields to the union is no less clear. Union of the free would put far greater power behind their freedom at far less cost in taxation. It would save billions on the navy alone.

The colossal power that union would bring the free in many other ways has been proved in detail in *Union Now*. It would be so great as to discourage aggression against the free by making attack hopeless; it would liberate them from war, if anything could.

Union is the only way by which free peoples can enormously increase their defensive power without increasing the power of government over themselves, or sacrificing any of their individual liberty. It also preserves them from the danger (inherent in separate diplomacy), of becoming divided against themselves over secondary issues, and thus falling prey to aggression.

No customs union has ever failed in the long run to increase the trade and prosperity, raise the standard of living of all the people in it and give them greater economic freedom. The imagination of even the economic expert cannot grasp all that the people, say, of the Atlantic democracies would gain by uniting in one free trade market as the forty-eight states have done.

The freedom that citizens of New York, Missouri and California gain from having the same currency indicates the freedom that a union currency would bring Americans, British, French. It would free them not only from the vexations of the present exchange system, but from the loss inherent in the existing currency uncertainties and dangers of depreciation.

It is no less obvious that union in the field of communications, measures and patents frees the individual in it from many vexations and fees and other barriers to business and pleasure. It cuts the cost of such communications, whether by rail or by road, sea or air, mail or electricity, and makes them safer, and more reliable and frequent.

The object in uniting, we need to remember, is not to see how much we can centralize government but rather how much we can decentralize it, or cut it out entirely as unnecessary. We transfer five rights to the union. This curbs the centralizing tendency fostered by possession of these rights in each of our nations. We create some new government in order to get rid of much more existing government, to gain more freedom from governmental interference in our lives.

The acme of decentralization is, after all, complete individual freedom. And to come nearer to the democratic ideal where each man governs himself so perfectly that no other government is needed, we see that free men need to federate in five fields at least.

The five rights that they transfer to their union are merely means of defending the individual, local and national rights that they now hold dear – means, that is, of defending what decentralization they have already attained. Far from weakening these dearer rights, they protect and strengthen them by this transfer. Failure to make this transfer forces each democracy to centralize, to reduce individual and local rights so as to keep these five national rights – to sacrifice the end to the means.

Union would give *de jure* status to all the existing decentralization that free men value – to national home rule for national political and economic affairs by whatever system of government and economy each nation desires. Similarly it would legalize each national language, each national educational system, each distinctive trait that makes each nation – the whole distinctive internal system of local liberties, customs and individual rights for which each nation stands.

These things now really have only *de facto* status, as regards the world outside each nation. Only by uniting to recognize and guarantee all these national, local and individual rights can free peoples legalize them, even in the democractic world. And the practical result of their doing this is to make these rights much more secure as regards outside nations, too.

(C. K. S.)

8   Who shall found the union?

If the *supreme* purpose of the free in forming any government is to preserve and promote human liberty, shall they, in forming an international federal union government, limit its founders to the free? We say, yes.

Given a choice in the matter, free men will not associate with other individuals in such a manner as to abridge their liberties in any unnecessary way. Being free, they are presumably free to associate among themselves in such a manner as to strengthen and preserve the rights they already have, to acquire new ones, and to extend them to other peoples.

It would be a denial of the freedom of free people to deny them the right to associate among themselves for the purpose of increasing human freedom. Moreover, only thus has freedom grown to the extent that it exists today.

One way to condemn unfree people to continued bondage is to insist that the free are not free to associate in such a way as will defend their freedom. The best promise of future freedom to those who do not enjoy it is the existence of a strong republic, well organized to preserve and increase individual liberties. This is all the truer when its avowed purpose is to admit other peoples to the advantages of union with it when they rid themselves of their dictators.

Clearly, it is a disservice to the unfree to insist that free people associate in any way that curtails liberty. Such freedom as the world knows today is a tremendous asset not only to the free but to those now in some form of bondage. The value of that asset can be increased only by doing as much as possible to strengthen freedom and to increase it – both in the amount of freedom enjoyed and the number who enjoy it.

This requires the uniting under federal government of the largest number of people enjoying the greatest individual liberty. Should the emphasis be on the maximum number of individuals or on the maximum degree of liberty?

Consideration of the basic principles involved will make our choice easier. We must bear in mind that what we contemplate is an international government, and that any government must operate directly on the individual. We must face the fact that international government thus offers almost unlimited possibilities for peace by oppression. Common sense would therefore seem to urge us to limit it to peoples with a maximum of experience in maintaining freedom through self-government.

A frailty of human nature is the desire to silence opposition. We have all heard of the 'castor-oil treatment' for those who disagreed with [Mussolini's] Black Shirts – a mild method compared to those used by the German Nazis. Even US apologists for Soviet tyranny admit that opposition is not tolerated in the USSR.

It is no answer to argue that such tyrannies are the work of a minority propped up by armed forces and a secret police. Even oppression of a minority by the majority is unjustifiable.

For the sake of democracy, the minority has to be given every opportunity to express itself freely. This means that even the timid shall feel free to speak up. Freedom of speech that can be exercised only at the risk of death will not be exercised very often by very many persons. Without a vigorous exchange of different opinions – particularly opinions that differ from those of the people in power – democracy cannot hope to maintain itself.

At present, a universal world government would be composed about seven to one of people inexperienced in political freedom. That would help those in power in it to entrench themselves through a super Gestapo, GPU, NKVD, or MVD. Would it console any person accustomed to freedom to know that this world tyranny had sole possession of atom bombs?

Such a situation would be even worse than anything we are likely to experience under the present division into many separate nations, because now the people of at least some nations enjoy a fairly high degree of freedom. In present circumstances, it is still possible for a victim to escape from a police state to a free country.[3]

But if the free join a supranational government which includes so many people without experience in maintaining freedom that the free lose the freedom they have, how shall they ever regain it? Remember, this world government would have not only atom bombs but an army, navy, and air force with which to suppress revolt.

When cave men were armed only with clubs and stones, every

rebel could find for himself the instruments of rebellion. But our highly advanced technology makes successful rebellion very difficult without the help of the armed force of the government. A dictator usually seeks first to assure himself of the loyalty of the army, navy, and air force.

Technological advances have already made revolt so difficult that we should exercise every caution to prevent control of an international government falling into unscrupulous hands. That means we must jealously guard such rights as freedom of the press, freedom of speech, religion, assembly, a free ballot.

The freedom we have is not ours alone. We hold it in trust for posterity, and for those unfortunate victims of the accident of birth who were born in lands where freedom is but a hope. It lives eternally in the hearts of the people, even there.

(J. F. S.)

9 No union with dictatorship

To continue the discussion of membership in the proposed international federal union: It is often said that a world government must permit the people of each member nation to live under a government of their own choosing, *even under a dictatorship if they so desire*. That assertion should be challenged whenever and wherever it appears. If a union is to maintain peace among its members, *no nation in the union can have a dictatorship form of government*.

It is the essence of a federal union that it maintains peace by operating on the individual person, according to general laws applied to each case by courts – by justice, in short. The alternative is to operate on nations as units – as does the United Nations and diplomacy. But to coerce a state by force is tantamount to war. Wars waged to execute the verdicts of international tribunals are undoubtedly superior morally to the jungle-law type of wars the world now suffers. But they remain wars – the opposite of peace.

To keep the peace, a world union composed of both dictatorships and democracies must operate on the citizen in both alike, through its courts. But how can it operate justly on the individuals under dictatorship without undermining the dictator's position? If the union's laws are to be respected, they must apply fairly equally to all persons in it, to the dictator and his secret police as much as to the people they oppress. Would any dictator accept this? Could any democrat accept less?

Dictators stay in power by suppressing opposition. They mislead public opinion by spreading lies among their subjects. They divert attention from domestic evils by calling attention to pretended dangers abroad. No dictatorship can be depended on for peace.

Where only the dictator's subjects are concerned, only they suffer. But in matters concerning the world as a whole, the whole world suffers when the dictator errs. Therefore, a world union is very much concerned with the kind of government that prevails in its member nations.

Although no nation should interfere in the domestic affairs of other nations, every free people has a sufficient interest in those internal affairs to be entitled to insist, before they federate with another nation, that its internal affairs shall be decided in accordance with the opinions of most of its citizens.

It is pertinent here to refer to article IV, section 4, of the US Constitution: 'The United States shall guarantee to every State in this Union a Republican Form of Government, and shall protect each of them against invasion; and on Application of the Legislature, or of the Executive (when the Legislature cannot be convened) against domestic Violence.'

In the Convention which drafted the Constitution, Randolph said this provision aimed: '1. To secure Republican [i.e. free representative] Government; 2. To suppress domestic commotions.'

There was considerable discussion over the exact wording. Inasmuch as the delegates wanted to avoid perpetuating those state constitutions which were considered bad, there was some sentiment for omitting the provision entirely. But an observation by Ghorum dispelled the belief that the matter could be ignored. As Madison noted:

Mr Ghorum thought it strange that a Rebellion should be known to exist in the Empire, and the General Government should be restrained from interposing to subdue it. At this rate an enterprising citizen might erect the standard of Monarchy in a particular State, might gather together partisans from all quarters, might extend his views from State to State, and threaten to establish a tyranny over the whole and the General Government be compelled to remain an active witness of its own destruction.

With regard to different parties in a State; as long as they confine their disputes to words, they will be harmless to the General Government and to each other. If they appeal to the sword, it will then be necessary for the General Government, however difficult it may be to decide on the merits of their contest, to interpose and put an end to it.

Supporters of universal union, embracing both the free and the unfree, sometimes argue for this on the ground that the United States itself includes examples of 'dictatorial' local governments. The analogy is unsound. About all the examples they can mention are corrupt municipal governments or city 'bosses'. The only dictatorial state government cited is the short-lived regime of the late Huey Long in Louisiana. No one who has lived under European dictatorships would call by that name the worst of these American departures from democracy. All the American bosses put together do not have, and never have had, the power that even a Perón exercises in Argentina.

It is essential to note that though one may dominate the local courts and press in a city in the United States, one cannot keep newspapers and magazines and speakers from other cities from entering that area, and reporting freely to its people and to all the union conditions in it.

For a sound analogy between the conditions in a world union today and the United States, one must imagine that at least as powerful a state as New York is governed as absolutely by a dictator as Russia is by Stalin. One must imagine rigid control of the New York press and radio, with rigid censorship of news from and to the rest of the United States. One must imagine also a ruthless, omnipresent secret police, spying on and clapping into its numerous concentration camps all New Yorkers who oppose the dictatorship. The same police would, of course, be spying on the few people from the rest of the United States whom it allowed to enter New York, and tightly limiting their movements.

New Yorkers – except for a few trusties of the dictator – would not be allowed to travel in Pennsylvania, Massachusetts, or other states. New Yorkers could vote only for the dictator's nominees for US President, Congress, and all other offices; and all of New York's votes in Congress would be cast as the dictator directed.

This paints only a feeble picture of what an attempt to federate real dictatorship with the Atlantic democracies would mean. But it should suffice to show the absurdity of the plans for a union of such conflicting systems.

For the same reasons that the Philadelphia Convention thought a guarantee of free representative government necessary, so must we consider free representative government necessary in each member nation of any international union we enter. It is, in fact, even more imperative that a world union insist on free representative government in its members. For if tyranny should ever spread from one member nation to cover all the world union, then freedom would probably be lost to the world for many generations, and perhaps even for all time.

(J. F. S.)

10   Self-governing peoples needed

Are the peoples who are not governed by a despot necessarily capable of entering into an international union of free men?

The answer is, *no*. The issue is not between dictatorship and its absence. It is between dictatorship and self-government. Only where there is a high degree of self-government can there be a high degree of genuine freedom.

The object of the free in establishing international self-government must be to preserve the freedom they now have, and extend it to still other fields and to an ever-increasing number of people. The free will defeat their purpose if they expand this union so fast, or include so many people at the outset, that freedom will be imperiled.

The free have a right to insist as a prerequisite to union that the people with whom they unite should be able to bring their collective judgment to bear on the issues. For this to be possible, the political structure of their governments must be such as to offer no obstacles – i.e. they must not be dictatorships. But the *possibility* of judging is not enough. The people must also have the *ability* to pass on major issues freely. This ability is mainly dependent on: (1) freedom of the press, (2) ability to read a free press, (3) freedom of speech to discuss the problems which are presented in the free press, and (4) freedom of assembly to make fullest use of freedom of speech.

If the people are to pass judgement on the solution of public problems, they must know what those problems are. Everyone must be free to set forth his own statement of the problem, whether as a newspaper editor, reporter, columnist, pamphleteer, writer or as the author of a letter to the editor. Obviously, this requires freedom of the press.

But what good will come from publication of the facts if a large proportion of the electorate is illiterate?

Clearly, then, no public can possibly reach a right conclusion unless it is well informed, and that requires both a free press and a literate electorate. This is well known to Jeffersonian democrats. Jefferson, with his faith in the common man, insisted: 'The functionaries of every government have propensities to command at will the liberty and property of their constituents. There is no safe deposit for these but with the people themselves; nor can they be safe with them without information. *Where the press is free, and every man able to read, all is safe'* (emphasis supplied).

Students of government may well argue that this last sentence somewhat oversimplifies the problem. It holds only providing that 'every man' is sufficiently interested to inform himself on the issues and the candidates and, in addition, exercises his sovereign rights by going to the polls to vote.

So much do we take our system of government for granted that we seldom stop to contemplate the difficulties of self-government. Government of, by, and for the *people* is extremely difficult – so difficult that we often witness failures or near-failures of self-government among ourselves. Fortunately, these examples occur as a rule on a small scale, as with the Pendergast, Kelly-Nash, Hague, and Huey Long 'machines'.

The advocates of *immediate universal* world federal government are always the first to point to American, British, or French failures in democracy when one insists on beginning world government with a union of the democracies. The argument goes something like this: 'You are a fine bunch of hypocrites to talk about our taking the leadership in forming a democratic international federal union, when we don't practice democracy even at home.'

It is ironical that those who point to the holes in the fabric of the best democracies should insist that peoples with no experience whatever in domestic self-government are as well suited to practice international self-government as are the most experienced.

True, people learn self-government by practising it. But the free people of today who have had several generations' experience with self-government should insist that the non-self-governing peoples of the world demonstrate their ability to practice self-government at home before they attempt to constitute it on an international scale.

It will accomplish nothing to insist on perfection. To insist on perfect democracy in the United States, Britain, Canada, or France as a prerequisite to their uniting to found a democratic international federal union would be as foolish as to insist on perfection in the domestic democratic government of nations who apply for admission to the international union once it is set up. For freedom's sake, free men ought to insist that so tremendous an undertaking begin with those most experienced with self-government at home.

In *World Order*, (London and Toronto: Oxford University Press, 1939) Lionel Curtis records the failure of the French Revolution to establish self-government in France in 1790: 'In destroying their monarchy the French destroyed the entire mechanism of their national life. To do all this was easier than to copy methods of government which Anglo-Saxons had practised for centuries.' As a consequence of their inexperience, the French did not succeed in establishing stable self-government at home until 1870.

Next, the world saw this phenomenon repeated in Russia. The relatively democratic regime of Kerensky, trying to work with people inexperienced in self-government, gave way to the dictatorship of the Bolshevist minority. Later, the German people, also inexperienced in self-government, lost to still another dictator.

Shall the free people of the world run this risk by entrusting their freedom to a world government composed of an overwhelming majority of illiterates and people with little or no experience in free self-government? That would be folly indeed.

(J. F. S.)

11   Nuclear union *vs* the universalist approach

The Hague Conferences, the League of Nations, and the United Nations exemplify the universalist method of organizing nations. It aims to begin with all or nearly all the nations.

There are three fallacious assumptions in this universalist theory. One is that a few nations cannot or should not be united more strongly than many nations. Another is that peace and liberty are endangered more by offending the nations who are excluded from a non-universal organization than by weakening its constitution and enfeebling its action by including too many diverse nations at the start. The third fallacy is that strength lies in numbers rather than in the degree of organization, that a body politic created by fifty nations or two billion [= 2 thousand million] people must necessarily be stronger than one created by fifteen nations or half a billion people.

The more numerous the founders of any organization are, the more diverse they are. The greater their diversity of development, backround, interests and purpose, the looser and weaker will be the organization they consent to create. Conversely, the more naturally coherent and congenial the founders are, the fewer they will be – and the more likely they are to form a strong organization.

Universal membership must, of course, be the goal of those who seek to establish peace through international federal union. This leads many to conclude that the more founder nations the union has, the sooner it will reach its goal. They forget that effective power is much more essential for such a union than is universal membership. The first and hardest step in federating nations is to get agreement on a sound, effective constitution. This difficulty increases in proportion to the number and diversity of the nations whose agreement is required for the drafting of a constitution. And the more universal in membership the constitutional convention is, the lower falls the average of the political understanding and experience available in it to meet the difficulties that this universality produces. Universality is the goal, but one does not really advance toward it by trying to make the last step the first step.

The failures of universalism have led to various attempts to achieve world organization on some restricted basis. One way is exemplified by the various proposals to federate Europe; another, by the recurrent attempts to organize merely the great powers. (The Dumbarton Oaks idea that the Big Three should first agree on the Charter of the United Nations, and the San Francisco decision to give each of the Big Five a veto, stem from the theory that produced the Holy Alliance, the Quadruple Alliance, the Concert of Powers, Mussolini's Four Power proposal and Munich.) Both these methods have two grave faults: (1) They limit membership by some factor – position on a certain continent or possession of great armed power – which keeps their membership for ever restricted and excludes the possibility of expansion to universality, and (2) they fail to reduce political, economic and social diversity in reducing the number of members.

There remains the method of the nucleus, proposed by *Union Now* in 1939. It alone combines the truth in the universalist approach with the truth in the restrictionist method, and it combines them in their common-sense order. It alone seeks to achieve universal membership by the normal principle of growth, after first taking care to select the best seed.

This nuclear method would have the nucleus of a free world federal union created by federating the few democracies best qualified to agree on a constitution that is sound, and capable of gaining universal jurisdiction through the peaceful admission of outside nations to the union as all concerned grow ripe for this. This method counts on the vitality of the nucleus and the nature of its principles to make it grow into universality – eventual world government.

For reasons already given, the nucleus must be limited to the peoples most experienced in free self-government. To try to get dictatorship and democracy to pull together is – as has been seen in the Big Three and the United Nations – to organize a tug of war, not a government. To invite to a constituent assembly all the nations that call themselves democracies is to burden the most capable with the least experienced. It is as well-intentioned and as foolish as trying to preserve the Bill of Rights for children by giving children the vote.

The nuclear method would turn to the leaders in the field of free government for leadership in the tremendously difficult task of getting a free world government constituted. It would at one stroke reduce the problem to soluble proportions and heighten the level of ability of those called on to solve it.

The best example of the nuclear method is the United States. Its Constitutional Convention, as David Cort pointed out in the *The Great Union*, (Washington, DC: Federal Union, Inc., 1944) did not include all the peoples on the North American continent. It excluded the British in Canada, the Spanish in Florida, the Indian nations. It did not include all the allies in the war: France was not invited. Nor was it restricted to the Big Three among the thirteen states – Virginia, Pennsylvania, Massachusetts. The Convention of 1787 was limited to the most experienced democracies in the world. They created a constitution so sound that it is now the oldest written one in the world. The nuclear union it formed has expanded peacefully since then as no government ever did before – from thirteen to forty-eight states [in 1950] – and has produced the freest, greatest power on earth. It has grown to include people of all nationalities. It has proved that once a sound, free federal union is constituted, it can safely extend the advantages of citizenship to millions of immigrants and slaves quite inexperienced in self-government. But such a constitution could never have been formed save by the few most experienced in this field. The astonishing success of this nuclear method in the United States makes it the hopeful way to achieve a free federal world government.

(J. F. S. and C. K. S.)

12   The nucleus of union now

When the nucleus has been formed by those peoples best qualified to constitute a sound union, it would then achieve universality by peacefully extending its federal principles to other nations as this became practicable.

But what is meant by the 'peoples who are best qualified'? Where to draw the line? Obviously, it cannot be drawn sharply. Nucleus implies that the founders of the union will be relatively few in number. How few?

The term 'best qualified' refers of course to the ability to govern itself in freedom which a people has shown. The more experience it has had with the federal system, the better qualified it will be to solve soundly the many knotty constitutional problems facing the formation of any international federation. But its qualifications in these respects must be considered in the light of power and other factors.

The nuclear approach keeps always in mind the extreme difficulty of getting *any* nations to federate by common consent. To overcome these difficulties, the nucleus must be such as to repay with great advantages those who undertake to create it. One of the greatest advantages they can hope to gain from this effort is peace. The best nucleus is therefore one whose power from the start is so great that no aggressor can dream of attacking it. Neither a Western European nor an Anglo-American union could give this guarantee.

Again, the more of a community the founders already form in spirit, in interests, and as a geographical region, the better qualified they will be to succeed in federating soundly.

The best nucleus, in short, will be formed of these democracies that have the most experience, the strongest existing bonds to help bring them closer together, and enough material and moral power to provide their union, as soon as it is formed, with such overwhelming power as to discourage any aggressor. . . .

(J. F. S. and C. K. S.)

16   Essentials in a federal executive

The essential characteristics of the executive in a federal union, which Hamilton listed in *The Federalist*, no. 70, may be reduced to these two: *energy*, or power to uphold the constitution and enforce the laws, and *responsibility to the people*.

These characterize the executive in any democratic republic, even the most centralized ones; they are not peculiar to the federal system. Whereas a federal union differs on the legislative side from both a league and a unitary state, one may say that on the executive side, the essential is that it resembles the latter and differs only from the former. There is this exception, that the field of action of the unitary state's executive is much greater than that of the federal executive. But this limitation really results from the division of power between central and local governments that characterizes federal union.

Better understanding of the federal executive may be gained by considering the essential differences between a federal union and a league in this respect.

First, as regards *energy*. A league may have, on paper, power to act, as does the United Nations, as did the League of Nations. But the basic unit in a league – the sovereign state – makes this power illusory. States league together to preserve the sovereignty of each from invasion; that puts them in no mood to let their sovereignty be invaded by empowering any league organ to make them act without their consent.

A single executive is always the most energetic – but try to imagine the Kremlin letting the United States, France, Belgium,

Poland, any nation, have even for a month the executive power over it that it has over the states and people of the USSR. Or the US Government permitting Soviet Russia, or any other nation, to have over it the power the President has over the forty-eight states. Only one thing would be more abhorrent to the principle of national sovereignty. That would be to permit any man to have as a person – not as the embodiment of some nation's sovereignty – the power to uphold the UN Charter that any national executive has to uphold his country's constitution.

It is not surprising, then, that leagues never have, and cannot have, energy on the executive side. They can hardly be said to have a true executive organ. Their only permanent officials form merely a secretariat. Their presidents are but ephemeral figureheads. That was as true of the League of Friendship of the thirteen states as it is of the United Nations. There were fourteen 'Presidents of the United States' before Washington became its first federal executive, but who remembers them?

The nearest thing to an executive in the United Nations is the Security Council acting as a body. Though it seems at first glance to have more power than the Geneva League Council, it is really even feebler. For it cannot act legally against the worst crime in its calendar – aggression by a great-power member – as the Geneva Council did in Italy's case. It is no more authorized than that body was to execute minor league agreements within the territory of any member state.

The federal-union system was invented to save individual liberty from the anarchy that is inherent in a league, and it must therefore have an energetic executive. It succeeds in giving its executive the same effective power to act that the executive of any unitary state has because it is founded on the same basic unit – the individual citizen.

The essential in the federal system is that the executive should have this effective power to uphold the constitution and enforce the laws – not the exact form of the executive. It is not essential that executive power be confined to one person alone, as in the United States, for it to be effective. The Canadian federal union, for example, has a double executive; that is, the functions of the US President are divided between an hereditary king (acting through his viceroy) who is the ceremonial head of the state, and a prime minister whose tenure in office depends upon his retaining the confidence of parliament. The Swiss federal union, again, follows the US system of giving the executive a fixed, four-year term of office, but divides executive power equally among the seven members of the Federal Council, each of whom rotates in the purely ceremonial office of President of Switzerland. All three types of federal executive have worked effectively. The combination of them that *Union Now*[4] suggested for a federation of the democracies shows there are still other ways to ensure energy in a federal executive.

There remains the other essential, *responsibility to the people*. What passes for an executive in a league is by its nature as lacking in this respect as in energy. The nations composing the UN Security Council are, as a body, responsible to no one; even the elected members are not responsible to the Assembly. The delegates are responsible only to their own governments, not to their people.

To be responsible to the people of the union as a whole, it is essential that a federal executive should not depend, in any sense, on the government of any state member. The executive, however, need not be directly elected by the people of the union – as he practically is in the United States – to be responsible to them. He can be made even more abruptly subject to dismissal by public opinion through the British parliamentary system, as in Australia or Canada. By this method, the prime minister is a member of parliament who need be elected to that office merely by the voters of his district, but who holds the office of chief executive only so long as he has a majority in parliament. In the Swiss federal union, the two-house legislature, the National Assembly, elects the executive council, which is not subject to a vote of confidence, but is subject to re-election – an essential factor in assuring responsibility to the people. And it should be remembered that in no nation is government more directly in the hands of the people than in Switzerland, pioneer of the initiative and referendum.

One may argue the merits of the various existing federal executives, or improve on them; the only essentials are that the executive have effective power, safeguarded by effective responsibility to the people of the union.

(C. K. S.)

AUTHORS' NOTES

1. For fuller proof that the League failed *because* of its basic principles, see *Union Now* (New York: Harper and Brothers, 1939, 1940, 1949), esp. 4, 6 and 7.
2. The term, 'federal union', was occasionally used in the Convention of 1787, however, to denote the United States under the Articles of Confederation.
3. See, for example, *I Chose Freedom* by Victor Kravchenko (New York: Charles Scribner's Sons, 1946).
4. *Union Now* (postwar edition, pp. 145–6, 208–9) proposed for the executive of the union a board of five persons, each elected for five years, one each year, or each elected for ten years, one every other year, to 'assure constant change in the Board and constant stability'. Three would be elected by popular vote; the other two in between, by the Senate and by the House, respectively.

     The board would 'delegate most of its executive authority to a Premier who would exercise this power with the help of a Cabinet of his own choosing until he lost the confidence of either the House or the Senate, whereupon the Board would name another Premier.' The board would also have power to dissolve either house, or both of them, in order to call new elections. It would have the duties of reporting regularly on the state of freedom and of the union, and on the effects and need of change, and of recommending broad policies.

IV   ARNOLD TOYNBEE, 'TOWARDS A FUTURE WORLD ORDER'

In the final chapters of his massive *Study of History*, begun in 1934 and completed in 1961, Arnold Toynbee (1889–1975) devotes some attention to the international situation since the Second World War, trying to discern larger tendencies and possibilities emerging in the world. He portrays the citizens of the world in the 1950s as feeling caught between the two super-powers, the United States and the Soviet Union, locked in deadly struggle. He assumes that world government of some sort will be eventually necessary to avoid nuclear annihilation; and he argues that most men would prefer a world government under the leadership of the United States rather than the Soviet Union, and that the United States, if forced to assume the role of leadership, would not create a highly centralized super-government but a world federation. Toynbee dismisses (perhaps too easily) the possibility that the desired world federation might emerge out of the United Nations Organization. In *Change and Habit* (1966) Toynbee still argues for the possibility and the necessity of a world federation, but he is less definite about any leadership role of the United States. He also observes ominously that past history would lead us to look to the 'universal states' for leadership in world government, and that the only two extant 'universal states' are Russia and China.

The text below is reprinted from Arnold Toynbee, *A Study of History*, Somervell abridgement, II (London and New York: Oxford University Press, 1957) pp. 326–31.

By AD 1955 the abolition of War had, in fact, become imperative; but it could not be abolished unless the control of atomic energy could be concentrated in the hands of some single political authority. This monopoly of the command of the master weapon of the age would enable, and indeed compel, the authority to assume the role of a world government. The effective seat of this government, in the conditions of AD 1955, must be either Washington or Moscow; but neither the United States nor the Soviet Union was prepared to place itself at the mercy of the other.

In this awkward pass the traditional line of least psychological resistance would, no doubt, have been to resort to the old-fashioned expedient of ordeal by battle. A 'knock-out blow' had, as we have already seen, been the brutal means by which one broken-down civilization after another had passed out of its Time of Troubles into its universal state. But on this occasion the knock-out blow might knock out not only the antagonist but also the victor, the referee, the boxing-ring, and all the spectators.

In these circumstances the best hope for the future of Mankind lay in the possibility that the governments and peoples of the United States and the Soviet Union might have the patience to pursue a policy which had come to be called 'peaceful co-existence'. The greatest menace to the welfare and, indeed, to the continued existence of the Human Race was not the invention of atomic weapons but the rise in living human souls of a temper such as had once prevailed in an Early Modern Western world for about a hundred years beginning with the outbreak of the Western Wars of Religion *circa* AD 1560. At the opening of the second half of the twentieth century there were Capitalists and Communists who, like their Catholic and Protestant forerunners, felt it to be impracticable as well as intolerable to acquiesce in leaving the allegiance of Society divided for an indefinite time to come between the true faith (their own) and a damnable heresy (their adversary's). But the history of the Western Wars of Religion bore witness that spiritual issues could not be settled by force of arms; and Mankind's acquisition of atomic weapons gave warning that it would not be open to Capitalists and Communists to learn the futility of religious warfare by the empirical method of prolonged trial that had been practicable for Catholics and Protestants in an age in which Man's worst weapons had been swords, pikes, and muzzle-loading guns.

In circumstances so precarious and obscure, a dogmatic optimism was as unwarrantable as a dogmatic pessimism; and the living generation of Mankind had no choice but to reconcile itself, as best it could, to the knowledge that it was facing issues in which its very existence might be at stake, and that it was impossible to guess what the outcome was going to be. In AD 1955 these perennial waifs on board Noah's Ark were in the situation in which Thor Heyerdahl and his five fellow vikings on board a balsa-log raft had found themselves on the morning of 7 August 1947. On that fateful morning the westward-flowing current that had borne the raft *Kon-Tiki* 4300 miles across the Pacific Ocean was now carrying her towards the Raroia Reef. Beyond the line of surf breaking over this barrier the approaching seafarers could descry the feathery tops of palm-trees, and they knew that these palms bedecked idyllic isles set in a still lagoon; but between them and this haven ran the foaming and thundering reef 'in one line from horizon to horizon',[1] and the set of the current and the wind gave the voyagers no chance of circumnavigation. They were heading perforce towards an inevitable ordeal; and, though they might know what were the alternatives awaiting any voyagers in this plight, they could not guess which of these alternatives was to be the ending of their own saga.

If the raft were to disintegrate among the breakers, the crew would be torn in pieces by the knife-edged coral, unless they were saved by speedy drowning from that more painful death. If the raft were to hold together, and if its crew were to succeed in holding onto it until the breakers had defeated their own malice by washing the raft onto the reef high and dry, a shipwrecked crew might swim across the still lagoon beyond and reach one of the palm-crowned islands alive. If the moment of the raft's arrival at the reef should happen to coincide with the flood of one of those high tides that periodically submerged the reef to a depth that compelled the breakers to subside, the *Kon-Tiki* might, after all, clear the death-line in calm water, and so come through unscathed. In the event, a high tide did flow in to lift her battered frame off the reef into the lagoon some days after the surf had cast her up on to a bare coral scree; but on the morning of 7 August 1947 no man on board the

Kon-Tiki could tell which of these alternative destinies was going to be his.

The experience of these six young Scandinavian seafarers on that day was an apt allegory of an ordeal that still lay ahead of Mankind at the opening of the second half of the twentieth century of the Christian Era. An Ark of Civilization that had travelled a time-distance of some five or six thousand years across the ocean of History was making for a reef which its crew would not be able to circumnavigate. This unavoidable danger ahead was the perilous transition between a world partitioned into an American and a Russian sphere and a world united under the control of a single political authority which, in an age of atomic weapons, must supersede the present division of authority sooner or later in one way or another. Was the transition to be pacific or catastrophic, and, if catastrophic, was the catastrophe to be complete and irremediable, or would it be partial and leave behind it elements out of which a slow and painful recovery might ultimately be achieved? At the time when these words were being written no one could foreknow the outcome of the ordeal towards which the world was manifestly moving.

Without waiting, however, for a facile wisdom after the event, an observer might perhaps usefully speculate on the shape of things to come, so long as he confined his consideration of a future world order to elements which an ecumenical dispensation seemed likely to have in common with each of the two demi-mundane dispensations that had been crystallizing respectively round the United States and round the Soviet Union.

In so far as technology could, and did, supply facilities for transport, world government was already a quite practicable proposition. As soon, however, as we ascend – or descend – from the plane of technology to the plane of human nature, we find the earthly paradise skilfully assembled by the ingenuity of *Homo Faber* being reduced to a fool's paradise by the perversity of *Homo Politicus*. The 'Parliament of Man', whose inauguration the prophet Tennyson seemed to have synchronized approximately with the invention of the aeroplane, was now in being under the more prosaic name of the United Nations Organization; and UNO had not proved as ineffective as its critics sometimes asserted. On the other hand, UNO was evidently incapable of becoming the embryo of a world government. The realities of the distribution of power were not reflected in the clumsiness of a constitution that had embodied the unrealistic principle of 'one state, one vote', and had then found no better means of bringing a fictitious equality of states into line with a harsh reality than the concession to five powers, one of whom had since been reduced from China to Formosa, of a veto that was denied to their nominal peers. The best prospect in sight for the UNO was that it might evolve from being a forum into becoming a confederacy; but there is a great gulf between any confederacy of independent states and any confederation of peoples with a central government claiming and receiving the direct personal allegiance of every individual citizen of the union; and it was notorious that the history of political institutions knew of no case in which that gulf had been crossed by any other process than a revolutionary leap.

On this showing, UNO seemed unlikely to be the institutional nucleus out of which an eventually inevitable world government would grow. The probability seemed to be that this would take shape through the development, not of UNO, but of one or other of two older and tougher political 'going concerns', the Government of the United States or the Government of the Soviet Union.

If the living generation of Mankind had been free to choose between them, there could be little doubt in any Western observer's mind that a decisive majority of all living men and women that were competent to form any judgement on this issue would have opted for becoming subjects of the United States rather than of the Soviet Union. The virtues that made the United States incomparably preferable stood out conspicuously against a Communist Russian foil.

America's cardinal virtue in the eyes of her present and prospective subjects was her transparently sincere reluctance to be drawn into playing this role at all. An appreciable portion of the living generation of American citizens, as well as the ancestors of all American citizens who were not themselves immigrants, had been moved to pluck up their roots in the Old World and to start life again in the New World by a yearning to extricate themselves from the affairs of a continent whose dust they had demonstratively shaken from off their feet; and the buoyancy of the hope with which they had made their withdrawal was matched by the poignancy of the regret with which the living generation of Americans was making its compulsory return. The compulsion was, as we have seen, an aspect of that 'annihilation of distance' which was making the Old and the New World one and indivisible. But the ever-increasing clearness with which this compulsion was being recognized was not diminishing the reluctance with which it was being accepted.

The Americans' second outstanding virtue was their generosity. Both the United States and the Soviet Union were 'sated' powers, but their economic and social situations were identical only in the general sense that Russia, like America, commanded vast undeveloped resources. In contrast to America, Russia had hardly begun to exploit her potentialities, and the development that she had carried out, at such a cost in human effort and suffering, during the twelve years immediately preceding the German assault upon her in AD 1941, had been largely ruined by the invasion. Thereafter the Russians had taken an unjust advantage of finding themselves on the winning side by recouping themselves for a German destruction of Russian industrial plant by seizing and removing plant, not only from a guilty Germany, but also from East and Central European countries that the Russians professed to be liberating from the Nazis, and from Chinese provinces in Manchuria that they professed to be liberating from the Japanese. This was a contrast indeed to the American post-war reconstruction policy, implemented in the Marshall Plan and other measures, in which a number of countries, whose life had been disorganized by the war, were set on their feet again with the help of money voted by the Congress at Washington with the goodwill of the American taxpayer, out of whose pockets all this money had to come. In the past it had been customary for victorious powers, not to give, but to take, and there had been no departure from this evil custom in the policy of the Soviet Union. The Marshall Plan set a new standard for which there was no comparable historical precedent. It might be said that this generous policy was in America's own interests, on a long and enlightened view; but good deeds are not the less good for being, at the same time, wise.

Citizens of West European countries were, however, now haunted by fears that some American decision, in which the West European peoples might have had no say, might bring Russian atomic weapons down upon their heads as unintended by-products of some impulsive American retort to Russian provocation. Though the satellite states of the American Union enjoyed, in most respects, an enviable freedom of action that was entirely denied to the satellites of the Soviet Union, they did find themselves in much the same helpless plight in these matters of life and death.

In AD 1895, in connection with an Anglo-American dispute about the location of the frontier between British Guiana and Venezuela, an American Secretary of State, Richard Olney, had issued a resonant dispatch which had secured for his name such immortality as it still enjoyed.

'To-day the United States is practically sovereign on this continent, and its fiat is law upon the subjects to which it confines its interposition. Why? It is not because of the pure friendship or good will felt for it. It is not simply by reason of its high character as a civilized state, nor because wisdom and justice and equity are the invariable characteristics of the dealings of the United States. It is because, in addition to all other grounds, its infinite resources, combined with its isolated position, render it master of the situation and practically invulnerable as against any or all other Powers.

This dictum had not lost any of its cogency in coming to be applicable to a far wider sphere of hegemony than Latin America alone, and, though a non-American might resign himself to the fact that American whips were preferable to Russian scorpions, a 'philosopher' might (in Gibbonian parlance) 'be permitted to enlarge his views' by observing that the virtual monopoly, by a paramount power, of the determination and execution of policies in which the lives and fortunes of satellite peoples were at stake, was pregnant with a constitutional problem which could be solved only by some form of federal union. The constitutional issues raised by the advent of a supernational order were not likely to be settled easily or rapidly, but at least it was a good omen that the United States was already committed by its own history to an approval of the federal principle.

AUTHOR'S NOTE

1. Thor Heyerdahl, *Kon-Tiki* (Chicago: Rand McNally, 1950) p. 242.

3

Peace through Distributive Justice

Numerous books have been written to explain, or try to explain, how so many law-abiding and basically moral citizens in Germany in the 1930s could have rallied behind the bizarre and militaristic Nazi regime. One of the more probable explanations is that the German people were incensed and rankling over the perceived injustices of the Treaty of Versailles, which were imposed on them rather arbitrarily at the conclusion of the First World War. In many wars it is not as easy to determine overt aggression as in the case of the Second World War, but it would seem that, in cases where wars begin with aggression on the part of one nation against another, the aggression is often the result of injustices which the aggressor nation perceives itself to have received from another nation in the past – for instance, unrecognized border claims, unpaid debts, failure to keep pacts and harsh punishments for past offences. If this is the case, it might seem to be merely a matter of prudence that anyone working for peace should turn his attention first to questions of justice – perhaps with the optimistic expectation that the solution of problems of injustice will facilitate the solution of the problem of war. The authors represented in this chapter are characteristic of this approach, and this emphasis.

I   JEREMY BENTHAM, 'A PLAN FOR A UNIVERSAL AND PERPETUAL PEACE' (extracts)

Jeremy Bentham (1748–1832) is best known for some of his foundational works in utilitarian ethics, and his plan for international peace reflects some assumptions of utilitarianism. The 'greatest happiness' principle of utilitarianism is reflected here in Bentham's appeal to arrangements which will be conducive to the greatest happiness of the 'citizens of the world', rather than to the designs or convenience of sovereign governments. The utilitarian presupposition of a *laissez-faire* system of economics and an interest in distributive justice consonant with capitalist economics are also reflected in the concrete proposals he makes for the perpetuation of international peace. In line with these presuppositions he proposes, among other things, the disengagement of European powers from colonialism, which militates against the welfare not only of colonized peoples but also of the colonizers; the lifting of artificial governmental trade restrictions and preferences, which militated against the free trade and commerce that the capitalist theorist Adam Smith considered inimical to the prosperity of the masses as well as of business and industry; cutbacks in the troops maintained by each nation, not just to reduce the burden on taxpayers but to avoid military clashes and thus create the proper atmosphere for trade within and among nations; and the creation of a common court of adjudication, in order to further the cause of justice in the international sphere.

The essay was written in 1789 and first published in 1843. It is reprinted here abridged from Charles W. Everett, *Jeremy Bentham* (New York: Dell; London: Weidenfeld and Nicolson, 1966) pp. 195-7, 222-5, 227-9. Explanatory notes in square brackets have been added by the present editor.

The object of the present essay is to submit to the world a plan for an universal and perpetual peace. The globe is the field of dominion to which the author aspires – the press of the engine, and the only one he employs – the cabinet of mankind the theatre of his intrigue.

The happiest of mankind are sufferers by war; and the wisest, nay, even the least wise, are wise enough to ascribe the chief of their sufferings to that cause.

The following plan has for its basis two fundamental propositions: (1) the reduction and fixation of the force of the several nations that compose the European system; (2) the emancipation of the distant dependencies of each state.[1] Each of these propositions has its distinct advantages; but neither of them, it will appear, would completely answer the purpose without the other.

As to the utility of such an universal and lasting peace, supposing a plan for that purpose practicable, and likely to be adopted, there can be but one voice. The objection, and the only objection to it, is the apparent impracticability of it; that it is not only hopeless, but that to such a degree that any proposal to that effect deserves the name of visionary and ridiculous. This objection I shall endeavour in the first place to remove; for the removal of this prejudice may be necessary to procure for the plan a hearing.

What can be better suited to the preparing of men's minds for the reception of such a proposal than the proposal itself?

Let it not be objected that the age is not ripe for such a proposal: the more it wants of being ripe, the sooner we should begin to do what can be done to ripen it; the more we should do to ripen it. A proposal of this sort, is one of those things that can never come too early nor too late.

Who that bears the name of Christian can refuse the assistance of his prayers? What pulpit can forbear to second me with its eloquence – Catholics and Protestants, Church-of-England men and Dissenters, may all agree in this, if in nothing else. I call upon them all to aid me with their countenance and their support.

The ensuing sheets are dedicated to the common welfare of all civilized nations; but more particularly of Great Britain and France.

The end in view is to recommend three grand objects – simplicity of government, national frugality, and peace.

Reflection has satisfied me of the truth of the following propositions –

I   That it is not the interest of Great Britain to have any foreign dependencies whatsoever.

II   That it is not the interest of Great Britain to have any treaty of alliance, offensive or defensive, with any other power whatever.

III That it is not the interest of Great Britain to have any treaty with any power whatsoever, for the purpose of possessing any advantage whatsoever in point of trade, to the exclusion of any other nation whatsoever.

IV   That it is not the interest of Great Britain to keep up any naval force beyond what may be sufficient to defend its commerce against pirates.

V   That it is not the interest of Great Britain to keep on foot any regulations whatsoever of distant preparation for the augmentation or maintenance of its naval force; such as the Navigation Act, bounties on the Greenland trade, and other trades regarded as nurseries for seamen.

VI, VII, VIII, IX, and X   That all these several propositions are also true of France.

As far as Great Britain is concerned, I rest the proof of these several propositions principally upon two very simple principles.

1. That the increase of growing wealth in every nation in a given period, is necessarily limited by the quantity of capital it possesses at that period.
2. That Great Britain, with or without Ireland, and without any other dependency, can have no reasonable ground to apprehend injury from any one nation upon earth.

Turning to France, I substitute to the last of the two just-mentioned propositions the following:

3. That France, standing singly, has at present nothing to fear from any other nation than Great Britain: nor, if standing clear of her foreign dependencies, would she have anything to fear from Great Britain.

    XI   That supposing Great Britain and France thoroughly agreed, the principal difficulties would be removed to the establishment of a plan of general and permanent pacification for all Europe.

    XII   That for the maintenance of such a pacification, general and perpetual treaties might be formed, limiting the number of troops to be maintained.

    XIII   That the maintenance of such a pacification might be considerably facilitated, by the establishment of a common court of judicature for the decision of differences between the several nations, although such court were not to be armed with any coercive powers.

    XIV   That secrecy in the operations of the foreign department ought not to be endured in England; being altogether useless, and equally repugnant to the interests of liberty and to those of peace. . . .

Conquests made by New Zealanders have some sense in them; while the conquered fry, the conquerors fatten. Conquests made by the polished nations of antiquity – conquests made by Greeks and Romans – had some sense in them. Land, movables, inhabitants, everything went into the pocket. The invasions of France in the days of the Edwards and the Henries, had a rational object. Prisoners were taken, and the country was stripped to pay their ransom. The ransom of a single prisoner, a Duke of Orleans, exceeded one third of the national revenue of England.

Conquests made by a modern despot of the continent have still some sense in them. The new property; the inhabitants, as many as he thinks fit to set his mark upon, go to increase his armies; their substance, as much as he thinks fit to squeeze from them, goes into his purse.

Conquests made by the British nation would be violations of common sense, were there no such thing as justice. They are bungling imitations of miserable originals, [a]bating the essential circumstances. Nothing but confirmed blindness and stupidity can prompt us to go on imitating Alexander and Caesar, and the New Zealanders, and Catherine and Frederick, without the profit.

If it be the king alone who gets the appointment to the places [influential positions, franchises], it is a part of the nation, it may be said, that gets the benefit of filling them. A precious lottery! Fifty or one hundred millions the cost of the tickets. So many years purchase of ten or twenty thousand a year, the value of the prizes. This if the scheme succeed: what if it fail?

I do not say there are no shares in the plunder: it is impossible for the head of a gang to put the whole of it into his own pocket. All I contend for is, that robbery by wholesale is not so profitable as by retail: if the whole gang together pick the pockets of strangers to a certain amount, the ringleaders pick the pockets of the rest to a much greater. Shall I or shall I not succeed in persuading my countrymen that it is not their interest to be thieves?

'Oh, but you mistake!' cries somebody, 'we do not now make war for conquests, but for trade.' More foolish still. This is a still worse bargain than before. Conquer the whole world, it is impossible you should increase your trade one halfpenny: it is impossible you should do otherwise than diminish it. Conquer little or much, you pay for it by taxes: but just so much as a merchant pays in taxes, just so much he is disabled from adding to the capital he employs in trade. Had you two worlds to trade with, you could only trade with them to the amount of your capital, and what credit, you might meet with on the strength of it. This being true of each trader, is so of all traders. Find a fallacy in this short argument if you can. If you obtained your new right of trading given you for nothing, you would not be a halfpenny the richer: if you paid for them by war or preparations for war; by just so much as you paid for these you would be the poorer.

The good people of England, along with the right of self-government, conquered the prodigious right of trade. The revolution was to produce for them not only the blessings of security and power, but immense and sudden wealth. Year has followed after year, and to their endless astonishment, the progress to wealth has gone on no faster than before. One piece of good fortune still wanting, they have never thought of: that on the day their shackles were knocked off, some kind sylph should have slipped a few thousand pounds into every man's pocket. There is no law against my flying to the moon. Yet I cannot get there. Why? Because I have no wings. What wings are to flying, capital is to trade.

There are two ways of making war for trade – forcing independent nations to let you trade with them, and conquering nations, or pieces of nations, to make them trade with you. The former contrivance is to appearance the more easy, and the policy of it the more refined. The latter is more in the good old way, and the king does his own business and the nation's at the same time. He gets the naming to the places: and the nation cannot choose but join with him, being assured that it is all for the sake of getting them the trade. The places he lays hold of, good man, only out of necessity, and that they may not go a-begging: on his account, he has no more mind for them than a new-made bishop for the mitre, or a new-made speaker for the chair. To the increase of trade, both these plans of war equally contribute. What you get in both cases is the pleasure of the war.

The legal right of trading to part of America was conquered by France from Britain in the last war. What have they got by it? They have got Tobago [tobacco], bankruptcy, and a revolution, for their fifty millions. Ministers, who to account for the bankruptcy are forced to say something about the war, call it a national one: the king has not got by it – therefore the nation has. What has it got? A fine trade, were there but capital to carry it on. With such room for trade, how comes there to be no more to it? This is what merchants and manufacturers are putting themselves to the torture to account for. The sylph so necessary elsewhere, was still more necessary to France; since, over and above her other work, there was the fifty millions spent in powder and shot to replace.

The King of France, however, by getting Tobago, probably obtained two or three thousand pounds worth of places to give away. This is what he got, and this is all that anybody got for the nation's fifty millions. Let us go on as we have begun, strike a bold stroke, take all their vessels we can lay hold of without a declaration of war, and who knows but what we may get it back again.

With the advantages we now have over them, five times the success they are so pleased with, would be but a moderate expectation. For every fifty millions thus laid out, our king would get in places to the amount, not of two or three thousand pounds only, but say of ten, fifteen, or twenty thousand pounds. All this would be prodigious glory – and fine paragraphs and speeches, thanksgivings, and birthday odes, might be sung and said for it: but for economy, I would much rather give the king new places to the same amount at home, if at this price his ministers would sell us peace. . . .

Hitherto war has been the national rage: peace has always come too soon, war too late. To tie up the ministers' hands and make them continually accountable, would be depriving them of numberless occasions of seizing those happy advantages that lead to war: it would be lessening the people's chance of their favourite amusement. For these hundred years past, ministers, to do them justice, have generally been more backward than the people – the great object has rather been to force them into war, than to keep them out of it. Walpole and Newcastle were both forced into war.

It admits of no doubt, if we are really for war, and fond of it for its own sake, we can do no better than let things continue as they are. If we think peace better than war, it is equally certain that the law of secrecy cannot be too soon abolished.

Such is the general confusion of ideas – such the power of the imagination – such the force of prejudice – that I verily believe the persuasion is not an uncommon one; so clear in their notions are many worthy gentlemen, that they look upon war, if successful, as a cause of opulence and prosperity. With equal justice might they look upon the loss of a leg as a cause of swiftness.

Well, but if it be not directly the cause of opulence, it is indirectly; from the successes of war, come, say they, our prosperity, our greatness; thence the respect paid to us by foreign powers – thence our security: and who does not know how necessary security is to opulence?

No; war is, in this way, just as unfavourable to opulence as in the other. In the present mode of carrying on war – a mode which it is in no man's power to depart from, security is in proportion to opulence. Just so far then as war is, by its direct effects, unfavourable to opulence, just so far is it unfavourable to security.

Respect is a term I shall beg leave to change; respect is a mixture of fear and esteem, but for constituting esteem, force is not the instrument, but justice. The sentiment really relied upon for security is fear. By respect then is meant, in plain English, fear. But in a case like this, fear is much more adverse than favourable to security. So many as fear you, join against you till they think they are too strong for you, and then they are afraid of you no longer; meantime they all hate you, and jointly and severally they do you as much mischief as they can. You, on your part, are not behind-hand with them. Conscious or not conscious of your own bad intentions, you suspect theirs to be still worse. Their notion of your intentions is the same. Measures of mere self-defence are naturally taken for projects of aggression. The same causes produce, on both sides, the same effects; each makes haste to begin for fear of being forestalled. In this state of things, if on either side there happen to be a minister or a would-be minister, who has a fancy for war, the stroke is struck, and the tinder catches fire.

At school, the strongest boy may perhaps be the safest. Two or more boys are not always in readiness to join against one. But though this notion may hold good in an English school, it will not bear transplanting upon the theatre of Europe.

Oh! but if your neighbours are really afraid of you, their fear is of use to you in another way – you get the turn of the scale in all disputes. Points that are at all doubtful, they give up to you of course. Watch the moment, and you may every now and then gain points that do not admit of doubt. This is only the former old set of fallacies exhibited in a more obscure form, and which, from their obscurity only, can show as new. The fact is, as has been already shown, there is no nation that has any points to gain to the prejudice of any other. Between the interests of nations, there is nowhere any real conflict: if they appear repugnant anywhere, it is only in proportion as they are misunderstood. What are these points? What points are these which, if you had your choice, you would wish to gain of them? Preferences in trade have been proved to be worth nothing, distant territorial acquisitions have been proved to be worth less than nothing. When these are out of the question, what other points are there worth gaining by such means?

'Opulence' is the word I have first mentioned; but 'opulence' is not the word that would be first pitched upon. The repugnancy of the connection between war and opulence is too glaring: the term 'opulence' brings to view an idea too simple, too intelligible, too precise. 'Splendour', 'greatness', 'glory', these are terms better suited to the purpose. Prove first that war contributes to splendour and greatness, you may persuade yourself it contributes to opulence, because when you think of splendour you think of opulence. But splendour, greatness, glory, all these fine things, may be produced by useless success, and unprofitable and enervating extent of dominion obtained at the expense of opulence; and this is the way in which you may manage so as to prove to yourself, that the way to make a man run the quicker is to cut off one of his legs. And true enough it is, that a man who has had a leg cut off, and the stump healed, may hop faster than a man who lies in bed with both legs broken, can walk. And thus you may prove that Britain is in a better case after the expenditure of a glorious war, than if there had been no war; because France or some other country, was put by it into a still worse condition.

In respect, therefore, of any benefit to be derived in the shape of conquest, or of trade – of opulence or of respect – no advantage can be reaped by the employment of the unnecessary, the mischievous, and unconstitutional system of clandestinity and secrecy in negotiation.

AUTHOR'S NOTE

1. Two original writers have gone before me in this line, Dean Tucker and Dr Anderson. The object of the first was to persuade the world of the inutility of war, but more particularly of the war then raging when he wrote; the object of the second to show the inutility of the colonies.

II   PIERRE-JOSEPH PROUDHON, ['ON THE PRIMARY CAUSE OF WAR']

translated by Patrice O'Rourke and Howard P. Kainz

The anarchist Pierre-Joseph Proudhon (1809–65) is best known for his contention, 'Property is theft.' In maintaining that property is theft, he was referring not to individual possessions, but to property acquired by profiteers by exploitation of the impoverished working class. Karl Marx was somewhat influenced by Proudhon's ideas, but in the end broke ranks with him because of an apparent irreconcilability of goals. Proudhon, according to Marx, was speaking the language of 'justice and injustice', and asking for fair distribution of goods and profits *within* a capitalist system. But Marx believed that ideas of justice and injustice are created by economic systems, and that one objective should be to overthrow the present (capitalist) system entirely. Proudhon's views, with which many moderate socialists have found themselves in sympathy, gravitate towards the abolition of revolution and warfare, rather than the generation of revolutions and wars to overturn the entire system of economic relations.

The text below has been translated by Patrice O'Rourke and Howard P. Kainz from P.-J. Proudhon, *La Guerre et la paix: recherches sur le principe et la constitution du droit des gens* (Paris: Libraire des Sciences Politiques et Sociales, 1927), IV. 4: 'Influence du paupérisme sur l'état et les relations internationales'.

Is poverty the primary cause of war? How can people agitated by misery yet not content to blame their governments, their nobles, their clergy, their dynasties, their bourgeoisie, end up by accusing one another and produce for themselves war as blind as it is useless? I could, as so many others have done, castigate human madness, the bad advice of hunger and the Machiavellianism of princes and nobles, who have always seized the occasion to make war as a way of diverting popular restlessness and safeguarding their power. I do not deny that these considerations have their truth; nevertheless, they are not totally satisfying to the intellect. It is impossible, in good criticism, to attribute a phenomenon such as war – which, let us not forget, embraces the physiology and psychology of humanity, and which is ruled by a real law, the law of strength – to causes that are so inconsistent.

I have reached this conclusion by observing that the considerations of international law, upon which declarations of war rest almost exclusively, are linked in the most intimate way to economic considerations. The result of this is that, if political motives may be regarded as an apparent cause of war, then economic needs are the secret and first cause of it. On this fundamental point there can be no mistake.

It is a statistically recognized fact that property crime diminishes as the well-being of the masses increases. Whoever has enough to live on is little concerned with his neighbour. That is how people are. Thus there is no revolution in the state if the needs of the citizens have been satisfied; and there would be no war between states if they were not compelled by a dominating power. Guarantee a nation liberty, security and life, and it will not worry over what its neighbours do. It will not speak of union or incorporation or of adjusting the frontier; it will even make short shrift of its own nationality – witness the peasants of Galicia, happy to become Austrians to be delivered from their leaders; witness those of Lombardy, cursing their landowners and appealing to both the king and the emperor.

Alas, nationality comes into play, the spirit of war takes hold of the prince and the people, only when sustenance and property are at risk or land or markets are scarce. This is how the questions of pre-eminence, of the balance of power, of colonies, and so on, which . . . can be settled only by force, are posed.

Why conceal it? The law of incorporation or dismemberment, which we have seen play such a large role in politics and in history, appears under a completely different guise when, tracing back cause to cause, we seek out the hidden incentives. Likewise, the state – organ of collective force, incarnation of justice – is, in the last analysis, only an economic expression; and international relations, wars and peace treaties, despite all the majesty that the law of force confers upon them, are also economic expressions, monuments of our indigence. Worldly cupidity, the expectation of tribute, the ardent thirst for the foreigner's goods are concealed at the root of our diplomacy. We shall shortly see this more vividly when, taking leave of general considerations, we explore the facts.

We are now perfectly placed to distinguish between the first cause of war and its motives or secondary causes, the latter being of a purely political order, the former exclusively economic. It is perfectly possible that the political motives of war, more specious than real, leave the true cause to be discovered. This pre-eminence of the cause of war over its motives is . . . one of the characteristics of the present age. Is this a reason for always finding fault with the bad faith of princes, as historians do? (As if the heads of state, in the qualities that are of concern to us here, were not the representatives of their people, affected by the same poverty as their subjects!)

In general, the motives upon which declarations of war rest are serious and real; they translate a political necessity. But the first cause dominates them; and if it is possible always to contest, from the perspective of war, the legitimacy of such a cause, unfortunately there is no way to deny its existence. There is nothing on earth which is more constant and more implacable than the misery of the human species. *Ego sum pauper et dolens* ['I am poor and sorrowful', Psalm 69]; this, if warriors had as much philosophy as bravery, would be the motto they would inscribe on their banners.

Thus, the primary cause of all war is unique. It can vary in intensity and not be absolutely determining, but it is always present, always playing a part and, so far, indestructible. It breaks out through jealousies, rivalries, questions of borders, of slavery; questions, if I dare say so, of party divisions. This is where the responsibility of nations lies. Without this influence of poverty, without the disorder that produces economic disequilibrium in states, war would be impossible. No secondary motive would be capable of driving nations to arm themselves against each other. It is thus for nations to provide for their own economic well-being, and to insure themselves, through work, temperance and equilibrium of interests, against poverty, which is the one true cause of war.

But, if war, failing the ill-being that agitates nations, is impossible, like an effect without a cause, it only manages to seduce consciences and win acceptance by means of motives based on international law, which, prior to *raison d'état*, legitimates war. This is where the responsibility of political leaders begins, for they alone are capable of turning war from a possibility into a reality. It is a first and remarkable effect of the application of economic principles that nations which are economically stable can no longer spontaneously rush against each other. Massive invasions belong to the age of barbarism: the last act of forest and nomadic life. As people become more industrious and hard working, war becomes the prerogative of governments. It thus belongs to the men in power to determine when the annoyance caused by a threat from abroad has become insupportable. In such a case, the care of public security permits one power to avail itself of the rigour of international law against another and to call for a trial of strength. In all cases, the statesman must remember the full extent of his responsibility; that war, whatever he does, retains an odious side; that war is stimulated by poverty and all the vices that accompany it – cupidity, luxury, voluptuousness, all the corruptions and all the crimes that the craving for booty, along with scarcity, engenders.

Our conclusions about the primary cause of war place us in a new terrain, little known to the ancients – that of political economy. Here we make a further discovery. Henceforth it will be easy to predict – something the jurists of the old school would not suspect – that, where war is concerned, the rules of the law, sublime in theory, will be poor constraints for people who covet a prey or are concerned to defend their property. What can the laws of war [*la guerre dans les formes*] be for armies that march under the banner of famine? . . .

We conclude from this that philosophical and subjective knowledge of law is not enough to ensure justice in war and in peace. It is necessary to join to this philosophical knowledge a practical knowledge of the laws of production and exchange, for without this the application of law remains arbitrary and war inextinguishable.

III   JOHN RAWLS, ['THE ORIGINAL POSITION']

If one accepts the arguments of a Bentham or a Proudhon that a system of international justice is fundamental to international peace, a problem still remains in defining 'justice'. A proponent of classical *laissez-faire*, for example, may believe that justice will best be served if the government promotes free-market relationships; while an extreme anarchist such as Proudhon may hold that only a specially designed credit system for the working man will bring about a just state of affairs. We turn thus to John Rawl's theory of distributive justice, one of the most elaborately thought-out schemes to date. Although Rawls is not specifically concerned with the problem of peace here, his theory holds implications for anyone who would make peace dependent on justice, and his theory is particularly applicable to the international situation because it requires, by its very 'ground rules', that a state of abstraction from any particular concrete society be presumed. In other words, it asks us to assume an 'original position' prior to our own inclusion in any society. From that position we are to work out the basic structures of 'justice as fairness' that we should want to live under *if we did not know anything about our own relative position* or *advantages* in this society (Rawls calls this the 'veil of ignorance'). The following extract outlines the initial deliberations that one would go through in the 'original position'. The two basic principles that Rawls arrives at through these deliberations are (1) that certain basic rights and liberties, such as the rights of free speech and freedom of worship, would have to be guaranteed for all; and (2) that the distribution of unequal advantages or benefits – for example, of incentives for production or of income-tax exemptions – are only justified when they produce greater advantage to those who are worse off in any particular society. It is conceivable that the same principles, with appropriate modification, might be applicable to the inhabited world, as an ultimate 'society', as well as to societies in the more usual sense.

The text below is reprinted from John Rawls, *A Theory of Justice* (Cambridge, Mass.: Harvard University Press, 1971) section 3: 'The Main Idea of the Theory of Justice'. All ellipses indicate omission of cross-references to other sections.

My aim is to present a conception of justice which generalizes and carries to a higher level of abstraction the familiar theory of the social contract as found, say, in Locke, Rousseau, and Kant.[1] In order to do this we are not to think of the original contract as one to enter a particular society or to set up a particular form of government. Rather, the guiding idea is that the principles of justice for the basic structure of society are the object of the original agreement. They are the principles that free and rational persons concerned to further their own interests would accept in an initial position of equality as defining the fundamental terms of their association. These principles are to regulate all further agreements; they specify the kinds of social co-operation that can be entered into and the forms of government that can be established. This way of regarding the principles of justice I shall call 'justice as fairness'.

Thus we are to imagine that those who engage in social co-operation choose together, in one joint act, the principles which are to assign basic rights and duties and to determine the division of social benefits. Men are to decide in advance how they are to regulate their claims against one another and what is to be the foundation charter of their society. Just as each person must decide by rational reflection what constitutes his good, that is, the system of ends which it is rational for him to pursue, so a group of persons must decide once and for all what is to count among them as just and unjust. The choice which rational men would make in this hypothetical situation of equal liberty, assuming for the present that this choice problem has a solution, determines the principles of justice.

In justice as fairness the original position of equality corresponds to the state of nature in the traditional theory of the social contract. This original position is not, of course, thought of as an actual historical state of affairs, much less as a primitive condition of culture. It is understood as a purely hypothetical situation characterized so as to lead to a certain conception of justice.[2] Among the essential features of this situation is that no one knows his place in society, his class position or social status, nor does any one know his fortune in the distribution of natural assets and abilities, his intelligence, strength, and the like. I shall even assume that the parties do not know their conceptions of the good or their special psychological propensities. The principles of justice are chosen behind a veil of ignorance. This ensures that no one is advantaged or disadvantaged in the choice of principles by the outcome of natural chance or the contingency of social circumstances. Since all are similarly situated and no one is able to design principles to favour his particular condition, the principles of justice are the result of a fair agreement or bargain. For given the circumstances of the original position, the symmetry of everyone's relations to each other, this initial situation is fair between individuals as moral persons, that is, as rational beings with their own ends and capable, I shall assume, of a sense of justice. The original position is, one might say, the appropriate initial *status quo*, and thus the fundamental agreements reached in it are fair. This explains the propriety of the name 'justice as fairness': it conveys the idea that the principles of justice are agreed to in an initial situation that is fair. The name does not mean that the concepts of justice and fairness are the same, any more than the phrase 'poetry as metaphor' means that the concepts of poetry and metaphor are the same.

Justice as fairness begins, as I have said, with one of the most general of all choices which persons might make together, namely, with the choice of the first principles of a conception of justice which is to regulate all subsequent criticism and reform of institutions. Then, having chosen a conception of justice, we can suppose that they are to choose a constitution and a legislature to enact laws, and so on, all in accordance with the principles of justice initially agreed upon. Our social situation is just if it is such that by this sequence of hypothetical agreements we would have contracted into the general system of rules which defines it. Moreover, assuming that the original position does determine a set of principles (that is, that a particular conception of justice would be chosen), it will then be true that whenever social institutions satisfy these principles those engaged in them can say to one another that they are co-operating on terms to which they would agree if they were free and equal persons whose relations with respect to one another were fair. They could all view their arrangements as meeting the stipulations which they would acknowledge in an initial situation that embodies widely accepted and reasonable constraints on the choice of principles. The general recognition of this fact would provide the basis for a public acceptance of the corresponding principles of justice. No society can, of course, be a scheme of co-operation which men enter voluntarily in a literal sense; each person finds himself placed at birth in some particular position in some particular society, and the nature of this position materially affects his life prospects. Yet a society satisfying the principles of justice as fairness comes as close as a society can to being a voluntary scheme, for it meets the principles which free and equal persons would assent to under circumstances that are fair. In this sense its members are autonomous and the obligations they recognize self-imposed.

One feature of justice as fairness is to think of the parties in the initial situation as rational and mutually disinterested. This does not mean that the parties are egoists, that is, individuals with only certain kinds of interests, say in wealth, prestige, and domination. But they are conceived as not taking an interest in one another's interests. They are to presume that even their spiritual aims may be opposed, in the way that the aims of those of different religions may be opposed. Moreover, the concept of rationality must be interpreted as far as possible in the narrow sense, standard in economic theory, of taking the most effective means to given ends. I shall modify this concept to some extent, . . . but one must try to avoid introducing into it any controversial ethical elements. The initial situation must be characterized by stipulations that are widely accepted.

In working out the conception of justice as fairness one main task clearly is to determine which principles of justice would be chosen in the original position. To do this we must describe this situation in some detail and formulate with care the problem of choice which it presents. . . . It may be observed, however, that once the principles of justice are thought of as arising from an original agreement in a situation of equality, it is an open question whether the principle of utility would be acknowledged. Offhand it hardly seems likely that persons who view themselves as equals, entitled to press their claims upon one another, would agree to a principle which may require lesser life prospects for some simply for the sake of a greater sum of advantages enjoyed by others. Since each desires to protect his interests, his capacity to advance his conception of the good, no one has a reason to acquiesce in an enduring loss for himself in order to bring about a greater net balance of satisfaction. In the absence of strong and lasting benevolent impulses, a rational man would not accept a basic structure merely because it maximized the algebraic sum of advantages irrespective of its permanent effects on his own basic rights and interests. Thus it seems that the principle of utility is incompatible with the conception of social co-operation among equals for mutual advantage. It appears to be inconsistent with the idea of reciprocity implicit in the notion of a well-ordered society. Or, at any rate, so I shall argue.

I shall maintain instead that the persons in the initial situation would choose two rather different principles: the first requires equality in the assignment of basic rights and duties, while the second holds that social and economic inequalities, for example inequalities of wealth and authority, are just only if they result in compensating benefits for everyone, and in particular for the least advantaged members of society. These principles rule out justifying institutions on the grounds that the hardships of some are offset by a greater good in the aggregate. It may be expedient but it is not just that some should have less in order that others may prosper. But there is no injustice in the greater benefits earned by a few provided that the situation of persons not so fortunate is thereby improved. The intuitive idea is that since everyone's well-being depends upon a scheme of co-operation without which no one could have a satisfactory life, the division of advantages should be such as to draw forth the willing co-operation of everyone taking part in it, including those less well situated. Yet this can be expected only if reasonable terms are proposed. The two principles mentioned seem to be a fair agreement on the basis of which those better endowed, or more fortunate in their social position, neither of which we can be said to deserve, could expect the willing co-operation of others when some workable scheme is a necessary condition of the welfare of all.[3] Once we decide to look for a conception of justice that nullifies the accidents of natural endowment and the contingencies of social circumstance as counters in quest for political and economic advantage, we are led to these principles. They express the result of leaving aside those aspects of the social world that seem arbitrary from a moral point of view.

The problem of the choice of principles, however, is extremely difficult. I do not expect the answer I shall suggest to be convincing to everyone. It is, therefore, worth noting from the outset that justice as fairness, like other contract views, consists of two parts: (1) an interpretation of the initial situation and of the problem of choice posed there, and (2) a set of principles which, it is argued, would be agreed to. One may accept the first part of the theory (or some variant thereof), but not the other, and conversely. The concept of the initial contractual situation may seem reasonable although the particular principles proposed are rejected. To be sure, I want to maintain that the most appropriate conception of this situation does lead to principles of justice contrary to utilitarianism and perfectionism, and therefore that the contract doctrine provides an alternative to these views. Still, one may dispute this contention even though one grants that the contractarian method is a useful way of studying ethical theories and of setting forth their underlying assumptions.

Justice as fairness is an example of what I have called a contract theory. Now there may be an objection to the term 'contract' and related expressions, but I think it will serve reasonably well. Many words have misleading connotations which at first are likely to confuse. The terms 'utility' and 'utilitarianism' are surely no exception. They too have unfortunate suggestions which hostile critics have been willing to exploit; yet they are clear enough for those prepared to study utilitarian doctrine. The same should be true of the term 'contract' applied to moral theories. As I have mentioned, to understand it one has to keep in mind that it implies a certain level of abstraction. In particular, the content of the relevant agreement is not to enter a given society or to adopt a given form of government, but to accept certain moral principles. Moreover, the undertakings referred to are purely hypothetical: a contract view holds that certain principles would be accepted in a well-defined initial situation.

The merit of the contract terminology is that it conveys the idea that principles of justice may be conceived as principles that would be chosen by rational persons, and that in this way conceptions of justice may be explained and justified. The theory of justice is a part, perhaps the most significant part, of the theory of rational choice. Furthermore, principles of justice deal with conflicting claims upon the advantages won by social co-operation; they apply to the relations among several persons or groups. The word 'contract' suggests this plurality as well as the condition that the appropriate division of advantages must be in accordance with principles acceptable to all parties. The condition of publicity for principles of justice is also connoted by the contract phraseology. Thus, if these principles are the outcome of an agreement, citizens have a knowledge of the principles that others follow. It is characteristic of contract theories to stress the public nature of political principles. Finally there is the long tradition of the contract doctrine. Expressing the tie with this line of thought helps to define ideas and accords with natural piety. There are then several advantages in the use of the term 'contract'. With due precautions taken, it should not be misleading.

A final remark. Justice as fairness is not a complete contract theory. For it is clear that the contractarian idea can be extended to the choice of more or less an entire ethical system, that is, to a system including principles for all the virtues and not only for justice. Now for the most part I shall consider only principles of justice and others closely related to them; I make no attempt to discuss the virtues in a systematic way. Obviously if justice as fairness succeeds reasonably well, a next step would be to study the more general view suggested by the name 'rightness as fairness'. But even this wider theory fails to embrace all moral relationships, since it would seem to include only our relations with other persons and to leave out of account how we are to conduct ourselves toward animals and the rest of nature. I do not contend that the contract notion offers a way to approach these questions which are certainly of the first importance; and I shall have to put them aside. We must recognize the limited scope of justice as fairness and of the general type of view that it exemplifies. How far its conclusions must be revised once these other matters are understood cannot be decided in advance.

AUTHOR'S NOTES

1. As the text suggests, I shall regard Locke's *Second Treatise of Government*, Rousseau's *The Social Contract*, and Kant's ethical works beginning with *The Foundations of the Metaphysics of Morals* as definitive of the contract tradition. For all of its greatness, Hobbes's *Leviathan* raises special problems. A general historical survey is provided by J. W. Gough, *The Social Contract*, 2nd edn (Oxford: Clarendon Press, 1957), and Otto Gierke, *Natural Law and the Theory of Society*, tr. with an introduction by Ernest Barker (Cambridge: Cambridge University Press, 1934). A presentation of the contract view as primarily an ethical theory is to be found in G. R. Grice, *The Grounds of Moral Judgment* (Cambridge: Cambridge University Press, 1967). . . .

2. Kant is clear that the original agreement is hypothetical. See *The Metaphysics of Morals*, pt I (*Rechtslehre*), esp. sections 47, 52; and pt II of the essay 'Concerning the Common Saying: This May be True in Theory but it Does not Apply in Practice', in *Kant's Political Writings*, ed. Hans Reiss and tr. H. B. Nisbet (Cambridge: Cambridge Univer-

sity Press, 1970) pp. 73–87. See Georges Vlachos, *La Pensée politique de Kant* (Paris: Presses Universitaires de France, 1962) pp. 326–35; and J. G. Murphy, *Kant: The Philosophy of Right* (London: Macmillan, 1970) pp. 109–12, 133–6, for a further discussion.

3. For the formulation of this intuitive idea I am indebted to Allan Gibbard.

4

Peace through a Triumph of Religious or Spiritual Values

Off-hand one might hesitate to look to religion for any assistance in bringing about a state of worldwide peace. After all, have not the world's religions (with the possible exception of Buddhism) been responsible for some of the deepest, bitterest and most persistent rivalries in the history of mankind – Catholics against Protestants and Orthodox Christians, Muslims against Christians and Jews, Hindus against Muslims, and so on and so forth? On the other hand, there are mysterious commandments of universal love or compassion nesting at the heart of the world's religions, and it might seem that these, if only activated, would be the necessary and sufficient impetus for the inauguration of 'peace on earth'. Thus some thinkers have looked to religion, stripped of its accretions of dogma, superstition, taboo, rivalry and political connections, for the spiritual reserves necessary for overcoming the chronic conflict and discord of mankind. When religion comes into its own, they argue, a unified mankind will begin to emerge spontaneously without needing to be forged by force into unity by some totalitarian political leviathans.

I DESIDERIUS ERASMUS, *THE COMPLAINT OF PEACE*

The Dutch scholar Erasmus (1467–1534) published *The Complaint of Peace* in the same year as Martin Luther posted his ninety-five theses on the door of the cathedral church in Wittenberg, and just a few years after Niccolò Machiavelli had written *The Prince*. Like Luther, he was incensed at abuses in the Catholic Church, and in particular at the long history of Church involvement in military pursuits. But, unlike Luther, he became an advocate of reform, not revolt; and in the interests of reform he appeals in the

Complaint to the simple message of peace which is inherent in the Christian Gospel, and which (he argues) has been essentially connected with the spirit of Christianity all along. Like Machiavelli, Erasmus had a passionate interest in politics, but, very much unlike Machiavelli, he does not think it useful or even possible to separate considerations of the affairs of state from religious and moral considerations. *The Complaint of Peace* is thus a call to Christian peoples to take their own spiritual heritage more seriously, and disengage themselves from the folly of war, which is the enemy of all true progress.

The text below is reprinted from *The Essential Erasmus*, ed. and tr. John P. Dolan (London and New York: New English Library and New American Library, 1964) pp. 174–204.

Peace speaks:

If mankind had rejected me for its own advantage, I would, it seems, have sufficient reason to regret both an undeserved injury and an injustice. However, since men have cast me out, who am the source of all their happiness, and in doing so have brought down calamity after calamity upon themselves, this situation becomes more an object of pity than of resentment on my part. My inclination toward angry retaliation gives way to one of sympathy. To repel one who loves you is certainly a breach of kindness, yet to act in this manner toward one who is the protector of the entire race is an out-and-out crime. Consider the insanity of those who deem themselves unworthy of the advantages I offer and exchange them for increasing evils. Evil in itself is worthy of any kind of suppression, but what can we do other than lament the fate of those who are completely obsessed with evil? Their failure to recognize their own unhappy lot only increases the need for such lamentation. One of the surest signs of convalescence is the recognition of the seriousness of the disease. Even this they fail to do.

As Peace, am I not praised by both men and gods as the very source and defender of all good things? What is there of prosperity, of security, or of happiness that cannot be ascribed to me? On the other hand, is not war the destroyer of all things and the very seed of evil? What is there of prosperity that it does not infect? What is secure or pleasant that it does not undermine? No greater enemy of goodness or of religion can be found. Though nothing is more odious to gods and harmful to man, yet it is incredible to see the tremendous expenditure of work and effort that intelligent beings put forth in an effort to exchange me for a heap of ruinous evils.

Actually it would be much easier for me to be rejected by wild beasts. This I could forgive on the grounds that they are lacking in intelligence. But we are dealing with men endowed with reason and enriched with the gifts of the Holy Spirit, which should incline them toward love and concord with their fellow men. It is a strange situation, indeed, that I should prefer to take up my abode among beasts rather than men.

If we look at the various solar systems and the stars in the firmament, we find, although there is a diversity of motion and power, one continuing harmony. The very forces of the elements about us, although often ranged in opposition to one another, actually through a shifting of pressures bring about and facilitate a great concord. If we turn to animal life, we see that there is here every evidence of agreement and collaboration for mutual ends. What can be more dissimilar than the body and the soul? Yet nature has bound them together in such a marvellous manner that only death can adequately illustrate it. Life itself is nothing other than a union of body and soul, and health is based upon a working together of the various parts of the body. The various species of the animal kingdom live everywhere in peaceful communities. Take, for example, the behaviour of elephant herds, of swine and sheep pasturing together. Cranes and jays flock together. Storks noted for their parental care have their well-known roosts. Dolphins are known to defend one another, bees and ants demonstrate great community efforts.

Thus far I have spoken of creatures that lack intelligence but are nevertheless equipped with sense perception. Yet even members of the vegetable world, trees and herbs, show an attraction toward others of the same species. Vines embrace elms, peaches welcome the encirclement of vines. The world of the insensible appreciates the benefits of peace. Possessing life, they come close to the power of sense perception. Lifeless stones have a sense of peace and concord, as for example the magnet attracts and holds metal. Among themselves wild beasts exhibit basic agreement. Lions are wont to act civilly toward fellow lions, a boar will not threaten one of his own kind with its tusks, there is peace in the lynx family. Dragons refuse cruelty to fellow dragons, and the behaviour of wolves has been praised in proverbs. It may amaze you to note that even the diabolic spirits who first broke the peace and continue to create discord among men and angels are joined together in an effort to defend their tyranny.

Unanimity is of absolute necessity for man, yet neither nature, education, nor the rewards of concord and the disadvantages of disunity seem to be able to unite mankind in mutual love. Man possesses a unifying principle in the fact that he is moulded to the same figure and form and endowed with the same power of speech. Whereas beasts differ in the variety of their shapes, man is identical with fellow man in possessing speech and reason. It is this that distinguishes him from the beast. His ability to speak enables him above all to cultivate friendship. We find in him the seeds of all virtue, a ready disposition toward mutual benevolence, and a delight in helping others. Yet he appears to have been corrupted and to be prone to fall to the very level of beasts. What the common people call humanness and gentility we prefer to term benevolence. To all of this nature has added the gift of tears. Should any offence be committed or friendship darkened, the shedding of tears often rectifies the situation. Although nature has provided so many means for securing concord, she has not done so merely to afford pleasantries but rather because amity is of necessity as far as man is concerned. The very make-up of man is such that regardless of how well he may be endowed with various gifts of mind and body, he even requires the aid and assistance of his inferiors. This very fact that various men have diversified gifts indicates the need for mutual love and friendship. The variety of products of different nations lends itself to this need for reciprocity. Whereas nature has equipped the animal kingdom with various sorts of armour and means of defence, man's lack of these means necessitates mutual assistance. Necessity has invented cities, constructed for the purpose of repelling the attacks of beasts and brigands through the combined efforts of its citizenry.

The nature of things is such that were it not for the concord of the matrimonial state man would perish at birth without the care of his parents. As a matter of fact he would not have been born at all without parental effort and care. His infancy is a period demanding the solicitude of nurses and midwives. To this nature adds the love of children for their parents as it supports them in a mutual way during their helplessness. This the Greeks call ἀντιπελάργωσις, or mutual compensation of benefits. We can add to this the bonds of kinship and affinity. Some display a similarity of natural dispositions, similar tastes and interests that are a sure means of mutual love. Many possess a certain unanimity or mutual attraction that the ancients were wont to consider a special gift of God.

Thus we see that nature has amply provided man with inducements to peace and concord. With how many different arguments
does she not attract us? With how many means does she not
actually compel us to concord? Yet it appears that some diabolical
fiend has taken over the very heart of man and forced him to reject
and destroy these inclinations to tranquillity with an insatiable
desire for fighting. Had not continual strife and discord dulled our
sense of concord, who could believe that man endowed with
reason could perpetrate with continual strife such crime, bloodshed,
and destruction of places sacred and profane? No combination of
efforts, however holy, is able to prevent them from destroying
each other. If affairs were as they should be, the very nature of
mankind would be sufficient to bring some kind of agreement. Yet
as things now stand, nature, such a force in the animal world, is of
no avail among men. But can we say that Christ is of no consequence
among men? Why is it that his most cogent doctrine, that of peace,
has no effect among men? If nature is inadequate, then why is the
more powerful teaching of Christ also ineffective? Why does
his urging to mutual benevolence not deter them from the madness of war? When I hear the expression 'man', I run joyfully to his
company since it was for him that I was created and I hope to find
an abode in his midst. This is particularly true in the case of
Christian men. Yet I find that Christians are actually worse than
the heathen. Things are actually so bad that whereas in former
times lawyers were the bane of the ordinary man hauled into
court, they are now the least of the evils he has to encounter facing
trial.

I see a city and hope that there at least a single wall enclosing a
common code of laws might govern a society peacefully and with
co-operation. Yet the city is so filled with dissension that it appears
that here I have been completely proscribed.

I take my leave of the common people, who are as turbulent as
the stormy seas, to go to the courts of the princes. Here I expect to
find a sure haven since princes are wiser than the common people,
and they have received a commission from the Prince of Peace,
Who sends peace to all men but especially to princes.

Everything appears in order here, kind greetings, embraces,
merry banquets and all of the amenities. Yet it is all a façade, a
mere shadow of true peace and concord. Peace is but a pretence
covering factions and secret dissensions. The courts of princes are
not the home of peace but rather the real source of war.

Where shall I turn? Hope has too often deceived me! Princes display brawn rather than intelligence and are led by cupidity rather than reason. I will join the company of scholars. Good letters produce men; philosophy, more than men; theology, gods. I will be able to rest with these men after having been driven from all other areas. What a disillusion!

Here is a new kind of warfare, not as bloody but just as foolish. As if the truth were changed by its location, some doctrines do not cross the sea, do not pass the Alps, or do not swim the Rhine. In the same university logicians war with rhetoricians, theologians dispute with lawyers. In the same profession the Scotist fights with the Thomist, the Nominalist with the Realist, the Platonist with the Peripatetic. They disagree on the smallest matters and are frequently incensed over nothing at all. They fight until the heat of argument leads to slanders and to blows. Their weapons are not daggers but venomous pens. They tear one another with taunts. They attack the reputations of their opponents with the deadly darts of their tongues. After this deception where shall I turn? What remains but religion? Though religion is common to all Christians, the clergy, as their title, apparel, and ceremonies indicate, are more completely committed to it. Their profession of religion gives me hope of finding a haven among them. Their garments are of white, my own colour, a fact that pleases me. I perceive crosses, the symbols of peace. I hear the name of brother, a sign of love. I hear salutations of peace happily pronounced. I see all things held in common, a united chapter, a single Church, a common set of laws, and daily exercises. Who would not expect to discover good here? Yet the chapter rarely agrees with the bishop. This would not matter so much if the chapter members agreed among themselves. How many priests are there who do not tangle with fellow priests? Paul says that Christians should not take fellow Christians to court. Should a priest wage war with a priest or a bishop with a bishop? Perhaps these men should be forgiven because custom has brought them into the company of laymen who have corrupted them. Let them defend what has by now become their right.

There is one type of man who is bound to religion as closely as a turtle is to its shell. The tie is permanent. I had hoped to find a place among these, but my hopes again proved false. They were included since I did not wish to leave any stone unturned. I departed from nowhere more gladly than from the abode of the monks. What could I hope for when one order does not agree with another? There are as many factions as there are communities. The Dominicans wrangle with the Minorites; the Benedictines with the Bernardines. Community practices and ceremonies are as different as their purposes. Pleased with their own, they condemn all others. The same communities are divided into factions. Observants speak evil of Coletani, and they both attack the Conventuals. There is absolutely no agreement among them.

No longer trusting anything, I decided to hide myself in some little monastery that I felt was truly peaceful. What I found was most unpleasant. Would to God it were not true! I found no monastery that was not infected with hatred and disorder. Older men, revered for their wisdom, excited unprofitable debates on trifles. Yet in their own eyes they were fonts of wisdom and piety. A fading hope remained that perhaps in marriage I might find an abode. For do not a common home, a common bed, and common children promise peace? Certainly a union that binds two bodies into one promises it. Yet strife creeps in. Disagreement in outlook soon divides those otherwise so closely bound. Yet it would be more likely for me to find a place of abode among these than among those who with so many ceremonies profess absolute charity. Finally, desiring a place in at least one individual, I failed to discover even one who did not fight within himself. Reason wars with inclinations; inclination struggles against inclination; piety goes one way, cupidity another; lust desires one thing, anger another; ambition wants this, covetousness that.

Men who are not ashamed to be called Christians act in total disagreement with what is most important to Christ. Consider His life. What is it other than a doctrine of concord and love? What do His commandments and parables teach? Peace and charity. Did the prophet Isaiah, when he foretold of the coming of Christ, promise that He should be a ruler of cities or a warrior? No! What then did he promise? A Prince of Peace. Isaiah named Him after what he judged to be best since he wanted Him to be understood to be the finest of all things. It is not marvellous that it should seem so to Isaiah, when Silius, the pagan poet, wrote of me: 'Peace is the best of all things, which nature gives to man.' The Psalmist agrees, 'His seat is made in peace.' He said, 'In peace' rather than among armies. He is a prince of peace and loves peace. He is offended by discord.

Isaiah calls peace a work of justice, meaning what Paul, the once turbulent Saul made peaceable, also signified. This doctor of peace, who preferred charity to all other gifts of the spirit, eloquently thundered out my praise to the Corinthians! Is it not to my glory to be praised by so laudable a man? Sometimes he calls Him the god of peace, sometimes the peace of God. He declares that these are so closely united that there can be no peace where God is not present, nor God where peace is not to be found.

We read in Holy Scripture that the angels of peace are called meek and the ministers of God. It is quite evident whom we understand by the angels of war. Under whose banner do these warriors fight? Under his who first sowed discord between God and man. Man should therefore ascribe every calamity he suffers to the devil's dissensions.

It is beside the point that some argue that God in Holy Scripture is called the God of armies and the God of vengeance. There is a great difference between the God revealed to the Jews and the God revealed to the Christians, though in nature He is one God. If we wish to retain old titles, let Him be called the God of armies if you understand armies to mean virtues united together with good men for the destruction of vice. Let Him be the God of vengeance if you take vengeance to be the correction of vice, and if you understand the bloody slaughters of men that fill the books of Hebrews, not as the tearing of men into pieces, but as the tearing of wicked affections out of their hearts.

To return to my topic. As often as Holy Scripture indicates absolute happiness it does so under the name of peace. Isaiah says, 'My people shall sit in the beautifulness of peace.' The Psalmist says, 'Peace upon Israel.' Isaiah marvels at the beauty of the feet of the messengers who announce peace and salvation. Whoever brings tidings of Christ brings tidings of peace. Whoever proclaims war proclaims him who is most unlike Christ.

Did not the Son of God come to earth to reconcile the world to the Father, to join men by indissoluble bonds of charity, and to make man His friend? He was an ambassador for me; He did my business. Solomon prefigured Him. Regardless of David's greatness, because he was a warrior defiled with blood, he was not permitted to build the House of God. He did not deserve in this to be a figure of a peaceable Christ.

Consider, O soldiers, if wars undertaken on the command of God profane, what is the result of wars undertaken for ambition or anger? If pagan blood pollutes the meek king, what does Christian blood do? I pray the true Christian prince to behold the image of his chief Prince. If he observes how Christ entered His Kingdom and how He departed the earth, he will understand how He would have him rule. Peace and concord should be the goal.

Did the angels sound military trumpets when Christ was born? The Jews, who were permitted war, heard the sound of such trumpets; they were allowed to hate their enemies. The angels of peace sing a different song to the people of peace. They do not call men to war. They proclaim peace and the oracles of the prophets. They proclaim peace, not to murderers and warmongers, but to those who in good will are inclined to concord.

Let men pretend what they will about their own injuries. If they did not love war, they would not war continually among themselves. What did Christ teach besides peace? What did He express Himself on besides peace? He saluted His disciples with, 'Peace be to you.' He prescribed it as the only worthy form of greeting for Christians. The Apostles, mindful of this, begin their epistles with wishes of peace to all and with peace to those whom they particularly love. He desires an excellent thing, who wishes for good health; but he who desires peace wishes the very totality of happiness.

Notice the care with which He, in departing from this world, commended the peace He frequently commended throughout His life. He said, 'Love ye one another as I have loved you', and 'I give you My peace, I leave you My peace.' Do you hear what He leaves us? Does He bequeath horses, an army, an empire, riches? No, none of these things. What then? He leaves peace – peace with His friends, peace with His enemies.

Consider His prayer to the Father at the Last Supper, when death was imminent. One would suppose that He would ask for something extraordinary since He knew that whatever He asked for He would obtain. He said, 'O Holy Father, keep them in My name that they may be one as We are one.' See what a noble union Christ asks for us. He said not that they might be of one mind but that they might be one, and not one in any manner but, 'as We are one'. We Who are one in a most perfect and ineffable manner. He declared that men could be saved only by nourishing among themselves peace and concord.

The princes of this world give a distinctive uniform to their men, particularly in time of war, that they may be distinguished from others. Take a look at the badge with which Christ has marked His followers. It is none other than the badge of mutual charity. He said, 'By this sign shall men know that you are My disciples', not if you wear such a uniform, or if you eat this or that food, or if you fast, or if you read psalms, but 'if you love one another as I have loved you'. The precepts of philosophers are innumerable, and the commandments of Moses and of kings are many; but He said, 'My precept is but one: that is that you love one another.'

In prescribing a form of prayer, does He not even at its beginning urge a remarkable concord? 'Our Father', He says. It is the common petition of all men; they are all one household, one family, dependent on one Father. How is it then that they make continual war amongst themselves? With what audacity do you call upon the common Father while thrusting your sword into your brother's vitals. This is the one thing He would have uppermost in the minds of His followers. In so many signs, parables, and precepts He emphasized this zeal for concord. He called Himself a shepherd and His servants sheep. Who has ever seen sheep fighting with sheep? What will the wolves do if the sheep tear at one another?

When the Vine calls Himself the roots and calls His followers the branches, what is He expressing but unanimity? It would be amazing for one branch of a vine to fight with another. Is it not a more monstrous thing for a Christian to fight with a Christian? If anything is sacred and holy to Christians, it should be Christ's last commandments. His last will and testament, so to speak, gave us what He wanted and hence should never be forgotten. What did He command if not mutual love among His followers? What does the communion of holy bread and cup decree but a new and indissoluble concord? When He perceived that peace could not stand up against competition for position, riches, glory, and the desire for vengeance, He forbade such aspirations to His followers. He called on them not to resist evil. He commanded them to do good even to those who did not deserve it and to pray for and wish well to those who were malevolent. Can we call them Christian who for every light injury plunge the greater part of the world into war?

He commands the prince to play the role of minister among his people, not to be superior in just anything but to surpass others in aiding those who need help. Yet for small territorial gain they are not ashamed to stir up widespread dissension. He teaches us to live without possessions like birds or lilies. He forbids us to be concerned about the morrow. It is His will that we all should depend upon heaven. Yet some men do not hesitate for the sake of a little unpaid money to shed much human blood even before payment is due. In these days this appears an extremely justifiable reason for declaring war.

Christ does nothing but command them to learn one lesson from Him: meekness and placidity. When He commands that the gift to be left before the altar be not offered until you are in friendship with your brother, is He not teaching us that concord is to be preserved above all other things and that no sacrifice is pleasing to God if offered in discord? God refused the Jew's gift, a sheep or a kid, if offered by those in disagreement. Dare Christian men while making war offer the Holy Sacrifice?

When He likens Himself to a hen gathering her chickens under her wings, how apt a symbol He uses to depict concord. He is a gatherer. Is it proper that we Christians should act like hawks? He is called the cornerstone. Is it right that His vicars should move the world to battle? Those who boast that they have that supreme moderation as their Prince cannot be reconciled to themselves. He reconciled Pilate and Herod, yet He cannot bring His followers to agreement. Peter, still half Jew, was ready to defend his Lord at the risk of his life; Christ rebuked him and told him to put up his sword. Yet among Christians the sword is drawn against Christians for any light matter. Would He be defended with the sword Who prayed for the authors of His death while dying?

All Christian doctrine in both the Old and New Testament calls for peace, yet Christian life is filled with warfare. What evil is there that cannot be overcome? Let them either relinquish the name of Christian or give expression to the doctrine of Christ by concord. How long shall theory and practice disagree? Adorn your house and your clothes with the image of the Cross as much as you please; Christ will never acknowledge any other sign but that which He Himself prescribed – concord.

The Apostles were commanded to wait for the Holy Spirit when they saw Christ ascending. He promised that He would be continually present among those of His followers who were assembled. Hence no man should expect Christ to be present in war.

What was that fiery and flaming Spirit but charity? Nothing is more common than fire. Fire is kindled with fire, just as the Spirit is the parent of concord. Yet look at the result. Christ claims that they were all of one heart and mind. Remove the spirit from the body and it decays. Take peace away from the Christian life and and it perishes. Many theologians affirm that the Spirit is infused by the sacraments. If they preach the truth, where is the effect of the Spirit – one heart and one mind? If these are fables, why do they pay such great honour to them? I write this in order that Christians might be ashamed of their lives, not that I would dishonour the sacraments.

Christians are called the Church. Does this not admonish us to unanimity? What agreement can there be between military forces and the Church? One points to dissension, the other to together-ness. If you take pride in being a member of the Church, what have you to do with war? If you are outside the Church, what have you to do with Christ?

Are you not received into the same household? Have you not the same Prince? Do you not strive for the same goal? Are you not consecrated by the same sacraments? Do you not enjoy the same gifts? Are you not nourished by the same food? Do you not desire the same reward? Then why do you cause such a disturbance? We notice agreement among mercenaries hired to slaughter because they wage war under the same banner. Cannot the benefits just mentioned unite pious men? Are so many sacraments able to accomplish nothing?

Baptism is the sacrament common to all. By it we are born again to Christ, cut off from the world and grafted as members of Christ. What can be as much itself as the members of a body? There is neither bond nor free, barbarian nor Greek, man nor woman. All are identical in Christ, Who reduces all things to concord.

A little blood tasted on both sides joins the Scythians so that they do not hesitate to die for their friends. Amity is a sacred and holy thing among pagans when a common table unites them. Shall not that heavenly bread and that mystical cup unite Christian men in charity when Christ has ordained it and they renew that sacrifice daily? If Christ has accomplished nothing, why these ceremonies? If He did something really important, why do we neglect it as if it were trivial? Does any man dare be so bold as to come to that table, the banquet of peace, who prepares to war against fellow Chris-tians, who prepares to destroy those for whom Christ died, who prepares to draw that blood for whom Christ shed His?

O hard hearts! In so many things there is fellowship, yet in life there is inexplicable tension. All men are born, must grow old, and die. We are all of the same species. Our religion is the work of one man. We are redeemed by the same sacrifice and nourished by the same sacraments. Whatever gifts come from this come from one source to all equally. We have one Church. All men will have the same reward. The Celestial Jerusalem Christians desire is called the vision of peace. The Church on earth is its prototype. How is it then that the Church differs so greatly from its exemplar? Has industrious nature accomplished so little? Has Christ with His commandments and mysteries accomplished nothing?

Vicious things, according to the proverb, attract to themselves more evil. What is more fragile than the life of man? What is shorter? How many infirmities is it not subject to? Being burdened themselves with more evil than they can bear, these madmen call down upon themselves the worst part of all evil. Blindness clouds their minds, and driven headlong, they break the bonds of nature, Christ, and every organization. They fight everywhere endlessly and without measure, nation against nation, city against city, one faction against another, one prince against another, continually destroying one another. For the foolish ambition of two men, who will shortly perish, human affairs are turned upside down.

I will not recall the tragedies of antiquity. Let us look at the last ten years. What land or what sea did not witness warfare? What region was not soaked with Christian blood? What river was not dyed with human blood? The cruelty of Christians surpasses that of heathens and beasts. The Jews' wars were against strangers and at God's command. Christians should war against vice. Yet they ally themselves with vice to war against men. All pretence aside, ambitions, anger, and the desire for plunder are at the base of Christian wars. The Jewish wars were against foreigners, yet Christians have allied themselves with the Turks to war with fellow Christians.

A desire for glory aroused heathen tyrants to war. When they subdued the barbarians, they treated them well and endeavoured to make the victory as bloodless as possible, thus increasing their own fame and rendering defeat more bearable.

It shames me to recall the vain and superficial reasons whereby Christian princes provoke the world to war. This particular prince finds or feigns an old title as if it mattered who ruled a kingdom so long as the welfare of the people was seen to. Another finds a trifling fault in some neighbouring confederation. A third is privately offended over some slight to someone's wife.

The most criminal of all causes of war is, of course, the desire for power. When certain princes see power slipping from them because a general peace has rendered them expendable, they stir up war in order to remain in power and oppress the people. Others are unable to find a place in peaceful society. What diabolical agents could have put such poison into Christian hearts? Who taught Christians this tyranny? No Dionysius or Mezentius can answer this. They are beasts, not men, and are noble only in tyranny. Their wisdom leads only to harm and misfortune. They are in agreement only to oppress the common good, yet they who do these things are accepted as Christians. Thus polluted they enter holy churches and approach our altars. They should be exiled as diseased persons to some remote corner of the globe.

If Christians are members of one body, why does not every man rejoice at another's fortune? Yet if a neighbouring kingdom is prosperous, this is considered a just cause for war.

What has moved or will move so many to tear at the kingdom of France except that it is prospering? There is no larger kingdom. Nowhere is there a nobler senate. No other country has such a famous university. Nowhere is there greater concord and therefore greater power. Nowhere is the law more respected. Religion itself is pure and free from corruption. It is not infected by the proximity of Turks or Moors as is Hungary or Spain. Germany (excluding Bohemia) is divided among so many princes that there is not even the semblance of a kingdom. France is the undefiled flower of the Christian commonwealth. Should a storm arise, France stands as a strong castle to be attacked with cunning and deceit, and this very fact other Christians delight in. They use their own title as an excuse for wickedness. They enlarge the empire of Christ. Nonsense! They believe the common good is not well provided for unless they overthrow the most beautiful and most fortunate part of Christendom.

Indeed, in doing these things they surpass beasts in cruelty. Not every kind of beast fights. The conflicts of animals are against other beasts. This we cannot overemphasize. A snake does not bite a snake nor a lynx tear a lynx to pieces. When beasts fight, they use their own weapons. Nature has armed them, but man she has left defenceless. O God! With what weapons does anger not arm mankind? Christians attack Christians with the very weapons of hell. Who could believe that man invented explosives?

Beasts do not fight collectively. Who has ever seen ten lions fight ten bulls? Yet how often do 20,000 armed Christians fight 20,000 armed Christians? Is it such a pleasant affair to injure your fellow man? Beasts fight only when motivated by hunger or when fear for their young has enraged them. Actually, what injury is there important enough to cause war between Christians?

The vulgar crowd can claim ignorance for acting thus; the young, lack of knowledge, criminals, their delinquency. However, the seed of war actually springs from those who by age, experience, and wisdom should overcome the ignorance of the common people and the inexperience of the young. The common people construct excellent cities, rule them peacefully, and enrich them. Governors and rulers, like wasps and drones, creep into those cities and secretly steal that which was provided by other men's industry. What many have gathered is wasted by a few; what was well constructed is ruined. If you will not remember things long past, remember the battles and the wars fought during the past ten years. You will find that they were fought for causes that did not concern the common man.

Among the heathens it is a shameful thing for an old man to be obliged to go to war. Among Christians it has become praiseworthy. An old soldier is a shameful thing for [Ovid's] Naso. Yet today we praise men in military service who are over seventy.

The priests, who in times past under the bloody law of Moses were not permitted to be defiled with blood, are no longer ashamed to fight. Theologians, masters of the Christian life, are not ashamed, nor are religious, bishops, and even cardinals. The vicars of Christ do not hesitate to instigate that very thing that Christ so detested.

What do mitres and helmets have in common? What has a crosier to do with a sword? What has a Bible to do with a shield? How can one reconcile a salutation of peace with an exhortation to war; peace in one's mouth and war in one's deeds? Do you praise war with the same mouth that you preach peace and Christ? Do you herald with the same trumpet both God and Satan? Do you, wearing a cowl, incite the simple to murder, believing you are preaching the Gospel? Do you in the place of the Apostles teach what is contrary to the precepts of the Apostles? Are you not afraid that what was spoken of by Christ's messengers – how good the [feet] of those who spread peace and salvation – will be contradicted? What filth is the tongue of a priest who exhorts war, evil, and murder!

Among pagan Romans, whoever became Pontifex Maximus took an oath to keep his hands free from blood and, if he should injure anyone, never to excuse his action. Titus Vespasian, the pagan emperor, kept the oath constantly and was praised by pagan writers. Yet priests dedicated to God as well as monks, who should be even more holy, now inflame men to murder. They make the trumpet of the Gospel the trumpet of Mars. They forget their dignity and stop at nothing in their warmongering. Through these clergy normally peaceful princes are incited to war by the men whose duty it is to divert them from warfare. Priests fight for things condemned even by the pagan philosophers, a contempt that should be strongly evident among followers of the Apostles.

A few years ago, when the world was violently drawn into war, those Gospel-preachers, the Grey and Black Friars, stirred up to a greater tempo men already so inclined. They encouraged Frenchmen against Englishmen; Englishmen against Frenchmen. Only one or two, whom I cannot name for fear of causing them great difficulties, fought for peace. Holy bishops, forgetting their dignity and calling, ran hither and thither vexing an already troubled world. On the one hand they urged Pope Julius to war and on the other they pressured the national leaders, as if kings were not of themselves bellicose enough. All this madness we cloak with fine-sounding terms.

For purposes of war, not only laws, the writings of pious men, but the Scriptures themselves are compromised. It has come to the point where it is considered folly to express yourself against war or to praise what Christ Himself praised. Whoever gives advice to the common people appears to neglect the rulers in recommending what is salutary.

Priests follow the armies. Bishops leave their diocese to perform the business of war. Mars consecrates priests, bishops, and cardinals. The honourable title of military legate is esteemed as a term indicating a successor of the Apostles. Any attempt to remedy this situation is concealed under the guise of piety. Their standards are adorned with crosses, and mercenaries hired to murder carry before them the same symbol. That alone which can dissuade men from war has become its banner. O wicked soldiers! What have you to do with the sign of the Cross? Your actions are more in line with those of ferocious beasts. This is the sacred symbol of Christ whose triumph was in death rather than war. The Cross is a warning against your real enemy and a means of victory over him.

You soldiers with the sign of salvation emblazoned on your banners hasten to destroy those who were saved by the very same sign of the Cross. What a terrible thing it is that men receive the sacraments now administered in the camps and then rush out to combat. The sacrament is the principal symbol of Christian union. Yet Christ, if He is present, is made to witness swords drawn against fellow men in a demonstration that is above all acceptable to the forces of evil. And, finally, what is more horrible than the fact that the Cross is honoured in both camps and in both lines of battle. Does the Cross fight the Cross, and does Christ fight against Christ? The sign of the Cross once terrified its enemies. Why do men now fight against that which they adore and worship? What is the prayer of the soldier during the service? 'Our Father'. How can you dare to call Him Father as you go forth to slay your brother? 'Hallowed be Thy name.' How could the name of God be more dishonoured than by your fighting? 'Thy Kingdom come.' Are you praying that so much shedding of blood aid tyranny? 'Thy will be done on earth as it is in heaven.' His will is to preserve the peace and you prepare for war. You ask for daily bread from our Father and at the same time you destroy the crops of your brother and hope their destruction will hasten his death. How can you repeat, 'and forgive us our trespasses as we forgive those who trespass against us', when you rush out to slay your brother? With danger to yourself and your neighbour you ask to avoid the dangers of temptation. You ask deliverance from evil and yet at the instigation of the Evil One you prepare evil for your brother.

Plato in the *Republic* denounces any war of Greek against Greek and calls it sedition. Christians consider war to be sacred even when the causes are not proportionate to the means used. The pagans of old were wont to sew into a bag anyone who had bloodied his sword with the blood of his brother and cast him into the water. What is the difference between blood brothers and those who are brothers in Christ? In this case both the victor and the vanquished are guilty of parricide. Such is the misery of war.

In spite of this they detest and curse the Turk as foreign to Christ. They do this because they assume themselves to be Christian. Yet what could be more pleasant in the sight of the Turk than to see Christians engaged in internecine warfare? The Turk offers sacrifice to Satan, but the behaviour of Christians toward Christians must certainly fulfil the same purpose. In this case there is a double sacrifice. The excuses that are made to explain warfare are well known to me. They protest that their action is not in the least voluntary. It is high time they threw aside the mask and dropped their pretences. If they examined their consciences, they would find that the real reasons are anger, ambition, and stupidity. If these constitute necessity, you ought to re-evaluate them.

The populace ought to be reminded that God is not mocked, nor is He deceived with pretences. Meanwhile solemn prayers and processions are undertaken and peace is prayed for with loud supplications. 'Grant us peace, we beseech Thee, hear us.' God can justly answer us with, 'Why do you laugh me to scorn? You ask me to avoid what you yourselves are the authors of.' If each and every offence is a sufficient cause for war, then who is there who has not been offended? How often are not offences between husband and wife condoned that mutual love be preserved? If offence be given to this or that prince, is this cause for war? There are laws, learned men, pious abbots, and reverend bishops whose mature counselling can bring these matters to a peaceful solution. Let these be the arbiters, and even though the decisions arrived at be somewhat unjust, they are much to be preferred to the evil of war. No peace, regardless of the injustice it involves, should be passed over in favour of war. A sober consideration of the results of any war will weigh the scales in favour of peace. The Pope would be an excellent authority in this matter. But when man has been engaged for so long a time in violent struggle, what happens to his authority? Where is that power that is, after Christ, the most potent? In this matter it would be demonstrated were it not hampered by worldly considerations. When the Pope issues a summons to war, men obey. Why is it that they cannot exhibit a similar obedience when he calls for peace? If they prefer peace, why did they obey Pope Julius, the author of war? Hardly anyone has obeyed Pope Leo in his exhortation to peace. If the Pope's authority is sacred, then certainly it should be obeyed whenever it is voiced. This is especially true when it voices what Christ most particularly exhorted. Those who listened to Julius' war cries explain that they cannot hear Leo's proposals of peace under the same false guise of religion. Under pretence of serving the Church they have satisfied their own malicious ambitions.

Let me give a few words on the defence of peace and concord to those of you who actually despise war. Peace is not to be found in various leagues or confederations of men, which are oft-times the very source and cause of wars. We must look for peace by purging the very sources of war, false ambitions and evil desires. As long as individuals serve their own personal interests, the common good will suffer. No one achieves what he desires if the methods employed be evil. The princes should use their wisdom for the promotion of what is good for the entire populace. The measure of their majesty, happiness, renown, and riches should be what actually makes great men outstanding. Let their attitude toward the common good be that of a father toward his family. The mark of a great and noble king is that he so acts and governs as to make his subjects honest, content, and wealthy. In this he should respect the wealth of his richer citizens, the freedom of his city-dwellers, and above all he should take care that peace flourish in all places. His subordinates should imitate their king and take special care that the common good of all be protected. In this way they will insure their own office of state. Will a king that is of this mind hand over the money of his subjects to strange and barbarous mercenaries? Will he expose them to famine and hunger to provide pay for hired captains? Will he risk the lives of his people with many dangers? We do not think so.

In his performance of kingly duties let him bear always in mind that as a man he is dealing with fellow men, that as a free citizen he is dealing with free citizens, and above all that as a Christian he is dealing with fellow Christians. The citizenry on their part must act in such a manner that their respect for the king be motivated also by the interests of the common good. No ruler can expect more than this. Consent and approval on the part of the citizens will be a curb to the aspirations of the prince. For both the ruler and the subject private gain should not be a consideration. Those who make it their purpose to do away with war and who extend every effort to secure peace and concord rather than mobilization should be shown the greatest honour. In this matter the case of Diocletian should be recalled to mind.

If war is unavoidable, then it should be conducted in such a way that the misfortunes resulting from it be dropped at the door of those who occasioned and caused it. In most wars the safety of the heads of government is assured and their captains stand to gain. It is the poor farmer and the common people who bear the brunt of the destruction, and they have hardly any interest in it and were certainly not its cause. Any prince is lacking in wisdom if he does not take this into consideration. Some kind of plan ought to be devised that will terminate this constant change of empire. Any kind of innovation or renewal brings in its wake uprisings and wars. One suggestion in this regard would be to have royal families marry within their own realms or at least within adjoining territories. This would lessen the problem of royal succession. It should be illegal to sell or alienate territories, as if free cities were up for sale. Kingship does not imply absolute ownership. This continual intermarriage between royal families could produce a situation similar to an Irishman ruling in India or a Syrian becoming king of England. Thus neither of them will have an adequate ruler for the one realm is abandoned and the other is in the hands of one from another world. While such a king is attempting to establish his regal right through conquest and bargaining, he wastes the resources of his former kingdom. Trying to rule two areas he loses both of them. There should be some kind of an agreement that once the borders of an empire have been determined they must remain inviolate and no alliance can be allowed to alter or destroy them. Once this has been established, each rule shall be expended toward the improvement of the realm to the end that the ruler's successors shall find it a richer and better place in which to dwell. In this way each and every territory will prosper. Among themselves their alliances must be based, not on covenants and federations, but on a sincere friendship that shares in efforts toward the common good of all. The question of succession should be determined either by blood or by a general election of the people. Honesty and personal integrity should be the criterion of promotion to lesser offices. Personal interests should in no way determine the preferences of the ruler but rather the common good. He should especially avoid travelling about and should confine his peregrinations to his own kingdom. Let him bear in mind the age-old adage: 'The forehead is more excellent than the hindhead.'

Let him consider himself enriched only when he amasses wealth of his own and not of his neighbours. When confronted with the decision to declare war, he should have as his consultants neither young men, whose inexperience finds war attractive, nor those who stand to profit by public disturbance, nor those who fatten their purses at the expense of civic disasters. Rather let him choose older men renowned by their mercy and benevolence. In no case should war, such a terrible thing once begun, be instigated because of the disagreement of one or two men. The common consent of all must be obtained.

A certain frankness must be observed in pointing to the causes and occasions for war. Yet there are certain incidents that must be overlooked, for forbearance generates forbearance. There are times when peace must be purchased. If one considers the tremendous destruction of men and property that the purchase avoids, it is cheap at any price. Meanwhile let bishops turn again to their obligations and let the clergy act in a priestly manner. Monks should be cognizant of their profession. Theologians should concern themselves with what is worthy of Christian study. In every area let there be a combined effort to establish peace. This should be the aim of preaching and teaching. It should preoccupy them privately and publicly. If these efforts fail, at least let them show their disdain and disapproval by keeping themselves aloof from any association with its agents. It would be a good thing to prohibit the burial of those killed in battle in consecrated ground. Should there be any innocent in this group, this will hardly detract from their final reward. Such a prohibition would certainly have an effect on warmongers.

Of course I am speaking of those wars that Christians conduct among themselves. It is not our intention to condemn those who undertake legitimate war to repel barbarous invasions or defend the common good. Nowadays the trophies and souvenirs of their battles, dyed and stained with the blood of those for whom Christ shed His own blood, are exhibited in our churches along with relics of the Apostles and martyrs, as if it is a work of religion not only to be martyred but to perform the martyring. I feel it would be preferable to hang these trophies either in the courthouse or in some armoury. The church is hardly the place to exhibit anything that has been defiled with blood. Priests especially should do everything in their power to dissuade men from war. If they attack it with greater effort, there is no doubt their endeavours will bear fruit.

If, however, the disease of war is a malady of such a nature that it cannot possibly be extricated from men's minds, then let them expend their warlike efforts toward the extermination of the Turkish menace – although here again it would be much more in keeping with Christian principle to convert them with honest doctrine and good example. Would that there were some simpler means of solving disagreements among Christians. Certainly if mutual charity does not unite them, then some common enemy may perhaps do so. Yet, should this be effected, it can hardly be said that this concord would be the ideal.

Nothing is more conducive to genuine peace than a sincere desire that comes from the heart. Those who really favour it make it their duty to promote it at every opportunity. The obstacles to their endeavour they either circumvent or remove, even though this involves concessions on their part. Others not of this mind look for causes and excuses for war. The things that pertain to peace they either make light of or actually conceal. Whatever seems to promote war they advocate and favour with every assistance. It shames me to point out the trivial things they exaggerate and the conflagrations they enkindle. Once the flames of dissent appear, it is amazing the amount of forgotten injuries that are heaped upon it. So forgotten are the good deeds and blessings of the past that all seem to desire nothing other than war. How often it is that very insignificant matters of petty rulers are the causes of conflict, their true nature being withheld from the public. Lacking causes they use false propaganda to stir up the populace, nursing their grievances with all sorts of falsehood for no other purpose than personal gain. In this matter the clergy are not entirely blameless.

The English despise the French for no other reason than that they are French, the Scots are disliked because they are Scots, and the German is at odds with the Frenchman and both oppose the Spaniard. What can be more perverse than peoples being opposed to one another simply because of a dissimilarity of names? There are so many things that should bring them together. Why as men are they not benevolent to man, as Christians well disposed toward fellow Christians? Why is it that what is really of no great significance can dominate the minds of these men when the stronger forces of nature and of Christ seem to be powerless? Space can separate men's bodies but it cannot separate their minds. In previous centuries the Rhine separated the Gaul and the German, but it cannot be said to separate Christian from Christian. The Pyrenees divide the Spanish and the French, yet they do not divide the communion of the Church. The North Sea divides the French and the English, but hardly the society and fellowship of religion.

The Apostle Paul was disturbed to hear the early Christians say. 'I am Apollo's, I am a follower of Cephas', or 'I am Paul's disciple.' He violently opposed evil language as contrary to the mind of Christ. Yet empty words are today the reasons why nations turn against one another. Others, not finding this sufficient reason, seek even more subtle means of causing division. They partition France as neither the sea, the mountains, nor its natural provinces divide her. They disseminate the seeds of dissension so that friendship between France and Germany may not be based upon their common inheritance.

If judges in matters of divorce deliberate long and seriously, why do they not realize the seriousness of hasty judgement in affairs more grievous? Let them examine the self-evident fact that this world of ours is the fatherland of the entire race. If the same nationality binds together those born of the same forebears, if blood relationship fosters amity, if the Church is a great family common to all men, and if the same household can produce concord, is it not foolishness not to accept it everywhere? You can put up with your father-in-law because he is the parent of your wife. Then why not tolerate a little from him who is your brother in religion? The fellowship of Christ is the strongest bond of all.

Why do you dwell only on those things that embitter the heart? If you are seriously desirous of peace, let this be your manner of thought. 'Although he has offended me in this particular case, nevertheless on the other occasions he has been a real friend to me', or 'He did not harm me of his own accord but rather because someone else put him up to it.' In the case of the dissension between Agamemnon and Achilles the blame was laid at the feet of the goddess Ate. In these matters where we cannot find a real excuse, then let us blame it on Destiny, an evil god, and transfer our anger to this.

Why do men feel that wisdom lies in the self-destruction of their own faith, rather than in its defence? Why is evil, rather than the common good, such an obsession among men? Wise men deliberate when confronted with a personal affair. But these men charge aimlessly into war. They do not consider the fact that once a war has been viciously ignited, terminating it is a very difficult matter; evolving from insignificant skirmishes, it matures to full-scale battles, at the expense of many lives and much bloodshed.

It is the crucial duty of the prince and his nobility to perceive these possibilities if their subjects should overlook them. It is also the obligation of the clergy to continually promulgate and firmly insist upon these facts, regardless of the people's attitude. If the above method is diligently adhered to, there should be no fear concerning their effectiveness.

Are you preparing to wage war? The task is to define peace and war, carefully calculating the profits of peace and the chaos of war. If destruction and good sense require a war rather than peace, this will be evident. Consider for a moment a kingdom flourishing in every aspect, well-constructed cities, ruled by conscientious law-makers, well-cultivated fields, honest industry, and a pervading pious spirit. Consider this thought thoroughly: 'If I involve myself in war, I will inevitably disrupt this present concord.' Then consider the ruin of cities, the destruction of thoroughfares, the desolation of fields, and the insidious annihilation of churches. Seriously consider this: these are the fruits of war. If you are repulsed at the thought of bringing into your country wicked and filthy mercenaries whom you must support at the expense of your own people and at a great loss to yourself personally, then consider this as the price of war.

If you abhor theft, war necessarily demands it. If you detest parricide, it is readily accepted in war. Can someone be even minutely sensitive about killing one person when mass murder is his profession? If laws are totally neglected in peacetime, they are completely abolished in a time of war. If adultery, incest, and other insidious immoralities are wantonly favored by you, then war is the answer to your desire. The tempests of war completely disregard piety and religion, as impiety and neglect of religion are the roots of all evil.

If you perceive the state of your country to be such that evil conditions prevail, and men of questionable character are forcefully controlling the country, then you are in a condition of war, as under this condition the most deplored men rule. Those whose action would be staunchly condemned in peacetime are highly regarded in time of war. Who could more skilfully infiltrate a town with an army than one dedicated to theft and stealing? Who could with greater facility contemptuously pillage houses or destroy churches better than a professional soldier? Who will more maliciously smite his enemy and terminate their lives than someone skilled in weapons and all types of cold-blooded murder? Who is better qualified to reduce cities to mere ashes than someone experienced in the use of incendiaries? Who will better escape and unjustly survive the perils of floods and the sea than a well-seasoned pirate? If you desire fully to comprehend the destruction and agony of war, then consider well those who wage it.

Accepting the fact that a pious leader is primarily concerned with the safety and welfare of his people, he will most assuredly despise war. If the chief happiness of a ruler is that of his subjects, he must embrace peace. A good leader with the best interests of his subjects always in mind must vicariously detest war, which is the cesspool of all impiety. Since he will accept the possessions of his subjects as his own, he is morally obligated to make every attempt to prevent war. Otherwise the results of honest industry will be wasted on public executioners.

They must realize that every man's cause is a flattering of self and thus deceives him, especially when the cause is an evil one. But let us assume that the cause is a just one and the end victorious, then we must carefully weigh the advantages and the disadvantages involved and attentively judge whether the means justify the end.

Bloodless victories are few and far between. Your men will inevitably be contaminated with the blood of others. And at the same time earnestly consider the moral degeneration and absence of public discipline, whose restoration will be a very tedious matter. Your spoils are slothfully gluttoned; you pamper your people; those who are just are burdened; the malicious are enticed further, and after a victory their appetites are not easily quieted. Skilled labour, art, and commerce rapidly decay. The banks are closed. To contain the enemy, it is necessary to exclude yourself from many regions. Before this malignant conflict commenced, all territories adjacent to you were unrestricted, for peace made all things common by their exchange.

Behold what you have done; the territory that was yours is impossibly restricted. Debate the quantity of war materials necessary just to besiege a small town. In order to overthrow a town you must erect another, a sham town; yet you could erect your own town, a better town, with less labour and bloodshed. In order to prevent an enemy ambush you must uncomfortably camp in the open air. It would be cheaper to erect new walls than madly to batter down old ones and rebuild them elsewhere. I bring this to your attention, completely disregarding the graft that has fallen into the hands of the tax-collectors, receivers, and captain's purses.

Consider then what you would expend on war and if you find

that peace would have cost you more than a tenth of that expense, then I will willingly allow you to do away with me wherever you will. Yet if you remit even a small injury, you feel you are lacking in courage. There is no greater proof of a small mind than to seek revenge. You feel that it is an embarrassment to have to make some small allowance to a neighbour, or possibly a relative who once did you a favour. But you will humiliate yourself even further when you fill the pockets of the lowest dregs of society with gold that will never be repaid, or when you fawningly send ambassadors to the filthy and obnoxious Carians, entrusting the lives and possessions of your people to those who are absolutely lacking in trust and holiness.

If peace seems to be iniquitous for you, avoid thinking in this way, 'This I lose', but think instead, 'I buy peace for so much.' A more subtle approach would be, 'If it were mine, I would grant it, but I am a prince and rule a commonwealth.' No leader whose primary consideration is the public welfare will unwittingly enter in a war. Beyond all doubt quite the contrary is evident, and war is spooned by the food of wretched inhumanity. Will you defend to the death any portion of your country? What does his country hold for a man? Will you seek revenge on the one who has forsaken your daughter? What does revenge hold for the commonwealth? The consideration of these facts is the supreme proof of a very wise man and a noble prince.

Who has ever ruled more successfully than Octavius Augustus? He sought to give up his empire if he could find some other prince more deserving and in the better interests of the commonwealth. Many literary men have praised the one saying of an emperor, 'My children be lost to me if any other can better govern and counsel the commonwealth.' These well-meaning heathens demonstrate interest for the commonwealth. On the other hand, Christian leaders show little or no respect for their fellow man. They choose either to satiate their own cupidities or childishly pamper their egos by exacting the most grotesque violence on those who have slighted them.

I hear others say that their only safety lies in barbarically encountering the evil schemes of the wicked. Why were the Antonines, the meek, and the philosopher the sole emperors of Rome not attacked? It was because no man rules more efficiently and confidently than one who is prepared to give up his throne, contrary to his own interest, if it is for the common good of his people. If neither an earnest interest in humanity, nor a respect for piety, nor any calamity will move you, certainly the ill repute of a Christian name will shame you to human harmony. I ask you, what percentage of the world do Christians possess? This is the city situated well in the view of all and sinfully exhibited as a yardstick of human peace and tranquillity. How shall we interpret what the enemies of Christianity voice? What blasphemies will they spew forth before Christ, when they observe Christians bickering among themselves about more trivial matters than even the heathen, with more cruelty than the wicked, and with what machines of war?

Who invented artillery? Was it not Christians? They dedicate these inventions to the Apostles and carve their images on them so as to make them seem less treacherous. O cruel, contemptuous ridicule! Shall Paul, the faithful exhorter of peace, turn hellish war machines against the Christians?

If it is our aim to convert the Turks, we must first be Christians. They will inherently rebel against what we are trying to inculcate in them if they observe what Christ detests above all things thriving more among the Christians than any other people in the world.

Homer marvelled at satiability in such desirable things as sleep, meat, drink, dance, and music, but saw that war could never be satisfied. This stands out among those who ought to abominate war. Rome, the mighty conqueror of past centuries, would frequently bolt up the temple of Janus. Why is it that among us war never takes a recess? How can you dare to spread the Word of Christ, the Author of peace, when you constantly war among yourselves in perpetual dissension? Doesn't anyone realize that this chaotic spirit will give the Turks courage? Nothing is easier to defeat than a group divided amongst itself. If you wish to inspire them with fear, be at peace.

Why do you estimate yourselves so unworthy of life's pleasures? Will you retreat from the peace and contentment to come? Man encounters many misfortunes in a lifetime. Harmony softly displaces trouble and grief, so that if all are earnestly striving for harmony, one will be able to aid the other in a time of need. Whenever anything righteous and just occurs, greater concord is emanated. A faithful companion not only rejoices when his comrade is at peace, but he also grieves in the same way when his friend is grieved.

These incidents that arouse such great conflict among you are so petty and vain. Death continually threatens king and subject alike. What subversions shall an enemy of the state viciously incite, only to vanish shortly thereafter, as smoke from fire? Eternity is awaiting us. What point is there in grapling uselessly for these phantoms of the present as though this life were an eternity?

O pitiful mortals, you neither believe nor confidently aspire to the tranquil life of the righteous – foolish boasters who mistakenly promise themselves a peaceful way of life. The life of the just is really nothing other than an unspeakable gathering of happy souls who have a foretaste of that union that Christ requested in terms of the union between Himself and His Heavenly Father. How can you prepare for this final concord unless you now meditate upon it? As an angel is not abruptly transformed into a stinking glutton, so a companion of martyrs and saints is not suddenly transformed into a bloody warrior.

More than enough Christian blood has been shed. We have aimed furiously at destroying each other. We have unwittingly offered sufficient sacrifices to hell and the furies, and we have sufficiently nourished the appetites of the Turks. This beastly fable is through. Now that we have taxed the miseries of war, let us at least grow discreetly in wisdom. Whatever has been done foolishly in the past, let it willingly be imputed to destiny. Let Christian men happily rejoice, as did the pagans, that the past evils of life lay buried for ever in time. Faithfully give your attention to the study of peace, that it may fittingly be bound, not with weak hemp, but with a lasting cohesiveness.

I beseech you, princes, upon whose nod mortal affairs depend and who, among men, bear the image of Christ, willingly acknowledge the voice of your Creator, endlessly summoning you to peace. The whole world, wearied from war, mournfully petitions you to heed this cry for peace. If any single person is displeased with this, let the common good prevail. It is of the utmost urgency that we all undertake this project, rather than shunning it for more insignificant matters.

I beseech you, consecrated priests of God, unflinchingly promulgate that which you most certainly know to be most pleasing to Christ and exorcise that which is most hateful to Him.

I beseech you, theologians, fervently preach the gospel of peace, and unceasingly exhort the people to live by it.

I beseech you, bishops, who excel all others in ecclesiastical dignity, see that your authority is properly exercised to eternally bind peace to all. I beseech you, magistrates, to be uncompromisingly faithful to the wisdom of kings and the mercy of bishops. Now with no exceptions I beseech all Christians unselfishly to consent to universal peace and fervently to obey those who govern it. Illuminate the power of peace and tranquillity among all men, so as finally to terminate the tyranny of nobles.

For this purpose let everyone muster all that he possesses. May eternal concord, already established by nature, and more wondrously re-established by Christ, unite all things. And finally, let every man zealously aspire to that which pertains to the concord of all men. Every evidence points to peace: in the first place the very meaning of nature and humanity; secondly, Christ, the Prince of human concord; finally, the many fruitful advantages of peace and the many destructive disadvantages of war.

It is to this cause that the minds of princes, divinely inspired, beckon you. Behold the meek and peaceful Leo, piously reigning as the Vicar of Christ, who has set forth his ensign of peace, inviting all who join in its glory. If you are true sheep, follow your shepherd. Francis, most Christian King of France, not only in title, fraternally beckons you. He does not believe the peace negotiations to be nonsense. He is not at all concerned with his own well-being, which would selfishly prevent him from providing for the common good, but declares it to be a noble effort to propagate the common peace. The most noble Prince Charles, a young man of incorruptible disposition, convincingly summons you to peace. The Emperor Maximilian is abundantly in favour of it. King Henry of England does not refuse it. It is compelling that all men should follow the eminent example of such noteworthy princes.

Most people detest war and piously pray for peace. A few, whose wicked happiness thrives on public chaos, loathfully wish for war. Conscientiously judge whether it is right or wrong that their dishonesty should so heavily outweigh the earnest will of all good men.

Nothing is accomplished by confederations, alliances, violence, or revenge. On the other hand, be consciously aware of what placability and benevolence can do. War incessantly sows war, vengeance seethingly draws vengeance, kindness generously engenders kindness, favours will be abundantly returned by other favours, and he will humbly appear most righteous who, at all times, considers the rights of others first.

What is limitedly pursued by human effort does not succeed.

Christ shall divinely occasion good counsel to prosper. He will make His presence overwhelmingly known, and most favourably so. He will favourably breathe upon those who cherish what He most favours. Public welfare will shadow private interest.

While peace is fervently adhered to, every man's fortune will be increased. Princes' kingdoms will be carefully amplified if they conscientiously rule their subjects by laws rather than arms; the dignity accorded noblemen will be increased in sincerity; the leisure of priests more tranquil; the contentment of the people more productive and their productivity more quietly directed; the name of Christ will be more formidable to the enemies of the Cross; and finally everyone shall be fraternally affectionate to his fellow man and, above all, pleasing to Christ, the pleasing of Whom constitutes the greatest happiness. I rest my case.

II   LEO TOLSTOY, *THE KINGDOM OF GOD IS WITHIN YOU*

In the late 1870s the Russian novelist and social philosopher Tolstoy (1828–1910) underwent a powerful religious conversion, and his writings thereafter, including *The Kingdom of God is Within You* (1893), reflect a view of reality which contrasts sharply with the view implicit in, say, Tolstoy's earlier novel *War and Peace*. In *The Kingdom of God is Within You* Tolstoy is concerned with the omnipresence of violence not only in war, but in multifarious aspects and roles of 'civilized' life. He calls attention to an awakening of Christian consciousness, which has already begun and needs only to be encouraged to gather momentum. Towards the end of the essay he offers practical suggestions concerning ways in which people from all walks of life might contribute to the advancement of the cause of non-violence, and possibly even the elimination of the habits of violence from Christian societies dominated by oppressive regimes.

The text below is reprinted from Leo Tolstoy, *The Kingdom of God and Peace Essays*, ed. and tr. Aylmer Maude, World's Classics No. 445 (London: Oxford University Press, 1936) pp. 316–34, 434–44.

11   A Christian public opinion has already come to life in our society and will inevitably end the present order of life based on violence. When will that be?

The position of Christian humanity with its prisons and gallows, its factories and accumulations of capital, its taxes, churches, drink-shops and licensed brothels, its ever-increasing armaments and millions of stupefied men ready, like chained dogs, to attack those against whom their master may set them, would be terrible indeed were it the product of violence. But it is chiefly the product of public opinion. And what has been established by public opinion not only can be destroyed by it, but is being destroyed by it.

Hundreds of millions of money and tens of millions of disciplined troops, marvellous efficiency in weapons of destruction, with an organization carried to the utmost point of perfection and with whole bodies of men whose vocation it is to delude and hypnotize the people, and by means of electricity which abolishes distance, all this under the control of men who consider such an organization of society not merely advantageous to themselves, but one without which they would inevitably perish, and who therefore exert all their ingenuity for its maintenance – what an invincible power that would seem to be!

And yet we need only realize what is happening, and what no one can prevent – namely, that a Christian public opinion is replacing the pagan one and is being established with the same strength and universality, and that the majority of men today are as much ashamed to take part in and profit by violence as they are of swindling, thieving, begging, or cowardice – and at once, without strife or violence, that complex and seemingly powerful organization of life will be destroyed without a struggle.

And for this to happen it is not necessary that anything new should be brought to people's consciousness. Only let the mist evaporate that hides from men the true meaning of certain deeds of violence, and the Christian public opinion that is growing up will overcome the obsolescent pagan public opinion that permits and justifies deeds of violence.

It is only necessary for people to become as much ashamed of participating in deeds of violence and profiting by them, as they now are of being, or being considered, swindlers, thieves, cowards, or beggars. And that is just what is beginning to occur. We do not notice it, just as people fail to notice their movement when they and all that surrounds them are in motion.

It is true that the order of society in its chief features is still the same violent order that it was a thousand years ago, and in some respects (especially in preparations for war and in war itself) it appears even more cruel. But Christian public opinion – the same that at a certain stage of development must replace the pagan order of our life – already begins to make itself felt. The dead tree stands apparently as firmly as ever – it even seems firmer because it is harder – but it is already rotten at the core and ready to fall. So it is with the present order of society based on violence. The external aspect is as before: some exercise violence and others are subject to it. But neither these nor those any longer have the same view of the significance and dignity of their respective positions.

Those who do violence (that is, those who take part in government) and those who profit by violence (that is, the rich) no longer represent, as used to be the case, the flower of our society and the ideal of human well-being and grandeur towards which all the violated used formerly to strive. Now very often the oppressed do not strive to gain the position of the oppressors or try to imitate them. On the contrary, users of violence often voluntarily renounce the advantages of their position, choose the condition of the oppressed, and try to resemble them in the simplicity of their life.

Not to speak of the now openly despised duties and occupations – such as those of spies, agents of the secret police, usurers, and publicans – a large number of professions held by users of violence which used to be considered honourable (such as those of police officials, courtiers, officers of the law, administrative functionaries, the clergy, the military, the monopolists and bankers) are not only no longer accounted honourable by everyone, but are even condemned by a certain much respected section of people. There are already people who voluntarily abandon these positions which were once accounted irreproachable, and prefer less advantageous positions not connected with violence.

And apart from men in governmental positions, there are already some rich people who, not through religious sentiment as used to happen, but simply through special sensitiveness to the public opinion that is coming to life, relinquish property they inherit, believing that a man can only justly avail himself of what he has gained by his own labour.

The position of a government official or of a rich man no longer presents itself as used to be the case and is the case even now among the non-Christian peoples, as indubitably honourable, deserving of respect, and blessed by God.

The most morally sensitive people (who for the most part are also the most cultivated) avoid such positions and prefer humbler ones that are not dependent on the use of violence.

At the age when still uncorrupted by life and choosing a career,

the best of our young people prefer the callings of doctors, techno-
logists, teachers, artists, writers, or even simple tillers of the soil
living by their own labour, rather than legal, administrative, ecclesiastical or military positions in the pay of the government, or
even to living on their private incomes.

Nowadays monuments are not usually erected in commemora-
tion of statesmen or generals, still less to rich men; they are erected
to the learned, to artists, to inventors, to men who not only have
had nothing in common with the government and rulers but have
often even been in conflict with them. It is not so much state
functionaries and the rich, as learned men and artists, who are
represented in sculpture, sung in poetry, and honoured by solemn
jubilees.

The best men of our time seek these esteemed positions and the
circle from which the governing class and the wealthy come is
decreasing both in quantity and in quality, so that in intellect and
culture and especially in moral qualities, the rich men and those
who now stand at the head of governments no longer constitute
the flower of society as in olden times, but on the contrary are
below the average.

In Russia and Turkey, as in France and America, in spite of the
constant change of government officials, the majority of these are
self-seeking and venal men of such a low moral standard that they
do not even satisfy the low demand of simple integrity expected of
them. Nowadays one may often hear ingenuous regrets expressed
by persons in authority, that the best men – by some strange
chance as it seems to them – are always to be found in the opposite
camp. It is as if one regretted that – by some strange chance –
executioners are always chosen from among men neither very
refined nor very kind.

In the same way the majority of rich people of today no longer as
formerly constitute the most refined and educated portion of
society, but are either coarse money-grubbers only concerned with
enriching themselves (frequently by shady methods) or else the
degenerate heirs of such money-grubbers, who far from playing
any prominent part in society are for the most part held in general
contempt.

But not only is the class of those from whom the servants of
governments and the wealthy are drawn growing ever smaller and
smaller and lower in calibre, they themselves no longer attribute
the same importance to their positions that they once did, but are

often ashamed of them, and do not perform the duties their positions demand.[1] Kings and emperors now scarcely govern at all and hardly ever decide upon an internal reform themselves, or any new departure in foreign policy, but generally leave the decision of these questions to governmental institutions or to public opinion. Their whole duty now amounts to representing the unity and power of the state. But they perform even that duty less and less successfully. The majority of them not only do not keep up their former unapproachable majesty, but become more and more democratic and even vulgar themselves, throwing aside the last of their prestige – that is, infringing the very thing they were called on to maintain.

It is the same with the army. Military men of the upper classes, instead of encouraging in their soldiers the harshness and brutality indispensable to their calling, themselves promote education and inculcate humanity among them, and often even themselves share the socialistic ideas of the masses and condemn war. In the last conspiracies against the Russian Government many of those concerned were military men. And the number of such military conspirators is ever increasing. And it often happens (as was the case the other day) that when called upon to suppress disturbances they refuse to fire. Military bravado is simply condemned by the military themselves and is often held up to ridicule. The judges whose business it is to try and to condemn criminals, conduct proceedings so as to acquit them, so that the Russian Government to secure the conviction of those it wants to punish, never now entrusts them to the ordinary courts but hands them over to a so-called military court, which is only the simulacrum of a court of justice.[2] So too with the public prosecutors, who often refuse to prosecute and even, by an evasion of the law, instead of prosecuting defend those they ought to accuse. Learned jurists whose business it is to justify the government violence are more and more disposed to deny the right of punishment, and substitute theories of irresponsibility and even advise not the correction but the cure of those they call criminals.

Warders and governors of prisons frequently become the protectors of those they ought to torture. Gendarmes and spies frequently assist the escape of those they are supposed to ruin. The clergy preach tolerance and sometimes even condemn the use of violence, and the more educated among them try in their sermons to avoid the very deception which furnishes the basis of their position and which it is their business to preach. Executioners refuse to carry out their functions, so that in Russia sentences of death can often not be carried out for want of an executioner, since despite the inducements offered to convicts to persuade them to become executioners, there are ever fewer and fewer willing to take up the duty.

Governors, police officials, and tax-collectors, pitying the peasants, often try to find pretexts for not collecting the taxes from them. Rich men are reluctant to use their wealth for themselves alone, and disburse it for public purposes. Landowners build hospitals and schools on their land, and some of them even renounce the ownership of land and transfer it to the tillers of the soil or establish communities on it. Mill-owners and manufacturers arrange hospitals, schools, savings-banks and pensions as well as dwellings for their work-people. Some of them form companies in which they share equally with the workers. There are capitalists who devote part of their capital to educational, artistic, philanthropic and other public institutions. Others, unable to bring themselves to part with their wealth during their lifetime, leave it to public institutions after their death.

All these facts might appear accidental did they not all come from one common cause, just as it might seem accidental that in spring the buds begin to swell on some of the trees, if we did not know that this is caused by the coming of spring generally, and that if the buds have begun to swell on some of the trees they will certainly do so on all of them.

It is the same with the manifestation of Christian public opinion in regard to violence and all that is based on it. If this public opinion already influences some sensitive people and causes them each in his own sphere to renounce the advantages that violence affords, then it will continue to act on others and will go on doing so until it transforms all the activity of men, and brings it into accord with the Christian consciousness which is already a driving force among the most advanced people.

And if already now there are rulers who refrain from taking decisions on their own authority and who try as far as possible to be unlike monarchs and as much like plain mortals as they can, and who express readiness to give up their prerogatives and to become simply the first citizens of their republics; and if there are now military men who understand all the evil and wickedness of war and do not want to shoot people, either of their own or of another nation; and if there are judges and public prosecutors who do not like to prosecute and condemn criminals; and if there are clergy who renounce their lies, and tax-gatherers who try to fulfil the duties laid upon them as little as possible; and if there are rich men who give up their wealth, then this will inevitably happen with other rulers, other soldiers, other judges, priests, tax-gatherers, and rich men. And when there are no longer men willing to occupy these positions, there will be none of these positions and no violence.

But this is not the only road by which public opinion leads men to the abolition of the existing order and the substitution of another. As positions based on the rule of violence become less and less attractive and there are fewer and fewer candidates to fill them, their uselessness will become more and more apparent.

In a Christian world there are the same rulers and governments and armies and law-courts and tax-gatherers and clergy and wealthy landowners, manufacturers and capitalists, as before, but humanity has quite another attitude towards them and they themselves have quite another attitude towards their own position.

The rulers still have meetings, interview one another, and go about. There are the same hunts, banquets, balls, and uniforms; the same diplomatists still talk about alliances and wars; there are the same parliaments, in which in the same way they discuss the Eastern question, and Africa, and alliances, and breaches of relations, and Home Rule, and the eight-hour day. And one ministry is replaced by another in the same way, and speeches and incidents go on as before. But to men who see how one newspaper article has more effect on the position of affairs than a dozen imperial interviews or sessions of parliament, it becomes more and more evident that these interviews and meetings and debates in parliament do not guide the affairs of men, but that they are guided by something independent of all these and not centered anywhere.

There are the same generals and officers and soldiers and cannon and fortresses and reviews and manoeuvres, but no war for a year, for ten years, for twenty years. Moreover it becomes less and less possible to rely on the military for the suppression of internal risings, and consequently more and more evident that the generals and officers are only puppets for pageantry and processions – the plaything of sovereigns, a sort of enormous and too costly *corps-de-ballet*.[3]

There are the same lawyers and judges and the same assizes, but it becomes more and more evident that since the civil courts decide cases on every consideration except that of justice, and that criminal trials have no sense because punishments do not attain the desired effect (as is admitted even by judges themselves), these institutions have no significance other than to provide a means of livelihood for men who are not fit for anything more useful.

There are the same priests, bishops, churches, and synods, but it becomes clearer and clearer that they themselves have long ceased to believe what they preach, and that therefore they cannot convince anyone else of the necessity of believing it.

There are the same tax-gatherers, but they grow less and less capable of taking people's property from them by force, and it becomes more and more evident that people can collect all that is necessary by voluntary subscription, without tax-gatherers.

There are the same rich people, but it becomes ever clearer and clearer that they can be useful only in proportion as they cease to be personal managers of their wealth and give the community all or at least part of it.

When all this becomes quite evident to everybody it will be natural for men to ask themselves: 'Why should we feed and maintain all these kings, emperors, presidents, and members of various chambers and ministries, since nothing comes of their meetings and talks? Would it not be better, as some humorist has said, to make an india-rubber queen?

'And what do we want armies for, with their generals, and bands, and cavalry, and drums? What are they wanted for when there is no war and no one wants to conquer anybody? And even if there were a war, other nations would not let us profit by it, and the army will not fire on its own people.

'And what are the judges and lawyers for, who in civil cases decide nothing according to justice, and in criminal affairs themselves recognize the uselessness of punishments?

'And what are the tax-gatherers for, who exact the taxes reluctantly while what is really needed is easily collected without them?

'And what is the use of the clergy, who have long since ceased to believe in what they have to preach?

'And what is the use of capital in private hands, if it can be useful only after becoming public property?'

And once they ask themselves these questions, men cannot fail to conclude that they ought not to support all these institutions which have become useless.

But not only will men who support these institutions decide to abolish them; men occupying these positions will themselves at the same time be brought to the necessity of giving them up, if indeed they have not done so sooner.

Public opinion condemns violence more and more, and so men, submitting more and more to public opinion, are less and less anxious to occupy positions depending on the use of violence. And if they do occupy such positions they are less and less willing to use violence, and consequently become more and more useless.

And this superfluity, which is more and more plainly felt both by those who support these positions and by those occupying them, will at last become so pronounced that men will no longer be found willing to support or occupy such positions.

I was once present in Moscow at a discussion about faith which was held, as is the custom, in the first week after Easter near the church in Hunter's Row. A group of some twenty people had collected on the sidewalk and a serious discussion about religion was going on. At the same time some concert or other was being held in the Assembly of the Nobility, and a police officer, noticing the group of people collected near the church, sent a mounted gendarme to order them to disperse. There was no need at all for the officer to disperse them, the twenty men who had collected were in nobody's way, but the officer had been standing there all the morning and wanted something to do. The young gendarme, his right arm swaggeringly akimbo, and clattering with his sabre, rode up to us and shouted sternly: 'Move on! What have you collected here for?' Everybody looked round at the gendarme and one of the speakers, a modest man in a peasant's coat, quietly and amiably said: 'We are speaking of serious matters and there is no reason for us to move on. You had better get down and listen to what is being said, young man. It will do you good.' And turning round he continued his discourse. The gendarme silently turned his horse round and rode off.

That is what ought to happen wherever violence is used. The officer feels dull. He has nothing to do. He has been put, poor fellow, in a position in which he has to give orders. He is shut off from all rational human existence. He can only look on and give orders, give orders and look on, though nobody needs either his orders or his attention. All our unfortunate rulers, ministers, members of parliament, governors, generals, officers, archbishops, bishops, priests, and even rich men, already find themselves partly, and soon will find themselves completely, in that position. They can do nothing but give orders, and so they make a fuss and send their subordinates about, as that officer sent the gendarme, to interfere with people. And as the people they interfere with ask them not to interfere, they imagine themselves to be quite indispensable men.

But a time is approaching and draws near when it will become perfectly evident to everyone that these people are of no use at all but are merely a hindrance, and those whom they interfere with will say amiably and quietly, like the man in the peasant's coat: 'Don't interfere with us, please!' And then all these emissaries, and those who send them, will have to follow that good advice, that is, cease to ride about with an arm akimbo hindering people, and get off their horses, doff their uniforms, listen to what is being said, and join with others in real human work.

A time is coming, and will inevitably come, when all institutions based on violence will disappear because it has become obvious to everyone that they are useless, stupid, and even wrong.

A time must come when the men of our modern world who fill offices dependent on violence will find themselves in the position of the Emperor in Andersen's fairy-tale, when the little child who saw him undressed naïvely exclaimed: 'Why, he has no clothes on!' And all the people, who had known it before but had not dared to say so, had to admit it too.

The tale is of a monarch fond of new clothes to whom two tailors came offering to make him some wonderful attire. He engaged them and they set to work, saying that the peculiarity of the garments was that no one who was unfit for the position he held could see them.

The courtiers came to look at the tailors' work, but could see nothing, as the tailors were plying their needles in empty space. But remembering the caution, they all pretended they saw the garments, and expressed admiration of them. It was the same with the Emperor himself. The day came for the procession in which he was to go in his new clothes. He undressed and put them on – that is to say, he remained naked and went naked through the town. But remembering the special property of the clothes, no one

ventured to say that he had nothing on till the little child exclaimed: 'Why, he has no clothes on!'

The same thing ought to happen with all those who by inertia
continue to fill positions that have long ceased to be useful. The
first man not interested in 'washing one hand with the other' as
the Russian proverb has it, and who therefore has no interest in
concealing the uselessness of these institutions, should point it out
and ingenuously exclaim: 'But these people have long ago ceased
to be of any use!'

The condition of Christian humanity, with its fortresses, cannon, dynamite, rifles, torpedoes, prisons, gallows, churches, factories, custom houses, and palaces, is really terrible. But neither
the fortresses nor the cannon nor the rifles will attack anyone of
themselves, the prisons will not of themselves lock anyone up, the
gallows will not of themselves hang anyone, nor will the churches
delude anyone or the custom houses hold anyone back, and the
palaces and factories do not build themselves or maintain themselves. All this is done by people. And if they once understand that
there is no necessity for all these things, these things will disappear.

And men already begin to understand. If they do not all understand, the leaders among them do – those whom the rest will
follow. And what the leaders have once understood they cannot
possibly cease to understand. And what the leaders have understood the rest of mankind not only can, but inevitably must,
understand too.

So that the prediction that a time will come when men will be
taught of God, will cease to learn war any more, and will beat their
swords into ploughshares and their spears into pruninghooks
(which translated into our own tongue means that all the prisons,
fortresses, barracks, palaces, and churches, will remain empty,
and that all the gallows, guns and cannon will remain unused), is
no longer a dream but a definite new form of life, to which
humanity is approaching with ever-increasing rapidity.

But when will this be realized?

Nineteen hundred years ago Christ replied to this question, that
the end of the present age (the end, that is, of the pagan organization of the world) would come when the calamities of mankind had
increased to the utmost, and when the good news of the Kingdom
of God (that is, the possibility of a new system of life free from

violence) had been proclaimed throughout the world (Matthew 24:3–28).

'Of that day and hour knoweth no man, but my Father only' (Matthew 24:36), said Christ then. For it can come at any minute, even when least expected.

To the question when that hour will come, Christ replied that we cannot know that, but for that very reason should always hold ourselves in readiness to meet it, as the goodman must be ready who guards his home, and as the virgins with their lamps must be ready to meet the bridegroom, and that we, too, must work for the coming of that hour with all the powers given us, as the servants worked with the talents entrusted to them (Matthew 24:43; 25:1–30). In reply to the question when the hour would come, Christ exhorted people to devote all their energies to hasten its coming.

And there can be no other reply. Men cannot possibly know at what day and hour the Kingdom of God will come, for its coming depends only on themselves.

The reply is like that which the sage gave when asked whether it was far to the town: 'Walk on!'

How can we tell whether it is far to the goal to which humanity aspires when we do not know how humanity will advance towards it – whether it will choose to move onwards or to stand still, to slacken its pace or increase it?

All we can know is what we (who constitute humanity) must do and must not do to bring about the Kingdom of God. And we all know that. Each of us has only to begin to do what he ought to do and cease doing the contrary. We need only each of us live according to the light that is in us to bring about the promised Kingdom of God towards which the heart of every man aspires.

12   Conclusion

vi

Bethink yourselves men, or believe the Gospel, the teaching of welfare. If you do not bethink yourselves you will all perish, like those whom Pilate slew, and like those upon whom the tower of Siloam fell, like millions and millions who have perished, slayers and slain, executioners and executed, torturers and tortured, and like that man who having filled his barns thinking to enjoy a long life, perished stupidly the very night he meant to begin living. 'Bethink yourselves and believe in the glad tidings,' said Christ nineteen hundred years ago, and he says so yet more convincingly now, because the wretchedness and irrationality of our life, which he foretold, has now reached its utmost limits.

Nowadays after so many centuries of fruitless efforts to make our life secure by the pagan organization of violence, it should be evident to everyone that efforts in that direction merely bring fresh dangers both into our personal and our social life instead of rendering it more secure.

By whatever names we dignify ourselves, in whatever apparel we attire ourselves, by whatever and before whatever priests we may be smeared with oil, however many millions we possess, however many special guards are stationed along our route,[4] however many policemen guard our wealth, however many so-called miscreant revolutionaries and anarchists we may execute, whatever exploits we ourselves may perform, whatever states we may found, whatever fortresses and towers we may erect – from the Tower of Babel to that of Eiffel – we are always all of us confronted by two inevitable conditions of life which destroy its whole meaning. There is first of all death, which may at any moment overtake any of us, and there is the transitoriness of all that we do and that is so quickly destroyed leaving no trace. Whatever we may do – found kingdoms, build palaces and monuments, compose poems and [novels] – everything is transitory, and soon passes leaving no trace. And therefore, however we may conceal it from ourselves, we cannot help seeing that the meaning of our life can be neither in our personal physical existence, subject to unavoidable sufferings and inevitable death, nor in any worldly institution or organization.

Whoever you may be who read these lines, consider your position and your duties – not the position of landowner, merchant, judge, emperor, president, minister, priest, or soldier, temporarily attributed to you by men, nor those imaginary duties imposed on you by that position – but your real position in eternity as a creature who by Someone's will has been called out of unconsciousness after an eternity of non-existence, to which by the same will you may at any moment be recalled. Think of your duties – not your imaginary duties as a landowner to your estate, as a merchant to your capital, as an emperor, minister, or official to the state – but those real duties which follow from your real position as a being called to life and endowed with reason and love.

Are you doing what He demands of you who sent you into the world and to whom you will soon return? Are you doing what He wills? Are you doing His will when as landowner or manufacturer you take the produce of the toil of the poor, arranging your life on that spoliation, or when as ruler or judge you do violence, sentencing men to execution, or when as soldiers you prepare yourselves for war, go to war, plunder and kill?

You say that the world is so made that this is inevitable, that you do this not of your own free will but because you are compelled. But is it possible that so strong an aversion for human suffering, for ill-treatment, for the killing of men, should have been so deeply implanted in you; that you should be so imbued with the need of loving your fellows and a still stronger need of being loved by them, that you see clearly that only by recognizing the equality of all men and by mutual service one of another can the greatest good that is accessible to man be realized; that the same thing is taught you by your heart, by your reason, by the faith you profess, and the same said by science – is it possible that despite all this you can by some very vague and complicated reasoning be forced to do everything directly opposed to it? Are you really, as landowner or capitalist, obliged to base your whole life on the oppression of the people; as an emperor or president are you really obliged to command armies – that is, to be the head and leader of murders; as a government official are you really forced to take by violence from the poor the money earned by the sweat of their brow, to avail yourself of it or hand it over to rich men; as judge or juryman are you really obliged to sentence erring men to ill-treatment and death because the truth has not been revealed to them; and above all (for on this the whole evil is based) are you – and every young man – really compelled to be a soldier, and renouncing your own will and all human sentiments, compelled to promise to kill all those whom men you do not know may order you to kill?

That cannot be!

If people tell you that all this is necessary for the maintenance of the existing order of life and that this social order, with its destitution, hunger, prisons, executions, armies and wars, is necessary for society, that still more miseries would ensue were that organization infringed; all *that* is said only by those who profit by such an organization. Those who suffer from it – and they are ten times as numerous – all think and say the contrary. And in the depth of your soul you yourself know it is untrue, you know that the existing organization of life has outlived its time and must inevitably be reconstructed on new principles, and that therefore there is no need to sacrifice all human feeling to maintain it.

Even admitting that the existing order is necessary, why do you believe that it is just your business to maintain it at the cost of all your best human feelings? Who has made you a nurse in charge of this sick system? Neither society, nor the state, nor anyone else has ever asked you to support the existing organization by occupying the position (of landowner, trader, emperor, priest, or soldier) that you occupy, and you know very well that you occupy your position not at all with the self-sacrificing aim of maintaining an order of life necessary for the welfare of mankind, but for yourself – for the sake of your covetousness, vanity, ambition, insolence, or cowardice. If you did not want that position you would not have done all that it constantly demands of you in order to retain it. Only try to stop doing those complex, cruel, cunning and contemptible things that you constantly do to retain your position and you will quickly be deprived of it. Only try, as a ruler or an official, to give up lying, acting meanly, and participating in acts of violence and executions; try as a priest to give up deception; try in the army not to kill; as a landlord or manufacturer try to cease protecting your property by violence and by the law-courts; and you will immediately lose the position which you pretend is forced upon you and which you pretend oppresses you.

It is impossible for a man to be placed against his will in a situation repugnant to his conscience.

If you are in such a position it is not because it is necessary for anybody, but because you yourself want it. And therefore knowing that your position is directly opposed to your heart, to your reason, to your religion, and even to science in which you believe, you cannot but reflect on the question as to whether by remaining in that position, and above all by trying to justify it, you are doing right.

It might be possible to risk making a mistake if you had time to see it and to retrieve your error and if you ran the risk for something of any importance. But when you know for certain that you may disappear at any moment without the least possibility of retrieving a mistake either for yourself or for others involved in it, and when you also know that whatever you may do in the external arrangement of the world will soon all disappear as certainly as you yourself and without leaving a trace, it is evident that there is no reason for you to risk making so terrible a mistake.

This would be quite simple and clear if only we did not by hypocrisy befog the truth indubitably revealed to us.

Divide up what you possess with others, do not gather riches, do not exalt yourself, do not steal, do not cause suffering, do not kill anyone, do not do to another what you would not have done to yourself, was said not only nineteen hundred but five thousand years ago. And there can be no doubt of the truth of this law, and but for hypocrisy it would be impossible for men – even if they themselves did not conform to it – to fail to recognize at least its necessity, and that he who does not do these things is doing wrong.

But you say there is a public welfare for the sake of which these rules may and should be infringed: for the public good it is permissible to kill, torture, and rob. You say, as Caiaphas did, that it is better for one man to perish than the whole nation, and you sign the death sentence of a first, a second, and a third man, load your rifle against this man who is to perish for the public welfare, put him in prison, and take his possessions. You say that you do these cruel things because as a member of society and of the state you feel that it is your duty to serve them; as a landowner, judge, emperor, or military man to conform to their laws. But besides belonging to a certain state and having duties arising from that position, you belong also to eternity and to God and have duties arising from that.

And as a man's duty to his family or class is always subordinate to his duty as citizen of a state, so that duty in its turn is of necessity subordinate to his duty in relation to the universal life and to God.

And as it would be irrational to cut down telegraph posts to obtain fuel for a family or a society to increase their welfare, thus infringing the laws which guard the welfare of the country as a whole, so also is it irrational to torture, execute, and kill a man in order to make the state secure and increase its welfare, thus violating the unquestionable laws which guard the welfare of the world.

The obligations which result from your citizenship of the state must be subordinate to your higher eternal obligations to the infinite life of the world and to God, and cannot contradict these, as Christ's disciples said nineteen hundred years ago: 'Whether it be right to hearken unto you more than unto God, judge ye' (Acts 4:19), and 'We ought to obey God rather than men' (Acts 5:29).

We are told that in order not to infringe the ever-changing system established yesterday by a few men in one particular corner of the world, we must do acts of violence, commit murder, and oppress men, thus violating the eternal and immutable order of the world established by God and by reason. Is that possible?

And therefore we cannot but reflect that our position as land-owner, trader, judge, emperor, president, minister, priest, or soldier, is bound up with oppression, violence, deceptions, and murder, and recognize that it is wrong.

I do not say that if you are a landowner you are bound immediately to give your land to the poor; if you are a capitalist to give your money or your factory to the workpeople; if you are a tsar, minister, official, judge, or general, that you should at once renounce your advantageous position; or if you are a soldier (if, that is to say, you occupy the position on which all violence is based) that you should immediately refuse military service despite all the danger of doing so.

Were you to do this you would be doing the very best thing possible, but it may be, as is most likely, that you have not the strength. You have ties; a family, dependents, and superiors; you are under such powerful influences that you are not strong enough to shake them off. But to recognize the truth as a truth and avoid lying about it is a thing you can always do. It is always in your power to cease asserting that you remain a landowner, a manufac-turer, a merchant, an artist, or a writer, because that is useful to mankind; that you are a governor, a public prosecutor, or tsar, not because it is agreeable to you and you are used to it, but for the public good; that you continue to be a soldier not from fear of punishment but because you consider the army necessary for the security of people's lives. It is always in your power to stop lying like that to yourself and to others, and you not only can but should do this, because in this alone – in freeing yourself from falsehood and confessing the truth – lies the sole welfare of your life.

You need only free yourself from falsehood and your situation will inevitably change of itself.

There is one and only one thing in life in which it is granted man to be free and over which he has full control – all else being beyond his power. That one thing is to perceive the truth and profess it.

And yet, just because other wretched, erring creatures like yourself assure you that you are a soldier, an emperor, a landowner, a rich man, a priest, or a general, you do evil deeds obviously contrary to your reason and your heart: you torment, plunder, and kill people, base your existence on their sufferings, and above all instead of fulfilling the one duty of your life – acknowledging and confessing the truth known to you – you carefully pretend not to know it and hide it from yourself and from others, acting thereby in direct opposition to that sole purpose to which you are called.

And in what circumstances do you do that? You who may die at any moment, sign death sentences, declare war, go to war, fleece the labourers, sit in judgement, and punish people; you live in luxury surrounded by the poor, and teach weak men who trust you that these things must be, and that such is the duty of men. And yet it may be that at the very moment you are doing these things a germ or a bullet may come in your direction and you will rattle in your throat and die and for ever lose the possibility of repairing the evil you have done to others and above all to yourself. You will have ruined the only life given to you in the whole of eternity, without having accomplished the one thing you unquestionably ought to have done.

However simple and however old it may be and however we may have stupefied ourselves by hypocrisy and the auto-suggestion resulting from it, nothing can destroy the certainty of this clear and simple truth, that no external efforts can safeguard our life which is inevitably attended by unavoidable sufferings and ends in yet more inevitable death, which may come to each of us at any moment, and that consequently our life can have no other meaning than the constant fulfilment of what is demanded of us by

That Power cannot want of us what is irrational and impossible – the establishment of our temporary carnal life, the life of society or of the state. It demands of us what alone is certain, rational, and the establishment of our temporary carnal life, the life of society or of the state. It demands of us what alone is certain, rational, and possible – the service of the Kingdom of God, that is, our co-operation in establishing the greatest possible unity among all living beings – a unity possible only in the truth. It therefore demands that we acknowledge and profess the truth revealed to us – the only thing that is always in our power.

'Seek ye first the Kingdom of God and his righteousness, and all these things shall be added unto you.'

The sole meaning of human life lies in serving the world by promoting the establishment of the Kingdom of God. This service can be accomplished only by the recognition and avowal of the truth by each separate individual.

'The Kingdom of God cometh not with outward show; neither shall they say, Lo here! or, lo there! for, behold, the Kingdom of God is within you.'

TRANSLATOR'S NOTES

1. When Tolstoy wrote this, there were many cases of Russian government officials being privately friendly to men in active opposition to the Government, and this friendliness influenced their official conduct.

2. Almost the last case in which a conspicuous political prisoner in Russia was allowed a public trial by jury before an ordinary criminal court, was that of Vera Zasulich (in 1878) who shot at Trepov, the Governor of St Petersburg, who had flogged a prisoner. She was acquitted by the jury, who sympathized with her.

3. It was another twenty-two years before the quite needless Russo-Japanese war occurred, and a further nine before the Great War broke out, and in both cases Russia would have fared better had she not fought, but Tolstoy's hope that war was obsolescent was premature if not mistaken.

4. These references are evidently to the procedure at the Tsar's coronation.

III   ALDOUS HUXLEY, 'TIME AND ETERNITY' (extract)

The Perennial Philosophy by Aldous Huxley (1894–1963) develops the theme that the world's great religions are all rooted in a basic transcendent experience, which frees man from subjection to time, although there is always a possibility that time-directed thinking will reassert its dominance over man and over man's religions. Huxley, who was an Anglican, discovers in his survey of Eastern and Western religions that the adherence to the transcendent or eternal dimension of religion predisposes the adherents of that religion towards peace and tolerance, while the reversion to time-centred thinking predisposes to intolerance, cruelty and war. *The Perennial Philosophy* was published during the heyday of Nazism, and Nazism is taken as an instance of a time-centred pseudo-religion. Christianity itself is rooted in an eternity philosophy, but has been often overlaid with a time-obsessed philosophy; and the result has been innumerable wars both among Christians and between Christians and other religions.

Huxley conjectures that, if the religions of the world would cultivate the eternity philosophy at their core, they would be able not only to attain unity among themselves, but also to initiate a gigantic impetus for peace in the world as a whole.

The text below is reprinted from Aldous Huxley, *The Perennial Philosophy* (London: Chatto and Windus; New York: Harper and Row, 1944) pp. 192–200 (part of ch. 12). The one footnote in this section (a reference to Haldane's *Marxist Philosophy*) has been placed in parenthesis and taken into the text.

[The] philosophy which affirms the existence and the immediate realizableness of eternity is related to one kind of political theory and practice; the philosophy which affirms that what goes on in time is the only reality, results in a different kind of theory and justifies quite another kind of political practice. This has been clearly recognized by Marxist writers (see, for example, Professor J. B. S. Haldane's *The Marxist Philosophy and the Sciences*), who point out that when Christianity is mainly preoccupied with events in time, it is a 'revolutionary religion', and that when, under mystical influences, it stresses the Eternal Gospel, of which the historical or pseudo-historical facts recorded in Scripture are but symbols, it becomes politically 'static' and 'reactionary'.

This Marxian account of the matter is somewhat oversimplified. It is not quite true to say that all theologies and philosophies whose primary concern is with time, rather than eternity, are necessarily revolutionary. The aim of all revolutions is to make the future radically different from and better than the past. But some time-obsessed philosophies are primarily concerned with the past, not the future, and their politics are entirely a matter of preserving or or restoring the *status quo* and getting back to the good old days. But the retrospective time-worshippers have one thing in common with the revolutionary devotees of the bigger and better future; they are prepared to use unlimited violence to achieve their ends. It is here that we discover the essential difference between the politics of eternity philosophers and the politics of time philosophers. For the latter, the ultimate good is to be found in the temporal world – in a future, where everyone will be happy because all are doing and thinking something either entirely new and unprecedented or, alternatively, something old, traditional and hallowed. And because the ultimate good lies in time, they feel justified in making use of any temporal means for achieving it. The Inquisition burns and tortures in order to perpetuate a creed, a ritual and an ecclesiastico-politico-financial organization regarded as necessary to men's eternal salvation. Bible-worshipping Protestants fight long and savage wars, in order to make the world safe for what they fondly imagine to be the genuinely antique Christianity of apostolic times. Jacobins and Bolsheviks are ready to sacrifice millions of human lives for the sake of a political and economic future gorgeously unlike the present. And now all Europe and most of Asia has had to be sacrificed to a crystal-gazer's vision of perpetual Co-Prosperity and the Thousand Year Reich. From the records of history it seems to be abundantly clear that most of the religions and philosophies which take time too seriously are correlated with political theories that inculcate and justify the use of large-scale violence. The only exceptions are those simple Epicurean faiths, in which the reaction to an all too real time is 'Eat, drink and be merry, for tomorrow we die.' This is not a very noble, nor even a very realistic kind of morality. But it seems to make a good deal more sense than the revolutionary ethic: 'Die (and kill), for tomorrow some one else will eat, drink and be merry.' In practice, of course, the prospect even of somebody else's future merriment is extremely precarious. For the process of wholesale dying and killing creates material, social and psychological conditions that practically guarantee the revolution against the achievement of its beneficent ends.

For those whose philosophy does not compel them to take time with an excessive seriousness the ultimate good is to be sought neither in the revolutionary's progressive social apocalypse, nor in the reactionary's revived and perpetuated past, but in an eternal divine now which those who sufficiently desire this good can realize as a fact of immediate experience. The mere act of dying is not in itself a passport to eternity; nor can wholesale killing do anything to bring deliverance either to the slayers or the slain or their posterity. The peace that passes all understanding is the fruit of liberation into eternity; but in its ordinary everyday form peace is also the root of liberation. For where there are violent passions and compelling distractions, this ultimate good can never be realized. That is one of the reasons why the policy correlated with eternity philosophies is tolerant and non-violent. The other reason is that the eternity, whose realization is the ultimate good, is a kingdom of heaven within. [In Hindu theology,] Thou art That; and though That is immortal and impassible, the killing and torturing of individual 'thous' is a matter of cosmic significance, inasmuch as it interferes with the normal and natural relationship between individual souls and the divine eternal Ground of all being. Every violence is, over and above everything else, a sacrilegious rebellion against the divine order.

Passing now from theory to historical fact, we find that the religions, whose theology has been least preoccupied with events in time and most concerned with eternity, have been consistently the least violent and the most humane in political practice. Unlike early Judaism, Christianity and Mohammedanism (all of them obsessed with time), Hinduism and Buddhism have never been persecuting faiths, have preached almost no holy wars and have refrained from that proselytizing religious imperialism, which has gone hand in hand with the political and economic oppression of the coloured peoples. For four hundred years, from the beginning of the sixteenth century to the beginning of the twentieth, most of the Christian nations of Europe have spent a good part of their time and energy in attacking, conquering and exploiting their non-Christian neighbours in other continents. In the course of these centuries many individual churchmen did their best to mitigate the consequences of such iniquities; but none of the major Christian churches officially condemned them. The first collective protest against the slave system, introduced by the English and the Spaniards into the New World, was made in 1688 by the Quaker Meeting of Germantown. This fact is highly significant. Of all Christian sects in the seventeenth century, the Quakers were the least obsessed with history, the least addicted to the idolatry of things in time. They believed that the inner light was in all human beings and that salvation came to those who lived in conformity with that light and was not dependent on the profession of belief in historical or pseudo-historical events, nor on the performance of certain rites, nor on the support of a particular ecclesiastical organization. Moreover their eternity philosophy preserved them from the materialistic apocalypticism of that progress-worship which in recent times has justified every kind of iniquity from war and revolution to sweated labour, slavery and the exploitation of savages and children – has justified them on the ground that the supreme good is in future time and that any temporal means, however intrinsically horrible, may be used to achieve that good. Because Quaker theology was a form of eternity philosophy,

Quaker political theory rejected war and persecution as means to ideal ends, denounced slavery and proclaimed racial equality. Members of other denominations had done good work for the African victims of the white man's rapacity. One thinks, for example, of St Peter Claver at Cartagena. But this heroically charitable 'slave of the slaves' never raised his voice against the institution of slavery or the criminal trade by which it was sustained; nor, so far as the extant documents reveal, did he ever, like John Woolman, attempt to persuade the slave-owners to free their human chattels. The reason, presumably, was that Claver was a Jesuit, vowed to perfect obedience and constrained by his theology to regard a certain political and ecclesiastical organization as being the mystical Body of Christ. The heads of this organization had not pronounced against slavery or the slave trade. Who was he, Pedro Claver, to express a thought not officially approved by his superiors?

Another practical corollary of the great historical eternity philosophies, such as Hinduism and Buddhism, is a morality inculcating kindness to animals. Judaism and orthodox Christianity taught that animals might be used as things, for the realization of man's temporal ends. Even St Francis' attitude towards the brute creation was not entirely unequivocal. True, he converted a wolf and preached sermons to birds; but when Brother Juniper hacked the feet off a living pig in order to satisfy a sick man's craving for fried trotters, the saint merely blamed his disciple's intemperate zeal in damaging a valuable piece of private property. It was not until the nineteenth century, when orthodox Christianity had lost much of its power over European minds, that the idea that it might be a good thing to behave humanely towards animals began to make headway. This new morality was correlated with the new interest in Nature, which had been stimulated by the romantic poets and the men of science. Because it was not founded upon an eternity philosophy, a doctrine of divinity dwelling in all living creatures, the modern movement in favour of kindness to animals was and is perfectly compatible with intolerance, persecution and systematic cruelty towards human beings. Young Nazis are taught to be gentle with dogs and cats, ruthless with Jews. That is because Nazism is a typical time philosophy, which regards the ultimate good as existing, not in eternity, but in the future. Jews are, *ex hypothesi*, obstacles in the way of the realization of the supreme good; dogs and cats are not. The rest follows logically.

'Selfishness and partiality are very inhuman and base qualities even in the things of this world: but in the doctrines of religion they are of a baser nature. Now, this is the greatest evil that the division of the Church has brought forth; it raises in every communion a selfish, partial orthodoxy, which consists in courageously defending all that it has, and condemning all that it has not. And thus every champion is trained up in defence of their own truth, their own learning and their own church, and he has the most merit, the most honour, who likes everything, defends everything, among themselves, and leaves nothing uncensored in those that are of a different communion. Now, how can truth and goodness and union and religion be more struck at than by such defenders of it? If you ask why the great Bishop of Meaux wrote so many learned books against all parts of the Reformation, it is because he was born in France and bred up in the bosom of Mother Church. Had he been born in England, had Oxford or Cambridge been his *Alma Mater*, he might have rivalled our great Bishop Stillingfleet, and would have wrote as many learned folios against the Church of Rome as he has done. And yet I will venture to say that if each church could produce but one man apiece that had the piety of an apostle and the impartial love of the first Christians in the first Church at Jerusalem, that a Protestant and a Papist of this stamp would not want half a sheet of paper to hold their articles of union, nor be half an hour before they were of one religion. If, therefore, it should be said that churches are divided, estranged and made unfriendly to one another by a learning, a logic, a history, a criticism in the hands of partiality, it would be saying that which each particular church too much proves to be true. Ask why even the best amongst the Catholics are very shy of owning the validity of the orders of our Church; it is because they are afraid of removing any odium from the Reformation. Ask why no Protestants anywhere touch upon the benefit or necessity of celibacy in those who are separated from worldly business to preach the Gospel; it is because that would be seeming to lessen the Roman error of not suffering marriage in her clergy. Ask why even the most worthy and pious among the clergy of the Established Church are afraid to assert the sufficiency of the Divine Light, the necessity of seeking only the guidance and inspiration of the Holy Spirit; it is because the Quakers, who have broke off from the Church, have made this doctrine their corner-stone. If we loved truth as such, if we sought for it for its own sake, if we loved our neighbour as ourselves, if we desired nothing by our religion but to be acceptable to God, if we equally desired the salvation of all men, if we were afraid of error only because of its harmful nature to us and our fellow creatures, then nothing of this spirit could have any place in us.

'There is therefore a catholic spirit, a communion of saints in the love of God and all goodness, which no one can learn from that which is called orthodoxy in particular churches, but is only to be had by a total dying to all worldly views, by a pure love of God, and by such an unction from above as delivers the mind from all selfishness and makes it love truth and goodness with an equality of affection in every man, whether he is Christian, Jew or Gentile. He that would obtain this divine and catholic spirit in this disordered, divided state of things, and live in a divided part of the Church without partaking of its division, must have these three truths deeply fixed in his mind. First, that universal love, which gives the whole strength of the heart to God, and makes us love every man as we love ourselves, is the noblest, the most divine, the Godlike state of the soul, and is the utmost perfection to which the most perfect religion can raise us; and that no religion does any man any good but so far as it brings this perfection of love into him. This truth will show us that true orthodoxy can nowhere be found but in a pure disinterested love of God and our neighbour. Second, that in this present divided state of the Church, truth itself is torn and divided asunder; and that, therefore, he can be the only true catholic who has more of truth and less of error that is hedged in by any divided part. This truth will enable us to live in a divided part unhurt by its division, and keep us in a true liberty and fitness to be edified and assisted by all the good that we hear or see in any other part of the Church. . . . Thirdly, he must always have in mind this great truth, that it is the glory of the Divine Justice to have no respect of parties or persons, but to stand equally disposed to that which is right and wrong as well in the Jew as in the Gentile. He therefore that would like as God likes, and condemn as God condemns, must have neither the eyes of the Papist nor the Protestant; he must like no truth the less because Ignatius Loyola or John Bunyan were very zealous for it, nor have the less aversion to any error, because Dr Trapp or George Fox had brought it forth.' (William Law)

Dr Trapp was the author of a religious tract entitled 'On the Nature, Folly, Sin and Danger of Being Righteous Overmuch'. One of Law's controversial pieces was an answer to this work.

Benares is to the East, Mecca to the West; but explore your own heart, for there are both Rama and Allah.   (Kabir)

Like the bee gathering honey from different flowers, the wise man accepts the essence of different Scriptures and sees only the good in all religions.   (From the *Srimad Bhagavatam*)

His Sacred Majesty the King does reverence to men of all sects, whether ascetics or householders, by gifts and various forms of reverence. His Sacred Majesty, however, cares not so much for gifts or external reverence as that there should be a growth in the essence of the matter in all sects. The growth of the essence of the matter assumes various forms, but the root of it is restraint of speech, to wit, a man must not do reverence to his own sect or disparage that of another without reason. Depreciation should be for specific reasons only; for the sects of other people all deserve reverence for one reason or another. . . . He who does reverence to his own sect, while disparaging the sects of others wholly from attachment to his own, with intent to enhance the glory of his own sect, in reality by such conduct inflicts the severest injury on his own sect. Concord therefore is meritorious, to wit, hearkening and hearkening willingly to the Law of Piety, as accepted by other people.   (Edict of Asoka)

It would be difficult, alas, to find any edict of a Christian king to match Asoka's. In the West the good old rule, the simple plan, was glorification of one's own sect, disparagement and even persecution of all others. Recently, however, governments have changed their policy. Proselytizing and persecuting zeal is reserved for the political pseudo-religions, such as Communism, Fascism and nationalism; and unless they are thought to stand in the way of advance towards the temporal ends professed by such pseudo-religious, the various manifestations of the Perennial Philosophy are treated with a contemptuously tolerant indifference.

The children of God are very dear but very queer, very nice but very narrow.   (Sadhu Sundar Singh)

Such was the conclusion to which the most celebrated of Indian converts was forced after some years of association with his fellow Christians. There are many honourable exceptions, of course; but the rule even among learned Protestants and Catholics is a certain blandly bumptious provincialism which, if it did not constitute such a grave offence against charity and truth, would be just uproariously funny. A hundred years ago, hardly anything was known of Sanskrit, Pali or Chinese. The ignorance of European scholars was sufficient reason for their provincialism. Today, when more or less adequate translations are available in plenty, there is not only no reason for it, there is no excuse. And yet most European and American authors of books about religion and metaphysics write as though nobody had ever thought about these subjects, except the Jews, the Greeks and the Christians of the Mediterranean basin and Western Europe. This display of what, in the twentieth century, is an entirely voluntary and deliberate ignorance is not only absurd and discreditable; it is also socially dangerous. Like any other form of imperialism, theological imperialism is a menace to permanent world peace. The reign of violence will never come to an end until, first, most human beings accept the same, true philosophy of life; until, second, this Perennial Philosophy is recognized as the highest factor common to all the world religions; until, third, the adherents of every religion renounce the idolatrous time philosophies, with which, in their own particular faith, the Perennial Philosophy of eternity has been overlaid; until, fourth, there is a worldwide rejection of all the political pseudo-religions, which place man's supreme good in future time and therefore justify and commend the commission of every sort of present iniquity as a means to that end. If these conditions are not fulfilled, no amount of political planning, no economic blueprints however ingeniously drawn, can prevent the recrudescence of war and revolution.

IV   PIERRE TEILHARD DE CHARDIN, 'THE HEART OF THE PROBLEM'

The French Jesuit palaeoanthropologist and philosopher Teilhard de Chardin (1881–1955) theorized that mankind was evolving towards a stage of great communality, which he called the 'collective consciousness'. He conceived this rather after the pattern of the 'mystical Body of Christ' described by St Paul – a collective incarnation of God in and among human beings. Marxism is portrayed by Teilhard as an authentic, para-religious attempt to achieve the communal vision of Christianity, after Christians themselves had demonstrated their inability to co-ordinate this vision with their transcendent or supernatural aspirations. But, paradoxically enough, the transcendent dimension is the one element needed to allow Marxism to fulfil its own most significant objectives. Teilhard's theme, developed in the 1949 essay 'The Heart of the Problem', is strangely and strikingly parallel to that of the German Marxist Ernst Bloch, although the latter's views apparently did not have any direct influence on Teilhard.

The text below is reprinted from Pierre Teilhard de Chardin, *The Future of Man*, tr. Norman Denny (London: Collins; and New York: Harper and Row, 1964) ch. 18.

Some say, 'Let us wait patiently until the Christ returns'. Others say, 'Let us rather finish building the Earth.' Still others think, 'To speed the Parousia, let us complete the making of Man on Earth.'

Introduction

Among the most disquieting aspects of the modern world is its general and growing state of dissatisfaction in religious matters. Except in a humanitarian form, which we shall discuss later, there is no present sign anywhere of faith *that is expanding*: there are only here and there, creeds that at the best are holding their own, where they are not positively retrogressing. This is not because the world is growing colder: never has it generated more psychic warmth! Nor is it because Christianity has lost anything of its absolute power to attract: on the contrary, everything I am about to say goes to prove its extraordinary power of adaptability and mastery. But the fact remains that for some obscure reason something has gone wrong between Man and God *as in these days He is represented to Man*. Man would seem to have no clear picture of the God he longs to worship. Hence (despite certain positive indications of rebirth which are, however, still largely obscured) the persistent impression one gains from everything taking place around us is of an irresistible growth of atheism – or more exactly, a mounting and irresistible de-Christianization.

For the use of those better placed than I, whose direct or indirect task it is to lead the Church, I wish to show candidly in this paper *where*, in my view, the root of the trouble lies, and *how*, by means of a simple readjustment at this particular, clearly localized point, we may hope to procure a rapid and complete rebound in the religious and Christian evolution of Mankind.

I say 'candidly'. It would be presumptuous on my part to deliver a lecture, and criticism would be out of place. What I have to offer is simply the testimony of my own life, a testimony which I have the less right to suppress since I am one of the few beings who can offer it. For more than fifty years it has been my lot (and my good fortune) to live in close and intimate professional contact, in Europe, Asia and America, with what was and still is most humanly valuable, significant and influential – 'seminal' one might say – among the people of many countries. It is natural that, by reason of the unusual and exceptional contacts which have enabled me, a Jesuit (reared, that is to say, in the bosom of the Church) to penetrate and move freely in active spheres of thought and free research, I should have been very forcibly struck by things scarcely apparent to those who have lived only in one or other of the two opposed worlds, so that I feel compelled to cry them aloud.

It is this cry, and this alone, which I wish to make heard here – the cry of one who thinks he sees.

1 A major event in human consciousness: the emergence of the 'ultra-human'

Any effort to understand what is now taking place in human consciousness must of necessity proceed from the fundamental change of view which since the sixteenth century has been steadily exploding and rendering fluid what had seemed to be the ultimate stability – our concept of the world itself. To our clearer vision the Universe is no longer an order but a process. The Cosmos has become a cosmogenesis. And it may be said without exaggeration that, directly or indirectly, all the intellectual crises through which civilization has passed in the last four centuries arise out of the successive stages whereby a static *Weltanschauung* has been and is being transformed, in our minds and hearts, into a *Weltanschauung* of movement.

In the early stage, that of Galileo, it may have seemed that the stars alone were affected. But soon the Darwinian stage showed that the cosmic process extends from sidereal space to life on earth; with the inevitable result that, in the present phase, Man finds himself overtaken and borne on the whirlwind which his own science has discovered and, as it were, unloosed. From the time of the Renaissance, in other words, the cosmos has looked increasingly like a cosmogenesis; and now we find that Man in his turn is tending to be identified with an anthropogenesis. This is a major event which must lead, as we shall see, to the profound modification of the whole structure not only of our thought but of our beliefs.

Many biologists, and not the least eminent among them (all being convinced, moreover, that Man, like everything else, emerged by evolutionary means, i.e. was *born* in Nature) undoubtedly still believe that the human species, having attained the level of *Homo sapiens*, has reached an upper organic limit beyond which it cannot develop, so that anthropogenesis is only of interest retrospectively in the past. But I am convinced that, in opposition to this wholly illogical and arbitrary idea of arrested hominization, a new concept is arising, out of the growing accumulation of analogies and facts, which must eventually replace it. This is that, under the combined influence of two irresistible forces of planetary dimensions (the geographical curve of the Earth, by which we are physically compressed, and the psychic curve of thought, which draws us closer together), the power of reflection of the human mass, which means its degree of *humanization*, far from having come to a stop, is entering a critical period of intensification and renewed growth.

What we see taking place in the world today is not merely the multiplication of *men* but the continued shaping of *Man*. Man, that is to say, is not yet zoologically mature. Psychologically he has not spoken his last word. In one form or another something ultrahuman is being born which, through the direct or indirect effect of socialization, cannot fail to make its appearance in the near future; a future that is not simply the unfolding of Time, but which is being constructed in advance of us . . . Here is a vision which Man, we may be sure, having first glimpsed it in our day, will never lose sight of.

This having been postulated, do those in high places realize the revolutionary power of so novel a concept (it would be better to use the word 'doctrine') in its effect on religious faith? For the spiritually minded, whether in the East or the West, one point has hitherto not been in doubt: that Man could only attain to a fuller life by rising 'vertically' above the material zones of the world. Now we see the possibility of an entirely different line of progress.

The long-dreamed-of Higher Life, the Union, the consummation that has hitherto been sought *Above*, in the direction of some kind of transcendent (*OY*, diagram): should we not rather look for it *Ahead*, in the prolongation of the inherent forces of evolution (*OX*, diagram)?

Above or Ahead – or both? . . .

This is the question that must be forced upon every human conscience by our increasing awareness of the tide of anthropogenesis on which we are borne. It is, I am convinced, the vital question, and the fact that we have thus far left it unconfronted is the root cause of all our religious troubles; whereas an answer to it, which is perfectly possible, would mark a decisive advance on the part of Mankind towards God. That is the heart of the problem.

2 At the source of the modern religious crisis: a conflict of faith between the above and the ahead

Arising out of what I have said, the diagram at the end of this chapter represents the state of tension which has come to exist more or less consciously in every human heart as a result of the seeming conflict between the modern forward impluse (*OX*), induced in us all by the newly born force of trans-hominization, and the traditional upward impulse of religious worship (*OY*). To render the problem more concrete it is stated in its most final and recognizable terms, the co-ordinate *OY* simply representing the Christian impulse and *OX* the Communist or Marxist impulse[1] as these are commonly manifest in the present-day world. The question is, how does the situation look, here and now, as between these opposed forces?

We are bound to answer that it looks like one of conflict that may even be irreconcilable. The line *OY*, faith in God, soars upward, indifferent to any thought of an ultra-evolution of the human species, while the line *OX*, faith in the World, formally denies (at least in words) the existence of any transcendent God. Could there be a greater gulf, or one more impossible to bridge?

Such is the appearance: but let me say quickly that it cannot be true, not finally true, unless we accept the absurd position that the human soul is so badly devised that it contradicts within itself its own profoundest aspirations. Let us look more closely at *OX* and *OY* and see how these two vectors or currents appear and are at present behaving in their opposed state. Is it not apparent that both suffer acutely from their antagonism, and therefore that there must be some way of overcoming their mutual isolation?

Where OX is concerned the social experiment now in progress abundantly demonstrates how impossible it is for a *purely immanent* current of hominization to live wholly, in a closed circuit, upon itself. With no outlet ahead offering a way of escape from total death, no supreme centre of personalization to radiate love among the human cells, it is a frozen world that in the end must disintegrate entirely in a Universe without heart or ultimate purpose. However powerful its impetus in the early stages of the course of biological evolution into which it has thrust itself, the Marxist anthropogenesis, because it rules out the existence of an irreversible Centre at its consummation, can neither justify nor sustain its momentum to the end.

Worldly faith, in short, is not enough in itself to move the earth forward: but can we be sure that the Christian faith in its ancient interpretation is still sufficient of itself to carry the world upward?

By definition and principle it is the specific function of the Church to Christianize all that is human in Man. But what is likely to happen (indeed, is happening already) if at the very moment when an added component begins to arise in the *anima naturaliter christiana*, and one so compelling as the awareness of a terrestrial 'ultra-human', ecclesiastical authority ignores, disdains and even condemns this new aspiration without seeking to understand it? This, and simply this, that Christianity will lose, to the extent that it fails to embrace as it should *everything that is human on earth*, the keen edge of its vitality and its full power to attract. Being for the time *incompletely humanized* it will no longer fully satisfy even its own disciples. It will be less able to win over the unconverted or to resist its adversaries. We wonder why there is so much unease in the hearts of religious and of priests, why so few deep conversions are effected in China despite the flood of missionaries, why the Christian Church, with all its superiority of benevolence and devotion, yet makes so little appeal to the working masses. My answer is simply this, that it is because at present our magnificent Christian charity lacks what it needs to make it decisively effective, the sensitizing ingredient of *human* faith and hope without which, in reason and in fact, no religion can henceforth appear to Man other than colourless, cold and inassimilable.

OY and *OX*, the Upward and the Forward: two religious forces, let me repeat, now confronted in the heart of every man; forces which, as we have seen, weaken and wither away in separation . . . Therefore, as it remains for me to show, forces which await one thing alone – not that we should choose between them, but that we should find the means of combining them.

3 The rebound of the Christian faith: Upward by way of Forward

It is generally agreed that the drama of the present religious conflict lies in the apparent irreconcilability of two opposed kinds of faith – Christian faith, which disdains the primacy of the ultrahuman and the Earth, and 'natural' faith, which is founded upon it. But is it certain that these two forces, neither of which, as we have seen, can achieve its full development without the other, are really so mutually exclusive (the one so anti-progressive and the other so wholly atheist) as we assume? Is this so if we look to the very heart of the matter? Only a little reflection and psychological insight is required to see that it is not.

On the one hand, neo-human faith in the World, to the extent that it is truly a faith (that is to say, entailing sacrifice and the final abandonment of self for something greater) necessarily implies an element of worship, the acceptance of something 'divine'.[2] Every conversation I have ever had with Communist intellectuals has left me with a decided impression that Marxist atheism is not absolute, but that it simply rejects an 'extrinsicist' form of God, a *deus ex machina* whose existence can only undermine the dignity of the Universe and weaken the springs of human endeavour – a 'pseudo-God', in short, whom no one in these days any longer wants, least of all the Christians.

And on the other hand Christian faith (I stress the word Christian, as opposed to those 'oriental' faiths for which spiritual ascension often expressly signifies the negation or condemnation of the Phenomenon), by the very fact that it is rooted in the idea of Incarnation, has always based a large part of its tenets on the tangible values of the World and of Matter. A too humble and subordinate part, it may seem to us now (but was not this inevitable in the days when Man, not having become aware of the genesis of the Universe in progress, could not apprehend the spiritual possibilities still buried in the entrails of the Earth?) yet still a part so intimately linked with the essence of Christian dogma that, like a living bud, it needed only a sign, a ray of light, to cause it to break into flower. To clarify our ideas let us consider a single case, one which sums up everything. We continue from force of habit to think of the Parousia, whereby the Kingdom of God is to be consummated on Earth, as an event of a purely catastrophic nature – that is to say, liable to come about at any moment in history, irrespective of any definite state of Mankind. This is one way of looking at the matter. But why should we not assume, in accordance with the latest scientific view of Mankind in an actual state of anthropogenesis,[3] that the parousiac spark can, of physical and organic necessity, only be kindled between Heaven and a Mankind which has biologically reached a certain critical evolutionary point of collective maturity?

For my own part I can see no reason at all, theological or traditional, why this 'revised' approach should give rise to any serious difficulty. And it seems to me certain, on the other hand, that by the very fact of making this simple readjustment in our 'eschatological' vision we shall have performed a psychic operation having incalculable consequences. For if truly, in order that the Kingdom of God may come (in order that the Pleroma may close in upon its fullness), it is necessary, as an essential physical condition,[4] that the human Earth should already have attained the natural completion of its evolutionary growth, then it must mean that the ultra-human perfection which neo-humanism envisages for Evolution will coincide in concrete terms with the crowning of the Incarnation awaited by all Christians. The two vectors, or components as they are better called, veer and draw together until they give a possible resultant. The super-naturalizing Christian Above is incorporated (not immersed) in the human Ahead! And at the same time faith in God, in the very degree in which it assimilates and sublimates within its own spirit the spirit of faith in the World, regains all its power to attract and convert!

I said at the beginning of this paper that the human world of today has not grown cold, but that it is ardently searching for a God proportionate to the new dimensions of a Universe whose appearance has completely revolutionized the scale of our faculty of worship. And it is because the total Unity of which we dream still seems to beckon in two different directions, towards the zenith and towards the horizon, that we see the dramatic growth of a whole race of the 'spiritually stateless – human beings torn between a Marxism whose depersonalizing effect revolts them and a Christianity so lukewarm in human terms that it sickens them.

But let there be revealed to us the possibility of believing *at the same time and wholly* in God *and* the World, the one through the other;[5] let this belief burst forth, as it is ineluctably in process of doing under the pressure of these seemingly opposed forces, and then, we may be sure of it, a great flame will illumine all things: for a faith will have been born (or reborn) containing and embracing all others – and, inevitably, it is the strongest faith which sooner or later must possess the Earth.

DIAGRAM ILLUSTRATING THE CONFLICT BETWEEN THE TWO KINDS OF FAITH IN THE HEART OF MODERN MAN

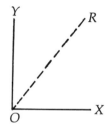

OY Christian faith in a personal transcendent, aspiring upward towards the Above.

OX Human faith in an ultra-human, driving forward towards the Ahead.

OR Christian faith, 'rectified' or 'made explicit', reconciling the two: salvation (outlet) at once Above and Ahead in a Christ who is both Saviour and Mover, not only of individual men but of anthropogenesis as a whole.

Let it be noted that by its construction OR is not a half-measure, a compromise between Heaven and Earth, but a resultant combining and fortifying, each through the other, two forms of detachment — that is to say, of 'sacrifice to that which is greater than self'.

AUTHOR'S NOTE

1. An unfavourable simplification where OX is concerned, inasmuch as Marxism and Communism (the latter a thoroughly bad, ill-chosen word, it may be said in passing) are clearly no more than an embryonic form, even a caricature, of a neo-humanism that is still scarcely born.
2. As in the case of biological evolutionary theory which also bore a materialist and atheist aspect when it appeared a century ago, but of which the spiritual content is now becoming apparent.
3. And, it may be added, in perfect analogy with the mystery of the first Christmas which (as everyone agrees) could only have happened between Heaven and an Earth which was *prepared*, socially, politically and psychologically, to receive Jesus.
4. But not, of course, sufficient in itself!
5. In a Christ no longer seen only as the Saviour of individual souls, but (precisely because He is the Redeemer in the fullest sense) as the ultimate Mover of anthropogenesis.

5

Peace through the Sublimation or Deflection of Aggression

It is well known that Karl Marx expressed an extraordinary optimism concerning the effects that the revolutionary overthrow of capitalistic economic relations might have. He visualized a new, co-operative, socialized man, no longer incited to anti-social or criminal activity, and, in short, largely freed from what we call the problem of aggression. Not so sure that a revolution would be enough to change patterns of aggression, the masters of Aldous Huxley's *Brave New World* encouraged occasional use of a drug called *soma* (a super-tranquillizer and super-mood-elevator) to guarantee the perpetuation of their own utopia. All of the following writers, like Marx and Huxley's masters, view aggression as a troublesome feature of human nature which must urgently be dealt with or channelled in some way, if mankind is to survive. They place little confidence, however, in drugs or revolutions, and have tried to work out a more natural and universal set of remedies or countermeasures, which would either channel aggression into sublimated forms of expression or deflect the full impact of aggressive tendencies by accentuating and encouraging other human tendencies.

I WILLIAM JAMES, 'THE MORAL EQUIVALENT OF WAR'

The philosopher and psychologist William James (1842–1910) was a pacifist, but was disturbed by an apparent weakness he noted in his fellow pacifists: they are continually forced into a merely negative position, arguing about the horrors and atrocities of war. They have nothing better to offer any potential reformed militarist than vague ideas of ease and abundance – objectives that are likely to seem rather dull and unattractive to someone who has been spurred on by patriotism, a love of the strenuous life, the

213

spirit of courage in the face of danger, the glory of victory, and so on. In short, there are powerfully attractive incentives to war for many men, incentives which render their life zestful and exciting in spite of the horror, and pacifists rather unreasonably just tell people that they must give up these attractions. Thus there are hardly any converts to pacifism from the militarist camp. But due attention to the demands of human nature would suggest that pacifists should offer some substitute for disciplined and dedicated militarism, some 'moral equivalent' of war. What substitute could be offered that would channel all these aggressive energies and the drive for glory and recognition into more socially useful channels? The only concrete suggestion James comes up with (a corps of youth to battle with Nature) seems patently weak, especially in an age of heightened ecological consciousness. Those of us who agree with James's general reasoning might tend to think of something like the American peace corps, albeit somewhat deficient in risk- and glory-value, as being at least one example of a viable 'moral equivalent' of war.

The text below is reprinted from *The Popular Science Monthly*, 77:28 (October 1910) pp. 400–10. A few references given as footnotes have been placed in parentheses and taken into the text.

The war against war is going to be no holiday excursion or camping-party. The military feelings are too deeply grounded to abdicate their place among our ideals until better substitutes are offered than the glory and shame that come to nations as well as to individuals from the ups and downs of politics and the vicissitudes of trade. There is something highly paradoxical in the modern man's relation to war. Ask all our millions, north and south, whether they would vote now (were such a thing possible) to have our war for the Union expunged from history, and the record of a peaceful transition to the present time substituted for that of its marches and battles, and probably hardly a handful of eccentrics would say yes. Those ancestors, those efforts, those memories and legends, are the most ideal part of what we now own together, a sacred spiritual possession worth more than all the blood poured out. Yet ask those same people whether they would be willing in cold blood to start another civil war now to gain another similar possession, and not one man or woman would vote for the proposition. In modern eyes, precious though wars may be, they must not be waged solely for the sake of the ideal harvest. Only when forced upon one, only when an enemy's injustice leaves us no alternative, is a war now thought permissible.

It was not thus in ancient times. The earlier men were hunting-men, and to hunt a neighbouring tribe, kill the males, loot the village and possess the females, was the most profitable, as well as the most exciting, way of living. Thus were the more martial tribes selected, and in chiefs and peoples a pure pugnacity and love of glory came to mingle with the more fundamental appetite for plunder.

Modern war is so expensive that we feel trade to be a better avenue to plunder; but modern man inherits all the innate pugnacity and all the love of glory of his ancestors. Showing war's irrationality and horror is of no effect upon him. The horrors make the fascination. War is the *strong* life; it is life *in extremis*; war taxes are the only ones men never hesitate to pay, as the budgets of all nations show us.

History is a bath of blood. The *Iliad* is one long recital of how Diomedes and Ajax, Sarpedon and Hector *killed*. No detail of the wounds they made is spared us, and the Greek mind fed upon the story. Greek history is a panorama of jingoism and imperialism – war for war's sake, all the citizens being warriors. It is horrible reading, because of the irrationality of it all – save for the purpose of making 'history' – and the history is that of the utter ruin of a civilization in intellectual respects perhaps the highest the earth has ever seen.

Those wars were purely piratical. Pride, gold, women, slaves, excitement, were their only motives. In the Peloponnesian war for example, the Athenians ask the inhabitants of Melos (the island where the 'Venus of Milo' was found), hitherto neutral, to own their lordship. The envoys meet, and hold a debate which Thucydides gives in full, and which, for sweet reasonableness of form, would have satisfied Matthew Arnold. 'The powerful exact what they can', said the Athenians, 'and the weak grant what they must.' When the Meleans say that sooner than be slaves they will appeal to the gods, the Athenians reply: 'Of the gods we believe and of men we know that, by a law of their nature, wherever they can rule they will. This law was not made by us; and we are not the first to have acted upon it; we did but inherit it, and we know that you and all mankind, if you were as strong as we are, would do as we do. So much for the gods; we have told you why we expect to stand as high in their good opinion as you.' Well, the Meleans still refused, and their town was taken. 'The Athenians', Thucydides quietly says, 'thereupon put to death all who were of military age and made slaves of the women and children. They then colonized the island, sending thither five hundred settlers of their own.'

Alexander's career was piracy pure and simple, nothing but an orgy of power and plunder, made romantic by the character of the hero. There was no rational principle in it, and the moment he died his generals and governors attacked one another. The cruelty of those times is incredible. When Rome finally conquered Greece, Paulus Aemilius was told by the Roman Senate to reward his soldiers for their toil by 'giving' them the old kingdom of Epirus. They sacked seventy cities and carried off a hundred and fifty thousand inhabitants as slaves. How many they killed I know not; but in Etolia they killed all the senators, five hundred and fifty in number. Brutus was 'the noblest Roman of them all', but to reanimate his soldiers on the eve of Philippi he similarly promises to give them the cities of Sparta and Thessalonica to ravage, if they win the fight.

Such was the gory nurse that trained societies to cohesiveness. We inherit the warlike type; and for most of the capacities of heroism that the human race is full of we have to thank this cruel history. Dead men tell no tales, and if there were any tribes of other type than this they have left no survivors. Our ancestors have bred pugnacity into our bone and marrow, and thousands of years of peace won't breed it out of us. The popular imagination fairly fattens on the thought of wars. Let public opinion once reach a certain fighting pitch, and no ruler can withstand it. In the Boer War both governments began with bluff but couldn't stay there, the military tension was too much for them. In 1898 our people had read the word 'war' in letters three inches high for three months in every newpaper. The pliant politician McKinley was swept away by their eagerness, and our squalid war with Spain became a necessity.

At the present day, civilized opinion is a curious mental mixture. The military instincts and ideals are as strong as ever, but are confronted by reflective criticisms which sorely curb their ancient freedom. Innumerable writers are showing up the bestial side of military service. Pure loot and mastery seem no longer morally avowable motives, and pretexts must be found for attributing them solely to the enemy. England and we, our army and navy authorities repeat without ceasing, arm solely for 'peace', Germany and Japan it is who are bent on loot and glory. 'Peace' in military mouths today is a synonym for 'war expected'. The word has become a pure provocative, and no government wishing peace sincerely should allow it ever to be printed in a newspaper. Every up-to-date dictionary should say that 'peace' and 'war' mean the same thing, now *in posse*, now *in actu*. It may even reasonably be said that the intensely sharp competitive *preparation* for war by the nations *is the real war*, permanent, unceasing; and that the battles are only a sort of public verification of the mastery gained during the 'peace' interval.

It is plain that on this subject civilized man has developed a sort of double personality. If we take European nations, no legitimate interest of any one of them would seem to justify the tremendous destructions which a war to compass it would necessarily entail. It would seem as though common sense and reason ought to find a way to reach agreement in every conflict of honest interests. I myself think it our bounden duty to believe in such international rationality as possible. But, as things stand, I see how desperately hard it is to bring the peace party and the war party together, and I believe that the difficulty is due to certain deficiencies in the programme of pacificism which set the militarist imagination strongly, and to a certain extent justifiably, against it. In the whole discussion both sides are on imaginative and sentimental ground. It is but one utopia against another, and everything one says must be abstract and hypothetical. Subject to this criticism and caution, I will try to characterize in abstract strokes the opposite imaginative forces, and point out what to my own very fallible mind seems the best utopian hypothesis, the most promising line of conciliation.

In my remarks, pacificist though I am, I will refuse to speak of the bestial side of the war regime (already done justice to by many writers) and consider only the higher aspects of militaristic sentiment. Patriotism no one thinks discreditable; nor does any one deny that war is the romance of history. But inordinate ambitions are the soul of every patriotism, and the possibility of violent death the soul of all romance. The militarily patriotic and romantic-minded everywhere, and especially the professional military class, refuse to admit for a moment that war may be a transitory phenomenon in social evolution. The notion of a sheep's paradise like that revolts, they say, our higher imagination. Where then would be the steeps of life? If war had ever stopped, we should have to reinvent it, on this view, to redeem life from flat degeneration.

Reflective apologists for war at the present day all take it religiously. It is a sort of sacrament. Its profits are to the vanquished as well as to the victor; and quite apart from any question of profit, it is an absolute good, we are told, for it is human nature at its highest dynamic. Its 'horrors' are a cheap price to pay for rescue from the only alternative supposed, of a world of clerks and teachers, of co-education and zoophily, of 'consumer's leagues' and 'associated charities', of industrialism unlimited, and femininism unabashed. No scorn, no hardness, no valour any more! Fie upon such a cattleyard of a planet!

So far as the central essence of this feeling goes, no healthy-minded person, it seems to me, can help to some degree partaking of it. Militarism is the great preserver of our ideals of hardihood, and human life with no use for hardihood would be contemptible. Without risks or prizes for the darer, history would be insipid indeed; and there is a type of military character which everyone feels that the race should never cease to breed, for everyone is sensitive to its superiority. The duty is incumbent on mankind, of keeping military characters in stock – of keeping them, if not for use, then as ends in themselves and as pure pieces of perfection – so that Roosevelt's weaklings and mollycoddles may not end by making everything else disappear from the face of nature.

This natural sort of feeling forms, I think, the innermost soul of army writings. Without any exception known to me, militarist authors take a highly mystical view of their subject, and regard war as a biological or sociological necessity, uncontrolled by ordinary psychological checks and motives. When the time of development is ripe the war must come, reason or no reason, for the justifications pleaded are invariably fictitious. War is, in short, a permanent human *obligation*. General Homer Lea, in his recent book *The Valor of Ignorance*, plants himself squarely on this ground. Readiness for war is for him the essence of nationality, and ability in it the supreme measure of the health of nations.

Nations, General Lea says, are never stationary – they must necessarily expand or shrink, according to their vitality or decrepitude. Japan now is culminating, and by the fatal law in question it is impossible that her statesmen should not long since have entered, with extraordinary foresight, upon a vast policy of conquest – the game in which the first moves were her wars with China and Russia and her treaty with England, and of which the final objective is the capture of the Philippines, the Hawaiian Islands, Alaska, and the whole of our coast west of the Sierra passes. This will give Japan what her ineluctable vocation as a state absolutely forces her to claim, the possession of the entire Pacific Ocean; and to oppose these deep designs we Americans have, according to our author, nothing but our conceit, our ignorance, our commercialism, our corruption, and our feminism. General Lea makes a minute technical comparison of the military strength which we at present could oppose to the strength of Japan, and concludes that the islands, Alaska, Oregon, and southern California would fall almost without resistance, that San Francisco must surrender in a fortnight to a Japanese investment, that in three of four months the war would be over, and our republic, unable to regain what it had heedlessly neglected to protect sufficiently, would then 'disintegrate', until perhaps some Caesar should arise to weld us again into a nation.

A dismal forecast indeed! Yet not unplausible, if the mentality of Japan's statesmen be of the Caesarian type of which history shows so many examples, and which is all that General Lea seems able to imagine. But there is no reason to think that women can no longer be the mothers of Napoleonic or Alexandrian characters; and if these come in Japan and find their opportunity, just such surprises as *The Valor of Ignorance* paints may lurk in ambush for us. Ignorant as we still are of the innermost recesses of Japanese mentality, we may be foolhardy to disregard such possibilities.

Other militarists are more complex and more moral in their considerations. The *Philosophie des Krieges*, by S. R. Steinmetz is a good example. War, according to this author, is an ordeal instituted by God, who weighs the nations in its balance. It is the essential form of the state, and the only function in which peoples can employ all their powers at once and convergently. No victory is possible save as the resultant of a totality of virtues, no defeat for which some vice or weakness is not responsible. Fidelity, cohesiveness, tenacity, heroism, conscience, education, inventiveness, economy, wealth, physical health and vigour – there isn't a moral or intellectual point of superiority that doesn't tell, when God holds his assizes and hurls the peoples upon one another. *Die Weltgeschichte ist das Weltgericht*; and Dr Steinmetz does not believe that in the long run chance and luck play any part in apportioning the issues.

The virtues that prevail, it must be noted, are virtues anyhow, superiorities that count in peaceful as well as in military competition; but the strain on them, being infinitely intenser in the latter case, makes war infinitely more searching as a trial. No ordeal is comparable to its winnowings. Its dread hammer is the welder of men into cohesive states, and nowhere but in such states can human nature adequately develop its capacity. The only alternative is 'degeneration'.

Dr Steinmetz is a conscientious thinker, and his book, short as it is, takes much into account. Its upshot can, it seems to me, be summed up in Simon Patten's word, that mankind was nursed in pain and fear, and that the transition to a 'pleasure economy' may be fatal to a being wielding no powers of defence against its disintegrative influences. If we speak of the *fear of emancipation from the fear regime*, we put the whole situation into a single phrase; fear regarding ourselves now taking the place of the ancient fear of the enemy.

Turn the fear over as I will in my mind, it all seems to lead back to two unwillingnesses of the imagination, one aesthetic, and the other moral; unwillingness, first to envisage a future in which army life, with its many elements of charm, shall be for ever impossible, and in which the destinies of peoples shall nevermore be decided quickly, thrillingly, and tragically, by force, but only gradually and insipidly by 'evolution'; and, secondly, unwillingness to see the supreme theatre of human strenuousness closed, and the splendid military aptitudes of men doomed to keep always in a state of latency and never show themselves in action. These insistent unwillingnesses, no less than other aesthetic and ethical insistencies, have, it seems to me, to be listened to and respected. One cannot meet them effectively by mere counter-insistency on war's expensiveness and horror. The horror makes the thrill; and when the question is of getting the extremest and supremest out of human nature, talk of expense sounds ignominious. The weakness of so much merely negative criticism is evident – pacificism makes no converts from the military party. The military party denies neither the bestiality nor the horror, nor the expense; it only says that these things tell but half the story. It only says that war is *worth* them; that, taking human nature as a whole, its wars are its best protection against its weaker and more cowardly self, and that mankind cannot *afford* to adopt a peace economy.

Pacificists ought to enter more deeply into the aesthetical and ethical point of view of their opponents. Do that first in any controversy, says J. J. Chapman, *then move the point*, and your opponent will follow. So long as anti-militarists propose no substitute for war's disciplinary function, no *moral equivalent* of war, analogous, as one might say, to the mechanical equivalent of heat, so long they fail to realize the full inwardness of the situation. And as a rule they do fail. The duties, penalties, and sanctions pictured in the utopias they paint are all too weak and tame to touch the military-minded. Tolstoy's pacificism is the only exception to this rule, for it is profoundly pessimistic as regards all this world's values, and makes the fear of the Lord furnish the moral spur provided elsewhere by the fear of the enemy. But our socialistic peace advocates all believe absolutely in this world's values; and instead of the fear of the Lord and the fear of the enemy, the only fear they reckon with is the fear of poverty if one be lazy. This weakness pervades all the socialistic literature with which I am acquainted. Even in Lowes Dickinson's exquisite dialogue (*Justice and Liberty*, New York, 1909), high wages and short hours are the only forces invoked for overcoming man's distaste for repulsive kinds of labour. Meanwhile men at large still live as they always have lived, under a pain-and-fear economy – for those of us who live in an ease economy are but an island in the stormy ocean – and the whole atmosphere of present-day utopian literature tastes mawkish and dishwatery to people who still keep a sense for life's more bitter flavours. It suggests, in truth, ubiquitous inferiority.

Inferiority is always with us, and merciless scorn of it is the keynote of the military temper. 'Dogs, would you live forever?' shouted Frederick the Great. 'Yes,' say our utopians, 'let us live forever, and raise our level gradually.' The best thing about our 'inferiors' today is that they are as tough as nails, and physically and morally almost as insensitive. Utopianism would see them soft and squeamish, while militarism would keep their callousness, but transfigure it into a meritorious characteristic, needed by 'the service', and redeemed by that from the suspicion of inferiority. All the qualities of a man acquire dignity when he knows that the service of the collectivity that owns him needs them. If proud of the collectivity, his own pride rises in proportion. No collectivity is like an army for nourishing such pride; but it has to be confessed that the only sentiment which the image of pacific cosmopolitan industrialism is capable of arousing in countless worthy breasts is shame at the idea of belonging to *such* a collectivity. It is obvious that the United States of America as they exist today impress a mind like General Lea's as so much human blubber. Where is the sharpness and precipitousness, the contempt for life, whether one's own, or another's? Where is the savage 'yes' and 'no', the unconditional duty? Where is the conscription? Where is the blood tax? Where is anything that one feels honoured by belonging to?

Having said thus much in preparation, I will now confess my own utopia. I devoutly believe in the reign of peace and in the gradual advent of some sort of a socialistic equilibrium. The fatalistic view of the war function is to me nonsense, for I know that war-making is due to definite motives and subject to prudential checks and reasonable criticisms, just like any other form of enterprise. And when whole nations are the armies,and the science of destruction vies in intellectual refinement with the sciences of production, I see that war becomes absurd and impossible from its own monstrosity. Extravagant ambitions will have to be replaced by reasonable claims, and nations must make common cause against them. I see no reason why all this should not apply to yellow as well as to white countries, and I look forward to a future when acts of war shall be formally outlawed as between civilized peoples.

All these beliefs of mine put me squarely into the anti-militarist party. But I do not believe that peace either ought to be or will be permanent on this globe, unless the states pacifically organized preserve some of the old elements of army discipline. A permanently successful peace economy cannot be a simple pleasure-economy. In the more or less socialistic future towards which mankind seems drifting we must still subject ourselves collectively to those severities which answer to our real position upon this only partly hospitable globe. We must make new energies and hardihoods continue the manliness to which the military mind so faithfully clings. Martial virtues must be the enduring cement; intrepidity, contempt of softness, surrender of private interest, obedience to command, must still remain the rock upon which states are built — unless, indeed, we wish for dangerous reactions against commonwealths fit only for contempt, and liable to invite attack whenever a centre of crystallization for military-minded enterprise gets formed anywhere in their neighbourhood.

The war party is assuredly right in affirming and reaffirming that the martial virtues, although originally gained by the race through war, are absolute and permanent human goods. Patriotic pride and ambition in their military form are, after all, only specifications of a more general competitive passion. They are its first form, but that is no reason for supposing them to be its last form. Men now are proud of belonging to a conquering nation, and without a murmur they lay down their persons and their wealth, if by so doing they may fend off subjection. But who can be sure that *other aspects of one's country* may not, with time and education and suggestion enough, come to be regarded with similarly effective feelings of pride and shame? Why should men not some day feel that it is worth a blood tax to belong to a collectivity superior in *any* ideal respect? Why should they not blush with indignant shame if the community that owns them is vile in any way whatsoever? Individuals, daily more numerous, now feel this civic passion. It is only a question of blowing on the spark till the whole population gets incandescent, and on the ruins of the old morals of military honour, a stable system of morals of civic honour builds itself up. What the whole community comes to believe in grasps the individual as in a vice. The war function has grasped us so far; but constructive interests may some day seem no less imperative, and impose on the individual a hardly lighter burden.

Let me illustrate my idea more concretely. There is nothing to make one indignant in the mere fact that life is hard, that men should toil and suffer pain. The planetary conditions once for all are such, and we can stand it. But that so many men, by mere accidents of birth and opportunity, should have a life of *nothing else* but toil and pain and hardness and inferiority imposed upon them, should have *no* vacation, while others natively no more deserving never get any taste of this campaigning life at all – *this* is capable of arousing indignation in reflective minds. It may end by seeming shameful to all of us that some of us have nothing but campaigning, and others nothing but unmanly ease. If now – and this is my idea – there were, instead of military conscription a conscription of the whole youthful population to form for a certain number of years a part of the army enlisted against *Nature*, the injustice would tend to be evened out, and numerous other goods to the commonwealth would follow. The military ideals of hardihood and discipline would be wrought into the growing fibre of the people; no one would remain blind as the luxurious classes now are blind, to man's relations to the globe he lives on, and to the permanently sour and hard foundations of his higher life. To coal and iron mines, to freight trains, to fishing-fleets in December, to dishwashing, clothes-washing, and window-washing, to road-building and tunnel-making, to foundries and stoke-holes, and to the frames of skyscrapers, would our gilded youths be drafted off, according to their choice, to get the childishness knocked out of them, and to come back into society with healthier sympathies and soberer ideas. They would have paid their blood tax, done their own part in the immemorial human warfare against nature; they would tread the earth more proudly, the women would value them more highly, they would be better fathers and teachers of the following generation.

Such a conscription, with the state of public opinion that would have required it, and the many moral fruits it would bear, would preserve in the midst of a pacific civilization the manly virtues which the military party is so afraid of seeing disappear in peace. We should get toughness without callousness, authority with as little criminal cruelty as possible, and painful work done cheerily because the duty is temporary, and threatens not, as now, to degrade the whole remainder of one's life. I spoke of the 'moral equivalent' of war. So far, war has been the only force that can discipline a whole community, and until an equivalent discipline is organized, I believe that war must have its way. But I have no serious doubt that the ordinary prides and shames of social man, once developed to a certain intensity, are capable of organizing such a moral equivalent as I have sketched, or some other just as effective for preserving manliness of type. It is but a question of time, of skilful propagandism, and of opinion-making men seizing historic opportunities.

The martial type of character can be bred without war. Strenuous honour and disinterestedness abound elsewhere. Priests and medical men are in a fashion educated to it, and we should all feel some degree of it imperative if we were conscious of our work as an obligatory service to the state. We should be *owned*, as soldiers are by the army and our pride would rise accordingly. We could be poor, then, without humiliation, as army officers now are. The only thing needed henceforward is to inflame the civic temper as past history has inflamed the military temper. H. G. Wells, as usual, sees the centre of the situation. 'In many ways,' he says

> military organization is the most peaceful of activities. When the contemporary man steps from the street of clamorous insincere advertisement, push, adulteration, underselling and intermittent employment into the barrack-yard, he steps on to a higher social plane, into an atmosphere of service and cooperation and of infinitely more honourable emulations. Here at least men are not flung out of employment to degenerate because there is no

immediate work for them to do. They are fed and drilled and trained for better services. Here at least a man is supposed to win promotion by self-forgetfulness and not by self-seeking. And beside the feeble and irregular endowment of research by commercialism, its little short-sighted snatches at profit by innovation and scientific economy, see how remarkable is the steady and rapid development of method and appliances in naval and military affairs! Nothing is more striking than to compare the progress of civil conveniences which has been left almost entirely to the trader, to the progress in military apparatus during the last few decades. The house-appliances of today for example, are little better than they were fifty years ago. A house of today is still almost as ill-ventilated, badly heated by wasteful fires, clumsily arranged and furnished as the house of 1858. Houses a couple of hundred years old are still satisfactory places of residence, so little have our standards risen. But the rifle or battleships of fifty years ago was beyond all comparison inferior to those we possess; in power, in speed, in convenience alike. No one has the use now for such superannuated things.   (*First and Last Things*, 1908, p. 215)

Wells adds (p. 226) that he thinks that the conceptions of order and discipline, the tradition of service and devotion, of physical fitness, unstinted exertion, and universal responsibility, which universal military duty is now teaching European nations, will remain a permanent acquisition, when the last ammunition has been used in the fireworks that celebrate the final peace. I believe as he does. It would be simply preposterous if the only force that could work ideals of honour and standards of efficiency into English or American natures should be the fear of being killed by the Germans or the Japanese. Great indeed is Fear; but it is not, as our military enthusiasts believe and try to make us believe, the only stimulus known for awakening the higher ranges of men's spritual energy. The amount of alteration in public opinion which my utopia postulates is vastly less than the difference between the mentality of those black warriors who pursued Stanley's party on the Congo with their cannibal war cry of 'Meat! Meat!' and that of the 'general staff' of any civilized nation. History has seen the latter interval bridged over: the former one can be bridged over much more easily.

II SIGMUND FREUD, *CIVILIZATION AND ITS DISCONTENTS*, CHAPTER 5 *(extract)*

Freud, like James, was concerned about the ever-menacing possibilities for eruptions of aggressive instincts in civilization; and, living after the First World War and writing during the period when tensions that would lead to Second World War were gathering momentum, Freud no doubt felt a certain urgency to offer some sort of general professional psychoanalytic counsel to his generation. In Freudian psychology, aggression (the death instinct) and eros or love (the life instinct) are opposed but paired within the human psyche. An acceptable civilized sublimation of aggression, according to Freud, is to be found in work. But he indicates that work alone is not enough to keep aggression within bounds. The ultimate solution to aggression devised by civilised man is through subtle encouragement of the extensions of eros beyond mere heterosexual, homosexual or autoerotic sexual gratification. Thus every civilization has inducements to 'aim-inhibited' love – the raising of a family, the initiation of friendships, and so on. The Christian religion, not content with enjoining men to love their neighbours as themselves, has even gone so far as to encourage them to love their enemies. If it were psychologically possible to fulfil injunctions like this, the final solution to the possibilities of wholesale aggression might be at hand. But Freud sees these ultimate extensions as unrealistic and counterproductive. So he leaves us with the question, what (if any) kind of channelling of aim-inhibited eros would be most conducive to civilizing the ineluctable constants of human aggression?

The text below is reprinted from the *Standard Edition of the Works of Sigmund Freud*, vol. 21, ed. and tr. James Strachey: *Civilization and its Discontents* (London: Hogarth Press, and New York: W. W. Norton, 1962) pp. 58–62. Freud's note is labelled 'a' to distinguish it from the translator's notes (1–3). All notes appear at the end of the section.

[M]en are not gentle creatures who want to be loved, and who at the most can defend themselves if they are attacked; they are, on the contrary, creatures among whose instinctual endowments is to be reckoned a powerful share of aggressiveness. As a result, their neighbour is for them not only a potential helper or sexual object, but also someone who tempts them to satisfy their aggressiveness on him, to exploit his capacity for work without compensation, to use him sexually without his consent, to seize his possessions, to humiliate him, to cause him pain, to torture and to kill him. *Homo homini lupus*.[1] Who, in the face of all his experience of life and of history, will have the courage to dispute this assertion? As a rule this cruel aggressiveness waits for some provocation or puts itself at the service of some other purpose, whose goal might also have been reached by milder measures. In circumstances that are favourable to it, when the mental counter-forces which ordinarily inhibit it are out of action, it also manifests itself spontaneously and reveals man as a savage beast to whom consideration towards his own kind is something alien. Anyone who calls to mind the atrocities committed during the racial migrations or the invasions of the Huns, or by the people known as Mongols under Jenghiz Khan and Tamerlane, or at the capture of Jesuralem by the pious Crusaders, or even, indeed, the horrors of the recent World War – anyone who calls these things to mind will have to bow humbly before the truth of this view.

The existence of this inclination to aggression, which we can detect in ourselves and justly assume to be present in others, is the factor which disturbs our relations with our neighbour and which forces civilization into such a high expenditure [of energy]. In consequence of this primary mutual hostility of human beings, civilized society is perpetually threatened with disintegration. The interest of work in common would not hold it together; instinctual passions are stronger than reasonable interests. Civilization has to use its utmost efforts in order to set limits to man's aggressive instincts and to hold the manifestations of them in check by psychical reaction formations. Hence, therefore, the use of methods intended to incite people into identifications and aim-inhibited relationships of love, hence the restriction upon sexual life, and hence too the ideal's commandment to love one's neighbour as oneself – a commandment which is really justified by the fact that nothing else runs so strongly counter to the original nature of man. In spite of every effort, these endeavours of civilization have not so far achieved very much. It hopes to prevent the crudest excesses of brutal violence by itself assuming the right to use violence against criminals, but the law is not able to lay hold of the more cautious and refined manifestations of human aggressiveness. The time comes when each one of us has to give up as illusions the expectations which, in his youth, he pinned upon his fellow men, and when he may learn how much difficulty and pain has been added to his life by their ill will. At the same time, it would be unfair to reproach civilization with trying to eliminate strife and competition from human activity. These things are undoubtedly indispensable. But opposition is not necessarily enmity; it is merely misused and made an *occasion* for enmity.

The Communists believe that they have found the path to deliverance from our evils. According to them, man is wholly good and is well-disposed to his neighbour; but the institution of private property has corrupted his nature. The ownership of private wealth gives the individual power, and with it the temptation to ill-treat his neighbour; while the man who is excluded from possession is bound to rebel in hostility against his oppressor. If private property were abolished , all wealth held in common, and everyone allowed to share in the enjoyment of it, ill will and hostility would disappear among men. Since everyone's needs would be satisfied, no one would have any reason to regard another as his enemy; all would willingly undertake the work that was necessary. I have no concern with any economic criticisms of the Communist system; I cannot enquire into whether the abolition of private property is expedient or advantageous.[a] But I am able to recognize that the psychological premisses on which the system is based are an untenable illusion. In abolishing private property we deprive the human love of aggression of one of its instruments, certainly a strong one, though certainly not the strongest; but we have in no way altered the differences in power and influence which are misused by aggressiveness, nor have we altered anything in its nature. Aggressiveness was not created by property. It reigned almost without limit in primitive times, when property was still very scanty, and it already shows itself in the nursery almost before property has given up its primal, anal form; it forms the basis of every relation of affection and love among people (with the single exception, perhaps, of the mother's relation to her male child[2]). If we do away with personal rights over material wealth, there still remains prerogative in the field of sexual relationships, which is bound to become the source of the strongest dislike and the most violent hostility among men who in other respects are on an equal footing. If we were to remove this factor, too, by allowing complete freedom of sexual life and thus abolishing the family, the germ cell of civilization, we cannot, it is true, easily foresee what new paths the development of civilization could take; but one thing we can expect, and that is that this indestructible feature of human nature will follow it there.

It is clearly not easy for men to give up the satisfaction of this inclination to aggression. They do not feel comfortable without it. The advantage which a comparatively small cultural group offers of allowing this instinct an outlet in the form of hostility against intruders is not be despised. It is always possible to bind together a considerable number of people in love, so long as there are other people left over to receive the manifestations of their aggressiveness. I once discussed the phenomenon that it is precisely communities with adjoining territories, and related to each other in other ways as well, who are engaged in constant feuds and in ridiculing each other – like the Spaniards and Portuguese, for instance, the North Germans and South Germans, the English and Scotch, and so on.[3] I gave this phenomenon the name of 'the narcissism of minor differences', a name which does not do much to explain it. We can now see that it is a convenient and relatively harmless satisfaction of the inclination to aggression, by means of which cohesion between the members of the community is made easier. In this respect the Jewish people, scattered everywhere, have rendered most useful services to the civilizations of the countries that have been their hosts; but unfortunately all the massacres of the Jews in the Middle Ages did not suffice to make that period more peaceful and secure for their Christian fellows. When once the Apostle Paul had posited universal love between men as the foundation of his Christian community, extreme intolerance on the part of Christendom towards those who remained outside it became the inevitable consequence. To the Romans, who had not founded their communal life as a state upon love, religious intolerance was something foreign, although with them religion was a concern of the state and the state was permeated by religion. Neither was it an unaccountable chance that the dream of a Germanic world dominion called for anti-semitism as its complement; and it is intelligible that the attempt to establish a new, Communist civilization in Russia should find its psychological support in the persecution of the bourgeois. One only wonders, with concern, what the Soviets will do after they have wiped out their bourgeois.

AUTHOR'S NOTE

a. Anyone who has tasted the miseries of poverty in his own youth and has experienced the indifference and arrogance of the well-to-do, should be safe from the suspicion of having no understanding or good will towards endeavours to fight against the inequality of wealth among men and all that it leads to. To be sure, if an attempt is made to base this fight upon an abstract demand, in the name of justice, for equality for all men, there is a very obvious objection to be made – that nature, by endowing individuals with extremely unequal physical attributes and mental capacities, has introduced injustices against which there is no remedy.

TRANSLATOR'S NOTES

1. 'Man is a wolf to man.' Derived from Plautus, *Asinaria*, II. iv. 88.
2. Cf. a footnote to chapter 6 of *Group Psychology* (1921), *Standard Edition of the Works of Sigmund Freud*, XVIII, 101n. A rather longer discussion of the point occurs near the end of Lecture XXXIII of the *New Introductory Lectures* (1933).
3. See *Group Psychology*, ch. 6; *Standard Edition*, XVIII. 101; and 'The Taboo of Virginity' (1918), *Standard Edition*, XI, 199.

III   KONRAD LORENZ, *ON AGGRESSION*, CHAPTER 14
(*conclusion*)

The Austrian ethologist Konrad Lorenz (born 1903), at the end of his book on aggression, here offers some final insights about steps mankind might take to deal with the ever present danger of outbreaks of aggression, especially in the form of militarism. He considers the role that may be played by art, science, medicine and humour in the overcoming of regional and national rivalries. Of particular interest are his speculations regarding the possible effects of formal or informal exchange programmes, and regarding international sporting-competitions (might not the Olympic Games play an increasingly significant role in defusing tensions among participant nations in the modern world, as they did for the Greek city states after 776 BC?). It is worth noting that Lorenz also touches on the possibility considered but rejected by Freud – the extension of the ideal of universal love throughout the human race – and finds the ideal much more psychologically feasible than did Freud.

The text below is reprinted from Konrad Lorenz, *On Aggression*, tr. Marjorie Kerr Wilson (New York: Harcourt, Brace and World; London: Methuen, 1966) pp. 275–99. Ellipses indicate the omission of cross-references. Square brackets outside quotations are editorial.

Redirection as a means of controlling the functions of aggression and other undischarged drives has been known to humanity for a long time. The ancient Greeks were familiar with the conception of catharsis, of purifying discharge, and psychoanalysis has shown very convincingly that many patterns of altogether laudable behaviour derive their impulses from the 'sublimation' of aggressive or sexual drives. Sublimation, however, must not be confounded with simple redirection of an instinctive activity toward a substitute object. There is a substantial difference between the man who bangs the table instead of hitting his antagonist, and the man who discharges the aggression aroused by an irritating family life by writing an enthusiastic pamphlet serving an altogether unconnected cause.

One of the many instances in which phylogenetic and cultural ritualization [has] hit on very similar solutions of the same problem concerns the method by which both have achieved the difficult task of avoiding killing without destroying the important functions performed by fighting in the interest of the species. All the culturally evolved norms of 'fair fighting', from primitive chivalry to the Geneva Conventions, are functionally analogous to phylogenetically ritualized combat in animals.

It was probably in highly ritualized but still serious hostile fighting that sport had its origin. It can be defined as a specifically human form of nonhostile combat, governed by the strictest of culturally developed rules. Sport is not directly comparable to the fighting-play of the higher vertebrates. The latter is never competitive, being essentially free from any appetitive or purposive tension. The enjoyable play of two dogs, however different in size and strength, is made possible only by the strict exclusion of all competitive elements. In sport, on the other hand, even in those kinds in which the enjoyment of skilled movements for their own sake predominates, as in skiing or skating, there is always a certain pride in doing it well, and there is no sport in which contests are not held. In this respect, human sport is more akin to serious fighting than animal play is; also, sport indubitably contains aggressive motivation, demonstrably absent in most animal play.

While some early forms of sport, like the jousting of medieval knights, may have had an appreciable influence on sexual selection, the main function of sport today lies in the cathartic discharge of aggressive urge; besides that, of course, it is of the greatest importance to keeping people healthy.

The value of sport, however, is much greater than that of a simple outlet of aggression in its coarser and more individualistic behaviour patterns, such as pummelling a punch-ball. It educates man to a conscious and responsible control of his own fighting-behaviour. Few lapses of self-control are punished as immediately and severely as loss of temper during a boxing-bout. More valuable still is the educational value of the restrictions imposed by the demands for fairness and chilvary which must be respected even in the face of the strongest aggression-eliciting stimuli.

The most important function of sport lies in furnishing a healthy safety valve for that most indispensable and, at the same time, most dangerous form of aggression that I have described as collective militant enthusiasm . . . . The Olympic Games are virtually the only occasion when the anthem of one nation can be played without arousing any hostility against another. This is so because the sportsman's dedication to the international social norms of his sport, to the ideals of chilvary and fair play, is equal to any national enthusiasm. The team spirit inherent in all international sport gives scope to a number of truly valuable patterns of social behaviour which are essentially motivated by aggression and which, in all probability, evolved under the selection pressure of tribal warfare at the very dawn of culture. The noble warrior's typical virtues, such as his readiness to sacrifice himself in the service of a common cause, disciplined submission to the rank order of the group, mutual aid in the face of deadly danger, and, above all, a superlatively strong bond of friendship between men, were obviously indispensable if a small tribe of the type we have to assume for early man was to survive in competition with others. All these virtues are still desirable in modern man and still command our instinctive respect. It is undeniable that there is no situation in which all these virtues shine so brilliantly as they do in war, a fact which is dangerously liable to convince quite excellent but naive people that war, after all, cannot be the absolutely abhorrent thing it really is.

Fortunately, there are other ways in which the above-mentioned, admittedly valuable virtues can be cultivated. The harder and more dangerous forms of sport, particularly those demanding the working together of larger groups, such as mountain-climbing, diving, offshore and ocean sailing, but also other dangerous undertakings, like polar expeditions and, above all, the exploration of space, all give scope for militant enthusiam, allowing nations to fight each other in hard and dangerous competition without engendering national or political hatred. On the contrary, I am convinced that of all the people on the two sides of the great curtain, the space pilots are the least likely to hate each other. Like the late Erich von Holst, I believe that the tremendous and otherwise not quite explicable public interest in space flight arises from the subconscious realization that it helps to preserve peace. May it continue to do so!

Sporting-contests between nations are beneficial not only because they provide an outlet for the collective militant enthusiasm of nations, but also because they have two other effects that counter the danger of war: they promote personal acquaintance between people of different nations or parties and they unite, in enthusiasm for a common cause, people who otherwise would have little in common. We must now discuss how these two measures against aggression work, and by what means they can be exploited to serve our purpose.

I have already said that we can learn much from demagogues who pursue the opposite purpose, namely to make peoples fight. They know very well that personal acquaintance, indeed every kind of brotherly feeling for the people to be attacked, constitutes a strong obstacle to aggression. Every militant ideology in history has propagated the belief that the members of the other party are not quite human, and every strategist is intent on preventing any 'fraternization' between the soldiers in confronting trenches. Anonymity of the person to be attacked greatly facilitates the releasing of aggressive behaviour. It is an observation familiar to anybody who has travelled in trains that well-bred people can behave atrociously toward strangers in the territorial defence of their compartment. When they discover that the intruder is an acquaintance, however casual, there is an amazing and ridiculous switch in their behaviour from extreme rudeness to exaggerated and shamefaced politeness. Similarly, a naïve person can feel quite genuine hatred for an anonymous group, against 'the' Germans, 'the' Catholic foreigners, etc., and may rail against them in public, but he will never dream of being so much as impolite when he comes face to face with an individual member. On closer acquaintance with one or more members of the abhorred group such a person will rarely revise his judgement on it as a whole, but will explain his sympathy for individuals by the assumption that they are exceptions to the rule.

If mere acquaintance has this remarkable and altogether desirable effect, it is not surprising that real friendship between individuals of different nationality or ideology [is] even more beneficial. No one is able to hate, wholeheartedly, a nation among whose numbers he has several friends. Being friends with a few 'samples' of another people is enough to awaken a healthy mistrust of all those generalizations which brand 'the' Russians, English, Germans, etc., with typical and usually hateful national characteristics. To the best of my belief, my friend Walter Robert Corti was the first to put into practice the method of subduing international hatred by promoting international friendships. In his famous children's village in Trogen, Switzerland, children and young people of all kinds of nations are living together in a friendly community. May this attempt find imitators on a grand scale!

What is needed is the arousal of enthusiasm for causes which are commonly recognized as values of the highest order by all human beings, irrespective of their national, cultural, or political allegiances. I have already called attention to the danger of defining a value by begging the question. A value is emphatically not just the object to which the instinctive response of militant enthusiasm becomes fixated by imprinting and early conditioning, even if, conversely, militant enthusiasm can become fixated on practically any institutionalized social norm or rite and make it appear as a value. Emotional loyalty to an institutionalized norm does not make it a value, otherwise war, even modern technical war, would be one. J. Marmor [*Bulletin of the Atomic Scientists*, March 1964, p. 21] has quite recently called attention to the fact that even today

> the history books of every nation justify its wars as brave, righteous, and honorable. This glorification is charged with overtones or patriotism and love of country. Virtues such as heroism and courage are regarded as being 'manly' and are traditionally associated with waging war. Conversely, the avoidance of war or the pursuit of peace are generally regarded as 'effeminate', passive, cowardly, weak, dishonorable or subversive. The brutal realities, even of traditional war, are glamorized and obscured by countless tales of heroism and glory, and the warnings of an occasional General Sherman that 'war is hell [and] its glory all moonshine' are disregarded.

I could not agree more with Dr Marmor when he discusses the psychological obstacles to the elimination of war as a social institution and counts among them the insidious effect of military toys and war games which all prepare the soil for a psychological acceptance of war and violence. I agree with Dr Marmor's assertion that modern war has become an institution, and I share his optimism in believing that, being an institution, war can be abolished.

However, I think we must face the fact that militant enthusiasm has evolved from the hackle-raising and chin-protruding communal defence instinct of our pre-human ancestors and that the key stimulus situations which release it still bear all the earmarks of this origin. Among them, the existence of an enemy, against whom to defend cultural values, is still one of the most effective. Militant enthusiasm, in one particular respect, is dangerously akin to the triumph ceremony of geese and to analogous instinctive behaviour patterns of other animals. The social bond embracing a group is closely connected with aggression directed against outsiders. In human beings, too, the feeling of togetherness which is so essential to the serving of a common cause is greatly enhanced by the presence of a definite, threatening enemy whom it is possible to hate. Also, it is much easier to make people identify with a simple and concrete common cause than with an abstract idea. For all these reasons, the teachers of militant ideologies have an enviably easy job in converting young people. We must face the fact that in Russia as well as in China the younger generation knows perfectly well what it is fighting for, while in our culture it is casting about in vain for causes worth embracing. The way in which huge numbers of young Americans have recently identified themselves with the rights of the American Negro is a glorious exception, though the fervour with which they have done so tends to accentuate the prevalent lack of militant enthusiasm for other equally just and equally important causes – such as the prevention of war in general. The actual warmonger, of course, has the best chances of arousing militant enthusiam because he can always work his dummy or fiction of an enemy for all it is worth.

In all these respects, the defender of peace is at a decided disadvantage. Everything he lives and works for, all the high goals at which he aims, are, or should be, determined by moral responsibility which presupposes quite a lot of knowledge and real insight. Nobody can get really enthusiastic about them without considerable erudition. The one and only unquestionable value that can be appreciated independently of rational morality or education is the bond of human love and friendship from which all kindness and charity springs, and which represents the great antithesis to aggression. In fact, love and friendship come far nearer to typifying all that is good, than aggression, which is identified with a destructive death drive only by mistake, comes to exemplifying all that is evil.

The champion of peace is debarred from inventing a sort of

dummy figure of evil for the purpose of arousing the militant enthusiasm or strengthening the bond between the fighters for the good cause. To attack just 'evil' is a questionable procedure, even with intelligent people. Evil, by definition, is that which endangers the good, and the good is that which we perceive as a value. Since for the scientist knowledge represents the highest of all values, he sees the lowest of all negative values in everything that impedes its progress. In my own case, the dangerous whispering of my aggression drive would probably persuade me to see the personification of evil in some philosophers who despise natural science, particularly in those who, for purely ideological reasons, refuse to believe in evolution. If I did not know all that I do about aggression and the compulsion of militant enthusiasm, I should perhaps be in danger of letting myself be inveigled into a religious war against anti-evolutionists. In other words, we had better dispense with the personification of evil, because it leads, all too easily, to the most dangerous kind of war: religious war.

If I have just said that considerable erudition is necessary for anyone to grasp the real values of humanity which are worthy of being served and defended, I certainly did not mean that it was a hopeless task to raise the education of average humanity to that level. I only wanted to emphasize that it was necessary to do so. Indeed, in our age of enlightenment, human beings of average intelligence are not so very far from appreciating real cultural and ethical values. There are at least three great human enterprises, collective in the truest sense of the word, whose ultimate and unconditional value no normal human being can doubt: art, the pursuit of beauty; science, the pursuit of truth; and, as an independent third which is neither art nor science, though it makes use of both, medicine, the attempt to mitigate human suffering.

Not even the most ruthlessly daring demagogues have ever undertaken to proclaim the whole art of an enemy nation or political party as entirely worthless. No normal educated human being can help appreciating the art of another culture however much he finds abhorrent in it in other respects. In addition, painting and music are unhindered by language barriers and are thus able to tell people on one side of a cultural barrier that on its other side, too, there are human beings serving the good and the beautiful. The universal appreciation of Negro music is perhaps an important step toward the solution of the burning racial problem in America. After Negroes had been robbed of their freedom and their own cultural traditions had been successfully extinguished, racial pride and prejudice have done their best, or to be more exact their worst, to prevent them from entering into the spirit and acquiring the basic social norms of Western culture. The only great cultural value which they were not prevented from making wholly their own was music. The indubitable creative power of Negro composers and musicians casts a strong doubt, to say the least, on the alleged lack of cultural creativity of their race.

Art is called upon to create supranational, suprapolitical values that cannot be denied by any narrowly national or political group. It turns traitor to its great mission when it allows itself to be harnessed to any political aim whatsoever. Propagandist tendency in any art, in poetry or in painting, means its final desecration and is altogether evil. Music, though supremely capable of whipping up militant enthusiasm, is fortunately quite unable to specify what the hearers are expected to get enthusiastic about. So the most feudalistic old aristocrat can appreciate the inspiring beauty of the 'Marseillaise', even though the text of the song suggests that his impure blood should be used as a fertilizer – *d'un sang impur abreuvez nos sillons*.

Science, which is closely akin to art in many other respects also, shares its mission of creating a value that no one can deny regardless of his national or political allegiance. Unlike art, science can only be communicated by language, and the truth of its results does not impress as immediately as the beauty of a work of art. On the other hand, opinions concerning the relative value of works of art may differ, and though the true and the false may also be distinguished in art, these words have a very different meaning when applied to the results of scientific research. Truth, in science, can be defined as the working hypothesis best fitted to open the way to the next better one. The scientist knows very well that he is approaching ultimate truth only in an asymptotic curve and is barred from ever reaching it; but at the same time he is proudly aware of being indeed able to determine whether a statement is a nearer or less near approach to truth. This determination is not furnished by any personal opinion nor by the authority of an individual, but by further research proceeding by rules universally accepted by all men of all cultures and all political affiliations. More than any other product of human culture, scientific knowledge is the collective property of all mankind.

Scientific truth is universal, because it is only discovered by the human brain and not made by it, as art is; even philosophy is certainly nothing other than poetry in the original sense of the word, which is derived from the Greek verb ποιεῖν, to make. Scientific truth is wrested from reality existing outside and independent of the human brain. Since this reality is the same for all human beings, all correct scientific results will always agree with each other, in whatever national or political surroundings they may be gained. Should a scientist, in the conscious or even unconscious wish to make his results agree with his political doctrine, falsify or colour the results of his work, be it ever so slightly, reality will put in an insuperable veto: these particular results will simply fail on practical application. For example, there was, a few years ago, a school of genetics in the Soviet Union which, from political and, I hope and believe, unconscious reasons, asserted that it had demonstrated the inheritance of acquired characters. These results could not be confirmed anywhere else in the world, and the situation was deeply disturbing to those who believe in the unity of science and its world-embracing mission. There is no more talk of this theory now; geneticists all over the world are again of one opinion. A small victory, indeed, but a victory for truth!

I need not say anything about the general recognition of the value of medicine. The sanctity of the Red Cross is about the only one of the laws of nations that has always been more or less respected by all nations.

Of course, education alone, in the sense of the simple transmission of knowledge, is only a prerequisite to the real appreciation of these and other ethical values. Another condition, quite as important, is that this knowledge and its ethical consequences should be handed down to the younger generation in such a way that it is able to identify itself with these values. I have already said what psychoanalysts have known for a long time, that a relation of trust and respect between two generations must exist in order to make a tradition of values possible. I have already said that Western culture, even without the danger of nuclear warfare, is more directly threatened by disintegration because of its failure to transmit its cultural and even its ethical values to the younger generation. To many people, and probably to all of those actively concerned with politics, my hope of improving the chances of permanent peace by arousing, in young people, militant enthusiasm for the ideals of art, science, medicine and the like, will appear unrealistic to the point of being fatuous. Young people today, they will argue, are notoriously materialistic and take an insuperably sceptical view of ideals in general and in particular of those that arouse the enthusiam of a member of the older generation. My answer is that this is quite true, but that young people today have excellent excuses for taking this attitude. Cultural and political ideas today have a way of becoming obsolete surprisingly fast; indeed there are few of them on either side of any curtain that have not already done so. To the extraterrestial observer in whose place we should be trying to put ourselves, it would seem a very minor issue whether capitalism or Communism will rule the world, since the differences between the two are rapidly decreasing anyhow. To such an observer, the great questions would be, firstly, whether mankind can keep its planet from becoming too radioactive to support life, and secondly whether mankind will succeed in preventing its population from 'exploding' in a way more annihilating than the explosion of the Bomb. Apart from the obvious obsolescence of most so-called ideals, we know some of the reasons why the younger generation refuses to accept handed-down customs and social norms . . . I believe that the 'angry young men' of Western civilization have a perfectly good right to be angry with the older generation, and I do not regard it as surprising if young people today are sceptical to the point of nihilism. I believe that their mistrust of all ideals is largely due to the fact that there have been and still are so many artificially contrived pseudo-ideals 'on the market', calculated to arouse enthusiam for demagogic purposes.

I believe that among the genuine values here discussed, science has a particular mission in vanquishing this distrust. Honest research must produce identical results anywhere. The verifiability of science proves the honesty of its work. There is no mystery whatsoever about its results; where they are met with obstinate incredulity they can be proved by incontestable figures. I believe that the most materialistic and the most sceptical are the very people whose enthusiasm could be aroused in the service of scientific truth and all that goes with it.

Of course, it is not to be suggested that all of the earth's population should engage in active scientific research, but scientific education might very well become general enough to exert a decisive influence on the social norms approved by public opinion. I am not speaking, at the moment, of the influence which a deeper understanding of the biological laws governing our own behaviour might have, a subject I shall discuss later on, but of the beneficial effect of scientific education in general. The discipline of scientific thinking rarely fails to imbue a good man not only with a certain ingrained habit of being honest, but also with a high appreciation of the value of scientific truth in itself. Scientific truth is one of the best causes for which a man can fight and although, being based on irreducible fact, it may seem less inspiring than the beauty of art or some of the older ideals possessing the glamour of myth and romance, it surpasses all others in being incontestable, and absolutely independent of cultural, national, and political allegiances.

Enthusiastic identification with any value that is ethical in the sense that its content will stand the test of Kant's categorical question, will act as an antidote to national or political aggression. Dr J. Hollo, an American physician, has pointed out that the militant enthusiasm by which a man identifies himself with a national or political cause, is dangerous mainly for the one reason that it excludes all other considerations the moment it is aroused . . . . A man really can feel 'wholly American' when thinking of 'the' Russians or *vice versa*. The single-mindedness with which enthusiasm eliminates all other considerations and the fact that the objects of identification happen, in this case, to be fighting-units, make national and political enthusiasm actually dangerous, to the point of its being ethically questionable.

Continuing Dr Hollo's argument, let us suppose that a man, whatever his political or national allegiance, also identifies with ideals other than national or political. Supposing that, being a patriot of my home country (which I am), I felt an unmitigated hostility against another country (which I emphatically do not), I still could not wish wholeheartedly for its destruction if I realized that there were people living in it who, like myself, were enthusiastic workers in the field of inductive natural science, or revered Charles Darwin and were enthusiastically propagating the truth of his discoveries, or still others who shared my appreciation of Michelangelo's art, or my enthusiasm for Goethe's *Faust*, or for the beauty of a coral reef, or for wildlife preservation or a number of minor enthusiasms I could name. I should find it quite impossible to hate, unreservedly, any enemy, if he shared only one of my identifications with cultural and ethical values.

Obviously, the number of cultural and ethical ideals with which people are able to identify irrespective of their national or political allegiance will be in direct proportion to their reluctance to follow the urge of single-minded national or political enthusiasm. It is only the education of all humanity that can increase the number of ideals with which every individual can identify. In this manner, education would become 'humanistic' in a new and wider sense of the word.

Humanistic ideals of this kind must become real and full-blooded enough to compete, in the esteem of young people, with all the romantic and glamorous stimulus situations which are, primarily, much more effective in releasing the old hackle-raising and chin-protruding response of militant enthusiasm. Much intelligence and insight, on the side of the educator as well as on that of the educated, will be needed before this great goal is reached. Indeed, a certain academic dryness, unavoidably inherent in humanistic ideals, might for ever prevent average humanity from recognizing their value, were it not that they have for their ally a heaven-sent gift of man that is anything but dry, a faculty as specifically human as speech or moral responsibility: humour. In its highest forms, it appears to be specially evolved to give us the power of sifting the true from the false. G. K. Chesterton has voiced the altogether novel opinion that the religion of the future will be based, to a considerable extent, on a more highly developed and differentiated, subtle form of humour. Though, in this formulation, the idea may appear somewhat exaggerated, I feel inclined to agree, answering one paradox with another by saying that we do not as yet take humour seriously enough. I should not write my avowal of optimism with so much conviction were it not for my confidence in the great and beneficial force of humour.

Laughter is not only the overt expression of humour, but it very probably constitutes the phylogenetic base on which it evolved. Laughter resembles militant enthusiasm as well as the triumph ceremony of geese in three essential points: all three are instinctive behaviour patterns, all three are derived from aggressive behaviour and still retain some of its primal motivation, and all three have a similar social function . . . Laughter probably evolved by ritualization of a redirected threatening movement, just as the triumph ceremony did. Like the latter, and like militant enthusiasm, laughter produces, simultaneously, a strong fellow feeling among participants and joint aggressiveness against outsiders. Heartily laughing together at the same thing forms an immediate bond, much as enthusiasm for the same ideal does. Finding the same thing funny is not only a prerequisite to a real friendship, but very often the first step to its formation. Laughter forms a bond and simultaneously draws a line. If you cannot laugh with the others, you feel an outsider, even if the laughter is in no way directed against yourself or indeed against anything at all. If laughter is in fact directed at an outsider, as in scornful derision, the component of agressive motivation and, at the same time, the analogy to certain forms of the triumph ceremony become greatly enhanced. In this case, laughter can turn into a very cruel weapon, causing injury if it strikes a defenceless human being undeservedly; it is criminal to laugh at a child.

Nevertheless laughter is, in a higher sense than enthusiasm, specifically human. The motor patterns of threatening underlying both have undergone a deeper change of form and function in the case of laughter. Unlike enthusiasm, laughter – even at its most intense – is never in danger of regressing and causing the primal aggressive behaviour to break through. Barking dogs may occasionally bite, but laughing men hardly ever shoot! And if the motor patterns of laughing are even more uncontrollably instinctive than those of enthusiasm, conversely its releasing mechanisms are far better and more reliably controlled by human reason. Laughter never makes us uncritical, while enthusiasm abolishes all thought of rational self-control.

Indeed, the reliable control exerted by reason over laughter allows us to use it in a way which would be highly dangerous if applied to militant enthusiasm. Both laughter and enthusiasm can, by appropriate manipulation, be used like aggressive dogs, that is, set on and made to attack practically any enemy that reason may choose. But while laughter, even in the form of the most outrageous and scornful ridicule, always remains obedient to reason, enthusiasm is always threatening to get out of hand and to turn on its master.

There is one particular enemy whom it is fair to attack to the barking tune of laughter, and that is a very definite form of lie. There are few things in the world so thoroughly despicable and deserving of immediate destruction as the fiction of an ideal cause artificially set up to elicit enthusiasm in the service of the contriver's aims. Humour is the best of lie-detectors, and it discovers, with an uncanny flair, the speciousness of contrived ideals and the insincerity of simulated enthusiasm. There are few things in the world so irresistibly comical as the sudden unmasking of this sort of pretence. When pompousness is abruptly debunked, when the balloon of puffed-up arrogance is pricked by humour and bursts with a loud report, we can indulge in uninhibited, refreshing laughter which is liberated by this special kind of sudden relief of tension. It is one of the few absolutely uncontrolled discharges of an instinctive motor pattern in man of which responsible morality wholly approves.

Responsible morality not only approves of the effects of humour, but finds a strong support in it. A satire is, by the definition of the *Concise Oxford Dictionary*, a poem aimed at prevalent vices and follies. The power of its persuasion lies in the manner of its appeal: it can make itself heard by ears which, through scepticism and sophistication, are deafened to any direct preaching of morality. In other words, satire is the right sort of sermon for today.

If, in ridiculing insincere ideals, humour is a powerful ally of rational morality, it is even more so in self-ridicule. Nowadays we are all radically intolerant of pompous or sanctimonious people, because we expect a certain amount of self-ridicule in every intelligent human being. Indeed, we feel that a man who takes himself absolutely seriously is not quite human, and this feeling has a sound foundation. That which, in colloquial German, is so aptly termed *tierischer Ernst* – that is, 'animal seriousness' – is an ever-present symptom of megalomania, in fact I suspect that it is one of its causes. The best definition of man is that he is the one creature capable of reflection, of seeing himself in the frame of reference of the surrounding universe. Pride is one of the chief obstacles to seeing ourselves as we really are, and self-deceit is the obliging servant of pride. It is my firm belief that a man sufficiently gifted with humour is in small danger of succumbing to flattering delusions about himself because he cannot help perceiving what a pompous ass he would become if he did. I believe that a really subtle and acute perception of the humorous aspects of ourselves is the strongest inducement in the world to make us honest with ourselves, thus fulfilling one of the first postulates of reasoning morality. An amazing parallel between humour and the categorical question is that both balk at logical inconsistencies and incongruities. Acting against reason is not only immoral but, funnily enough, it is very often extremely funny! 'Thou shalt not cheat thyself' ought to be the first of all commandments. The ability to obey it is in direct proportion to the ability of being honest with others.

It is not only because of these considerations that I regard humour as a force which justifies greater optimism. I also believe that humour is rapidly developing in modern man. Whether humour is becoming more effective because cultural tradition makes it more and more respected, or whether the instinctive drive to laugh is phylogenetically gaining power, is not the essential point; both processes probably are at work. In any case, there is no doubt that humour is rapidly becoming more effective, more searching, and more subtle in detecting dishonesty. I for one find the humour of earlier periods less effective, less probing, less subtle. Charles Dickens is the oldest writer I know whose satirical representation of human nature makes me really laugh. I can understand perfectly well at what particular 'prevalent vices and follies' the satires of late Roman writers or of Abraham a Sancta Clara are directed, but I do not respond to them with laughter. A systematic historical investigation of the stimulus situations that in different ages made people laugh might be extremely revealing.

I believe that humour exerts an influence on the social behaviour of man which, in one respect, is strictly analogous to that of moral responsibility: it tends to make the world a more honest and, therewith, a better place. I believe that this influence is rapidly increasing and, entering more and more subtly into the reasoning-processes, becoming more closely interwoven with and, in its effects, more akin to morality. In this sense, I absolutely agree with G. K. Chesterton's astonishing statement.

From the discussion of what I know I have gradually passed to the account of what I think probable and, finally, to a profession of what I believe. There is no law barring the scientist from doing so. I believe, in short, in the ultimate victory of truth. I know that this sounds rather pompous, but I honestly do think it is the most likely thing to happen. I might even say that I regard it as inevitable, provided the human species does not commit suicide in the near future, as well it may. Otherwise it is quite predictable that the simple truths concerning the biology of mankind and the laws governing its behaviour will sooner or later become generally accepted public property, in the same way as the older scientific truths . . . have done; they, too, were at first unacceptable to an all too complacent humanity because they disturbed its exaggerated self-esteem. Is it too much to hope that the fear of imminent self-destruction may have a sobering effect and act as a monitor of self-knowledge?

I do not consider in any way as utopian the possibility of conveying a sufficient knowledge of the essential biological facts to any sensible human being. They are indeed much easier to understand than, for instance, integral calculus or the computing of compound interest. Moreover, biology is a fascinating study, provided it is taught intelligently enough to make the pupil realize that he himself, being a living being, is directly concerned with what he is being told. *Tua res agitur*. [It is your interests that are being dealt with]. Expert teaching of biology is the one and only foundation on which really sound opinions about mankind and its relation to the universe can be built. Philosophical anthropology of a type neglecting biological fact has done its worst by imbuing humanity with that sort of pride which not only comes before, but causes, a fall. It is plain biology of *Homo sapiens* that ought to be considered the 'big science'.

Sufficient knowledge of man and of his position in the universe would, as I have said, automatically determine the ideals for which we have to strive. Sufficient humour may make mankind blessedly intolerant of phony, fraudulent ideals. Humour and knowledge are the two great hopes of civilization. There is a third, more distant hope based on the possibilities of human evolution; it is to be hoped that the cultural factors just mentioned will exert a selection pressure in a desirable direction. Many characters of man which, from the Palaeolithic to recent times, were accounted the highest virtues, today seem dangerous to thinking people and funny to people with a sense of humour. If it is true that, within a few hundred years, selection brought about a devastating hypertrophy of aggression in the Utes, that most unhappy of all peoples, we may hope without exaggerated optimism that a new kind of selection may, in civilized peoples, reduce the aggresive drive to a tolerable measure without, however, disturbing its indispensable function.

The great constructors of evolution will solve the problems of political strife and warfare, but they will not do so by entirely eliminating aggression and its communal form of militant enthusiasm. This would not be in keeping with their proven methods. If, in a newly arising biological situation, a drive begins to become injurious, it is never atrophied and removed entirely, for this would mean dispensing with all its indispensable functions. Invariably, the problem is solved by the evolution of a new inhibitory mechanism adapted to dealing specifically with the new situation and obviating the particular detrimental effects of the drive without otherwise interfering with its functions.

We know that, in the evolution of vertebrates, the bond of personal love and friendship was the epoch-making invention created by the great constructors when it became necessary for two or more individuals of an aggresive species to live peacefully together and to work for a common end. We know that human society is built on the foundation of this bond, but we have to recognize the fact that the bond has become too limited to encompass all that it should: it prevents aggression only between those who know each other and are friends, while obviously it is all active hostility between all men of all nations or ideologies that must be stopped. The obvious conclusion is that love and friendship should embrace all humanity, that we should love all our human brothers indiscriminately. This commandment is not new. Our reason is quite able to undertand its necessity as our feeling is able to appreciate its beauty, but nevertheless, made as we are, we are unable to obey it. We can feel the full, warm emotion of friendship and love only for individuals, and the utmost exertion of will power cannot alter this fact. But the great constructors can, and I believe they will. I believe in the power of human reason, as I believe in the power of natural selection. I believe that reason can and will exert a selection pressure in the right direction. I believe that this, in the not-too-distant future, will endow our descendants with the faculty of fulfilling the greatest and most beautiful of all commandments.

6

The Paradoxes of Contemporary Warfare

William James and Konrad Lorenz, in the pieces by them reprinted in Chapter 5, bring out very well the fact that there is a widespread, if not universal, attraction for war in mankind and that this must be dealt with if we are ever to succeed in abolishing war. The following extracts from T. H. White and Leonard Lewin carry this reasoning one final step further, indicating that human propensities for war may be intertwined with, and bolstered and fostered by, economic, social and political realities which render war a by-no-means dispensable luxury for mankind. These two selections are satirical in form. It sometimes happens with good satire that the persons satirized might conceivably read the portrayal of their ideas, and take the portrayal to be serious rather than satirical. This is certainly the case with Lewin's book, presented as a straightforward final report of a 'blue-ribbon' commission.

The final extract, from Jonathan Schell, is more serious and straightforward. It brings out directly and clearly some of the specific and peculiar paradoxes resulting from contemporary strategic nuclear armaments.

I   T. H. WHITE, 'THE PASSING OF CAMELOT' (extract)

The English novelist and satirist T. H. White (1906–64) wrote *The Book of Merlyn* in 1941 as the fifth volume of *The Once and Future King*, his series on the Arthurian legend. Most of *The Book of Merlyn* consists of a discourse on war. 'The Passing of Camelot' depicts a conversation of King Arthur with Merlyn the magician and with the animals with whom he served an apprenticeship as a child. In the following extract, Arthur at one final meeting of the Privy Council, in response to previous criticisms of war brought forth by Merlyn, suggests that their present discussion of the feasibility of war should begin with the arguments in favour of war. Merlyn does not wish to encourage war, but does what he can to present to the king the objective reasons for continuing to wage wars, as well as his 'committee's' plans for abolishing war.

The text below is reprinted from T. H. White, *The book of Merlyn: The Unpublished Conclusion to 'The Once and Future King'* (Austin: University of Texas Press; London: Collins, 1977) pp. 118–22.

'The second question deals with war. It has been suggested that we ought to abolish it, in one way or another, but nobody has given it the chance to speak for itself. Perhaps there is something to be said in favour of war. We would like to be told.'

Merlyn put his hat on the floor and whispered to the badger, who, after scuttling off to his pile of agenda, returned, to the wonder of all, with the proper piece of paper.

'Sir, this question has been before the attention of the committee, who have ventured to draw up a list of Pros and Cons, which we are ready to recite.'

Merlyn cleared his throat, and announced in a loud voice: 'PRO.'

'In favour of war', explained the badger.

'Number One', said Merlyn. 'War is one of the mainsprings of romance. Without war, there would be no Rolands, Maccabees, Lawrences or Hodsons of Hodson's Horse. There would be no Victoria Crosses. It is a stimulant to so-called virtues, such as courage and co-operation. In fact, war has moments of glory. It should also be noted that, without war, we should lose at least one half of our literature. Shakespeare is packed with it.

'Number Two. War is a way of keeping down the population, though it is a hideous and inefficient one. The same Shakespeare, who seems on the subject of war to have been in agreement with the Germans and with their raving apologist Nietzsche, says, in a scene which he is supposed to have written for Beaumont and Fletcher, that it heals with blood the earth when it is sick and cures the world of the pleurisy of people. Perhaps I may mention in parentheses, without irreverence, that the Bard seems to have been curiously insensitive on the subject of warfare. *King Henry V* is the most revolting play I know, as Henry himself is the most revolting character.

'Number Three. War does provide a vent for the pent-up ferocity of man, and, while man remains a savage, something of the sort seems to be needed. The committee finds from an examination of history that human cruelty will vent itself in one way, if it is denied another. During the eighteenth and nineteenth centuries, when war was a limited exercise confined to professional armies recruited from the criminal classes, the general mass of the population resorted to public executions, dental operations without anaesthetics, brutal sports and flogging their children. In the twentieth century, when war was extended to embrace the masses, hanging, hacking, cock-fighting and spanking went out of fashion.

'Number Four. The committee is at present occupied about a complicated investigation into the physical or psychological necessity. We do not feel that a report can be made at this stage with profit, but we think we have observed that war does answer a real need in man, perhaps connected with the ferocity mentioned in Article Three, but perhaps not. It has come to our notice that man becomes restless or dejected after a generation of peace. The immortal if not omniscient Swan of Avon remarks that peace seems to breed a disease, which, coming to a head in a sort of ulcer, bursts out into war. 'War', he says, 'is the imposthume of much wealth and peace, which only breaks, shewing no outward cause why the man dies.' Under this interpretation, it is the peace which is regarded as a slow disease, while the bursting of the imposthume, the war, must be assumed to be beneficial rather than the reverse. The committee has suggested two ways in which wealth and peace might destroy the race, if war were prevented: by emasculating it, or by rendering it comatose through glandular troubles. On the subject of emasculation, it should be noted that wars double the birth-rate. The reason why women tolerate war is because it promotes virility in men.

'Number Five. Finally, there is the suggestion which would probably be made by every other animal on the face of this earth, except man, namely that war is an inestimable boon to creation as a whole, because it does offer some faint hope of exterminating the human race.

'CON', announced the magician; but the king prevented him.

'We know the objections', he said. 'The idea that it is useful might be considered a little more. If there is some necessity for might, why is the committee ready to stop it?'

'Sir, the committee is attempting to trace the physiological basis, possibly of a pituitary or adrenal origin. Possibly the human system requires periodical doses of adrenalin, in order to remain healthy. (The Japanese, as an instance of glandular activity, are said to eat large quantities of fish, which, by charging their bodies with iodine, expands their thyroids and makes them touchy.) Until this matter has been properly investigated the subject remains vague, but the committee desires to point out that the physiological need could be supplied by other means. War, it has already been observed, is an inefficient way of keeping down the population: it may also be an inefficient way of stimulating the adrenal glands through fear.'

'What other ways?'

'Under the Roman Empire, the experiment of offering bloody spectacles in the circus was attempted as a substitute. They provided the Purgation which Aristotle talks about, and some such alternative might be found efficient. Science, however, would suggest more radical cures. Either the glandular deficiency might be supplied by periodical injections of the whole population with adrenalin – or with whatever the deficiency may prove to be – or else some form of surgery might be found effective. Perhaps the root of war is removable, like the appendix.'

'We were told that war is caused by national property: now we are told that it is due to a gland.'

'Sir, the two things may be related, though they may not be consequent upon one another. For instance, if wars were solely due to national property, we should expect them to continue without intermission so long as national property continued: that is, all the time. We find, however, that they are interrupted by frequent lulls, called peace. It seems as if the human race becomes more and more comatose during these periods of truce, until, when what you may call the saturation point of adrenalin deficiency has been reached, it seizes upon the first handy excuse for a good shot of fear stimulant. The handy excuse is national property. Even if the wars are dolled up as religious ones, such as crusades against Saladin or the Albigensians or Montezuma, the basis remains the same. Nobody would have troubled to extend the benefits of Christianity to Montezuma, if his sandals had not been made of gold, and nobody would have thought the gold itself a sufficient temptation, if they had not been needing a dose of adrenalin.'

'You suggest an alternative like the circus, pending the investigation of your gland. Have you considered it?'

Archimedes giggled unexpectedly.

'Merlyn wants to have an international fair, Sir. He wants to have a lot of flip-flaps and giant wheels and scenic railways in a reservation, and they are all to be slightly dangerous, so as to kill perhaps one man in a hundred. Entrance is to be voluntary, for he says that the one unutterably wicked thing about a war is conscription. He says that people will go to the fair of their own free will, through boredom or through adrenalin deficiency or whatever it is, and that they are likely to feel the need for it during their twenty-fifth, thirtieth, and forty-fifth years. It is to be made fashionable and glorious to go. Every visitor will get a commemorative medal, while those who go fifty times will get what he calls the DSO or the VC for a hundred visits.'

The magician looked ashamed and cracked his fingers.

'The suggestion', he said humbly, 'was more to provoke thought, than to be thought of.'

'Certainly it does not seem a practical suggestion for the present year of grace. Are there no panaceas for war, which could be used in the meantime?'

'The committee has suggested an antidote which might have a temporary effect, like soda for an acid stomach. It would be of no use as a cure for the malady, though it might alleviate it. It might save a few million lives in a century.'

'What is this antidote?'

'Sir, you will have noticed that the people who are responsible for the declaration and the higher conduct of wars do not tend to be the people who endure their extremes. At the battle of Bedegraine Your Majesty dealt with something of the same sort. The kings and the generals and the leaders of battles have a peculiar aptitude for not being killed in them. The committee has suggested that , after every war, all the officials on the losing side who held a higher rank than colonel ought to be executed out of hand, irrespective of their war guilt. No doubt there would be a certain amount of injustice in this measure, but the consciousness that death was the certain result of losing a war would have a deterrent effect on those who help to promote and to regulate such engagements, and it might, by preventing a few wars, save millions of lives among the lower classes. Even a Führer like Mordred might think twice about heading hostilities, if he knew that his own execution would be the result of being unlucky in them.'

'It seems reasonable.'

'It is less reasonable than it seems, partly because the responsibility for warfare does not lie wholly with the leaders. After all, a leader has to be chosen or accepted by those whom he leads. The hydra-headed multitudes are not so innocent as they like to pretend. They have given a mandate to their generals, and they must abide by the moral responsibility.'

'Still, it would have the effect of making the leaders reluctant to be pushed into warfare by their followers, and even that would help.'

'It would help. The difficulty would lie in persuading the leading classes to agree to such a convention in the first place. Also, I am afraid that you will find there is always a type of maniac, anxious for notoriety at any price, or even for martyrdom, who would accept the pomp of leadership with even greater alacrity because it was enhanced by melodramatic penalties. The kings of Irish mythology were compelled by their station to march in the forefront of the battle, which occasioned a frightful mortality among them, yet there never seems to have been a lack of kings or battles in the history of the Green Isle.'

'What about this new-fangled law', asked the goat suddenly, 'which our king has been inventing? If individuals can be deterred from murder by fear of a death penalty, why cannot there be an international law, under which nations can be deterred from war by similar means? An aggressive nation might be kept at peace by the knowledge that, if it began a war, some international police force would sentence it to dispersal, by mass transportation to other countries for instance.'

'There are two objections to that. First, you would be trying to cure the disease, not to prevent it. Second, we know from experience that the existence of a death penalty does not in fact abolish murder. It might, however, prove to be a temporary step in the right direction.'

The old man folded his hands in his sleeves, like a Chinaman, and looked round the council table, doggedly, waiting for further questions.

II   LEONARD C. LEWIN, *REPORT FROM IRON MOUNTAIN*
     ON THE POSSIBILITY AND DESIRABILITY OF PEACE,
     SECTIONS 4–8

Lewin's *Report from Iron Mountain* was first published during the intense national debate taking place in the 1960s concerning America's involvement in the Vietnam War; and it is more or less an attempt to respond to a question on the minds of many: are there possibly some important mechanisms that will lead a nation into fighting a war, even when the war is not in the nation's best interest, even when there is no hope of winning? Lewin's 'report' is in the format of a summary of results of a 'Special Study Group', commissioned to investigate the possibly traumatic effects of a transition from a state of war to a state of peace. In the course of their investigations they discover some essential functions of war which it may be difficult or even impossible to substitute for in a peacetime context. Nowhere in Lewin's book is it stated that the 'report' is fictional and satirical, but one presumes that it is. Or, at least, one hopes that it is.

The text below is reprinted from Leonard C. Lewin, *Report from Iron Mountain on the Possibility and Desirability of Peace* (New York: Dial Press, 1967) pp. 27–109. The one ellipsis indicates omission of a cross–reference; square brackets outside quotations are editorial.

4 War and peace as social systems

We have dealt only sketchily with proposed disarmament scenarios and economic analyses, but the reason for our seemingly casual dismissal of so much serious and sophisticated work lies in no disrespect for its competence. It is rather a question of relevance. To put it plainly, all these programmes, however detailed and well developed, are abstractions. The most carefully reasoned disarmament sequence inevitably reads more like the rules of a game or a classroom exercise in logic than like a prognosis of real events in the real world. This is as true of today's complex proposals as it was of the Abbé de Saint-Pierre's 'Plan for Perpetual Peace in Europe' 250 years ago.

Some essential element has clearly been lacking in all these schemes. One of our first tasks was to try to bring this missing quality into definable focus, and we believe we have succeeded in doing so. We find that at the heart of every peace study we have examined – from the modest technological proposal (e.g. to convert a poison-gas plant to the production of 'socially useful' equivalents) to the most elaborate scenario for universal peace in our time – lies one common fundamental misconception. It is the source of the miasma of unreality surrounding such plans. *It is the incorrect assumption that war, as an institution, is subordinate to the social systems it is believed to serve.*

This misconception, although profound and far-reaching, is entirely comprehensible. Few social clichés are so unquestioningly accepted as the notion that war is an extension of diplomacy (or of politics, or of the pursuit of economic objectives). If this were true, it would be wholly appropriate for economists and political theorists to look on the problems of transition to peace as essentially mechanical or procedural – as indeed they do, treating them as logistic corollaries of the settlement of national conflicts of interest. If this were true, there would be no real substance to the difficulties of transition. For it is evident that even in today's world there exists no conceivable conflict of interest, real or imaginary, between nations or between social forces within nations, that cannot be resolved without recourse to war – *if* such resolution were assigned a priority of social value. And if this were true, the economic analyses and disarmament proposals we have referred to, plausible and well conceived as they may be, would not inspire, as they do, an inescapable sense of indirection.

The point is that the cliché is not true, and the problems of transition are indeed substantive rather than merely procedural. Although war is 'used' as an instrument of national and social policy, the fact that a society is organized for any degree of readiness for war supersedes its political and economic structure. War itself is the basic social system, within which other secondary modes of social organization conflict or conspire. It is the system which has governed most human societies of record, as it is today.

Once this is correctly understood, the true magnitude of the problems entailed in a transition to peace – itself a social system, but without precedent except in a few simple pre-industrial societies – becomes apparent. At the same time, some of the puzzling superficial contradictions of modern societies can then be readily rationalized. The 'unnecessary' size and power of the world war industry; the pre-eminence of the military establishment in every society, whether open or concealed; the exemption of military or paramilitary institutions from the accepted social and legal standards of behaviour required elsewhere in the society; the successful operation of the armed forces and the armaments producers entirely outside the framework of each nation's economic ground rules: these and other ambiguities closely associated with the relationship of war to society are easily clarified, once the priority of war-making potential as the principal structuring-force in society is accepted. Economic systems, political philosophies, and *corpora jures* serve and extend the war system, not *vice versa*.

It must be emphasized that the precedence of a society's war-making potential over its other characteristics is not the result of the 'threat' presumed to exist at any one time from other societies. This is the reverse of the basic situation; 'threats' against the 'national interest' are usually created or accelerated to meet the changing needs of the war system. Only in comparatively recent times has it been considered politically expedient to euphemize war budgets as 'defence' requirements. The necessity for governments to distinguish between 'aggression' (bad) and 'defence' (good) has been a by-product of rising literacy and rapid communication. The distinction is tactical only, a concession to the growing inadequacy of ancient war-organizing political rationales.

Wars are not 'caused' by international conflicts of interest. Proper logical sequence would make it more often accurate to say that war-making societies require – and thus bring about – such conflicts. The capacity of a nation to make war expresses the greatest social power it can exercise; war-making, active or contemplated, is a matter of life and death on the greatest scale subject to social control. It should therefore hardly be surprising that the military institutions in each society claim its highest priorities.

We find further that most of the confusion surrounding the myth that war-making is a tool of state policy stems from a general misapprehension of the functions of war. In general, these are conceived as: to defend a nation from military attack by another, or to deter such an attack; to defend or advance a 'national interest' – economic, political, ideological; to maintain or increase a nation's military power for its own sake. These are the visible, or ostensible, functions of war. If there were no others, the importance of the war establishment in each society might in fact decline to the subordinate level it is believed to occupy. And the elimination of war would indeed be the procedural matter that the disarmament scenarios suggest.

But there are other, broader, more profoundly felt functions of war in modern societies. It is these invisible, or implied, functions that maintain war-readiness as the dominant force in our societies. And it is the unwillingness or inability of the writers of disarmament scenarios and reconversion plans to take them into account that has so reduced the usefulness of their work, and that has made it seem unrelated to the world we know.

5 The functions of war

As we have indicated, the pre-eminence of the concept of war as the principal organizing-force in most societies has been insufficiently appreciated. This is also true of its extensive effects throughout the many non-military activities of society. These effects are less apparent in complex industrial societies like our own than in primitive cultures, the activities of which can be more easily and fully comprehended.

We propose in this section to examine these non-military, implied, and usually invisible functions of war, to the extent that they bear on the problems of transition to peace for our society. The military, or ostensible, function of the war system requires no elaborations; it serves simply to defend or advance the 'national interest' by means of organized violence. It is often necessary for a national military establishment to create a need for its unique powers – to maintain the franchise, so to speak. And a healthy military apparatus requires regular 'exercise', by whatever rationale seems expedient, to prevent its atrophy.

The nonmilitary functions of the war system are more basic. They exist not merely to justify themselves but to serve broader social purposes. If and when war is eliminated, the military functions it has served will end with it. But its non-military functions will not. It is essential, therefore, that we understand their significance before we can reasonably expect to evaluate whatever institutions may be proposed to replace them.

Economic

The production of weapons of mass destruction has always been associated with economic 'waste'. The term is pejorative, since it implies a failure of function. But no human activity can properly be considered wasteful if it achieves its contextual objective. The phrase 'wasteful but necessary', applied not only to war expenditures but to most of the 'unproductive' commercial activities of our society, is a contradiction in terms. 'The attacks that have since the time of Samuel's criticism of King Saul been leveled against military expenditures as waste may well have concealed or misunderstood the point that some kinds of waste may have a larger social utility.'[1]

In the case of military 'waste', there is indeed a larger social utility. It derives from the fact that the 'wastefulness' of war production is exercised entirely outside the framework of the economy of supply and demand. As such, it provides the only critically large segment of the total economy that is subject to complete and arbitrary central control. If modern industrial societies can be defined as those which have developed the capacity to produce more than is required for their economic survival (regardless of the equities of distribution of goods within them), military spending can be said to furnish the only balance wheel with sufficient inertia to stabilize the advance of their economies. The fact that war is 'wasteful' is what enables it to serve this function. And the faster the economy advances, the heavier this balance wheel must be.

This function is often viewed, over-simply, as a device for the control of surpluses. One writer on the subject puts it this way: 'Why is war so wonderful? Because it creates artificial demand . . . the only kind of artificial demand, moreover, that does not raise any political issues: *war, and only war, solves the problem of inventory*'.[2] The reference here is to shooting war, but it applies equally to the general war economy as well. 'It is generally agreed', concludes, more cautiously, the report of a panel set up by the US Arms Control and Disarmament Agency, 'that the greatly expanded public sector since World War II, resulting from heavy defense expenditures, has provided additional protection against depressions, since this sector is not responsive to contraction in the private sector and has provided a sort of buffer or balance wheel in the economy.'[3]

The *principal* economic function of war, in our view, is that it provides just such a flywheel. It is not to be confused in function with the various forms of fiscal control, none of which directly engages vast numbers of men and units of production. It is not to be confused with massive government expenditures in social-welfare programmes; once initiated, such programmes normally become integral parts of the general economy and are no longer subject to arbitrary control.

But even in the context of the general civilian economy war cannot be considered wholly 'wasteful'. Without a long-established war economy, and without its frequent eruption into large-scale shooting war, most of the major industrial advances known to history, beginning with the development of iron, could never have taken place. Weapons technology structures the economy. According to the writer cited above,

Nothing is more ironic or revealing about our society than the fact that hugely destructive war is a very progressive force in it. . . . War production is progressive because it is production that would not otherwise have taken place. (It is not so widely appreciated, for example, that the civilian standard of living *rose* during World War II.)[4]

This is 'not ironic or revealing', but essentially a simple statement of fact.

It should also be noted that war production has a dependably stimulating effect outside itself. Far from constituting a 'wasteful' drain on the economy, war spending, considered pragmatically, has been a consistently positive factor in the rise of gross national product and of individual productivity. A former Secretary of the Army has carefully phrased it for public consumption thus: 'If there is, as I suspect there is, a direct relation between the stimulus of large defense spending and a substantially increased rate of growth of gross national product, it quite simply follows that defense spending per se might be countenanced *on economic grounds alone* [emphasis added] as a stimulator of the national metabolism.'[5] Actually, the fundamental non-military utility of war in the economy is far more widely acknowledged than the scarcity of such affirmations as that quoted above would suggest.

But *negatively* phrased public recognitions of the importance of war to the general economy abound. The most familiar example is the effect of 'peace threats' on the stock market, e.g. 'Wall Street was shaken yesterday by news of an apparent peace feeler from North Vietnam, but swiftly recovered its composure after about an hour of sometimes indiscriminate selling.'[6] Savings banks solicit deposits with similar cautionary slogans, e.g. 'If peace breaks out, will you be ready for it?' A more subtle case in point was the recent refusal of the Department of Defense to permit the West German Government to substitute non-military goods for unwanted armaments in its purchase commitments from the United States; the decisive consideration was that the German purchases should not affect the general (non-military) economy. Other incidental examples are to be found in the pressures brought to bear on the Department when it announces plans to close down an obsolete facility (as a 'wasteful' form of 'waste'), and in the usual coordination of stepped-up military activities (as in Vietnam in 1965) with dangerously rising unemployment rates.

Although we do not imply that a substitute for war in the economy cannot be devised, no combination of techniques for controlling employment, production, and consumption has yet been tested that can remotely compare to it in effectiveness. It is, and has been, the essential economic stabilizer of modern societies.

Political

The political functions of war have been up to now even more critical to social stability. It is not surprising, nevertheless, that discussions of economic conversion for peace tend to fall silent on the matter of political implementation, and that disarmament scenarios, often sophisticated in their weighing of international political factors, tend to disregard the political functions of the war system within individual societies.

These functions are essentially organizational. First of all, the existence of a society as a political 'nation' requires as part of its definition an attitude of relationship toward other 'nations'. This is what we usually call a foreign policy. But a nation's foreign policy can have no substance if it lacks the means of enforcing its attitude toward other nations. It can do this in a credible manner only if it implies the threat of maximum political organization for this pur- pose – which is to say that it is organized to some degree for war. War, then, as we have defined it to include all national activities that recognize the possibility of armed conflict, is itself the defining element of any nation's existence *vis-á-vis* any other nation. Since it is historically axiomatic that the existence of any form of weaponry ensures its use, we have used the word 'peace' as virtually syn- onymous with disarmament. By the same token, 'war' is virtually synonymous with nationhood. The elimination of war implies the inevitable elimination of national sovereignty and the traditional nation state.

The war system not only has been essential to the existence of nations as independent political entities, but has been equally indispensable to their stable internal political structure. Without it, no government has ever been able to obtain acquiescence in its 'legitimacy', or right to rule its society. The possibility of war provides the sense of external necessity without which no govern- ment can long remain in power. The historical record reveals one instance after another where the failure of a regime to maintain the credibility of a war threat led to its dissolution, by the forces of private interests, of reactions to social injustice, or of other disinte- grative elements. The organization of a society for the possibility of war is its principal political stabilizer. It is ironic that this pri- mary function of war has been generally recognized by historians only where it has been expressly acknowledged – in the pirate societies of the great conquerors.

The basic authority of a modern state over its people resides in its war powers. (There is, in fact, good reason to believe that codified law had its origins in the rules of conduct established by military victors for dealing with the defeated enemy, which were later adapted to apply to all subject populations.[7]) On a day-to-day basis, it is represented by the institution of police, armed organizations charged expressly with dealing with 'internal enemies' in a military manner. Like the conventional 'external' military, the police are also substantially exempt from many civilian legal restraints on their social behaviour. In some countries, the artificial distinction between police and other military forces does not exist. On the long-term basis, a government's emergency war powers – inherent in the structure of even the most libertarian of nations – define the most significant aspect of the relation between state and citizen.

In advanced modern democratic societies, the war system has provided political leaders with another political–economic function of increasing importance: it has served as the last great safeguard against the elimination of necessary social classes. As economic productivity increases to a level further and further above that of minimum subsistence, it becomes more and more difficult for a society to maintain distribution patterns ensuring the existence of 'hewers of wood and drawers of water.' The further progress of automation can be expected to differentiate still more sharply between 'superior' workers and what Ricardo called 'menials', while simultaneously aggravating the problem of maintaining an unskilled labour supply.

The arbitrary nature of war expenditures and of other military activities make[s] them ideally suited to control these essential class relationships. Obviously, if the war system were to be discarded, new political machinery would be needed at once to serve this vital sub-function. Until it is developed, the continuance of the war system must be assured, if for no other reason, among others, than to preserve whatever quality and degree of poverty a society requires as an incentive, as well as to maintain the stability of its internal organization of power.

Sociological

Under this heading, we will examine a nexus of functions served by the war system that affect human behaviour in society. In general, they are broader in application and less susceptible to direct observation than the economic and political factors previously considered.

The most obvious of these functions is the time-honoured use of military institutions to provide anti-social elements with an acceptable role in the social structure. The disintegrative, unstable social movements loosely described as 'fascist' have traditionally taken root in societies that have lacked adequate military or paramilitary outlets to meet the needs of these elements. This function has been critical in periods of rapid change. The danger signals are easy to recognize, even though the stigmata bear different names at different times. The current euphemistic cliches – 'juvenile delinquency' and 'alienation' – have had their counterparts in every age. In earlier days these conditions were dealt with directly by the military without the complications of due process, usually through press gangs or outright enslavement. But it is not hard to visualize, for example, the degree of social disruption that might have taken place in the United States during the last two decades if the problem of the socially disaffected of the post-World War II period had not been foreseen and effectively met. The younger, and more dangerous, of these hostile social groupings have been kept under control by the Selective Service System.

This system and its analogues elsewhere furnish remarkably clear examples of disguised military utility. Informed persons in this country have never accepted the official rationale for a peacetime draft – military necessity, preparedness, etc. – as worthy of serious consideration. But what has gained credence among thoughtful men is the rarely voiced, less easily refuted, proposition that the institution of military service has a 'patriotic' priority in our society that must be maintained for its own sake. Ironically, the simplistic official justification for selective service comes closer to the mark, once the non-military functions of military institutions are understood. As a control device over the hostile, nihilistic, and potentially unsettling elements of a society in transition, the draft can again be defended, and quite convincingly, as a 'military' necessity.

Nor can it be considered a coincidence that overt military activity, and thus the level of draft calls, tend to follow the major fluctuations in the unemployment rate in the lower age groups. This rate, in turn, is a time-tested herald of social discontent. It must be noted also that the armed forces in every civilization have provided the principal state-supported haven for what we now call the 'unemployable'. The typical European standing army (of fifty years ago) consisted of 'troops unfit for employment in commerce, industry, or agriculture, led by officers unfit to practice any legitimate profession or to conduct a business enterprise'.[8] This is still largely true, if less apparent. In a sense, this function of the military as the custodian of the economically or culturally deprived was the forerunner of most contemporary civilian social-welfare programmes, from the WPA to various forms of 'socialized' medicine and social security. It is interesting that liberal sociologists currently proposing to use the Selective Service System as a medium of cultural upgrading of the poor consider this a *novel* application of military practice.

Although it cannot be said absolutely that such critical measures of social control as the draft require a military rationale, no modern society has yet been willing to risk experimentation with any other kind. Even during such periods of comparatively simple social crisis as the so-called Great Depression of the 1930s, it was deemed prudent by the Government to invest minor make-work projects, like the 'Civilian' Conservation Corps, with a military character, and to place the more ambitious National Recovery Administration under the direction of a professional army officer at its inception. Today, at least one small Northern European country, plagued with uncontrollable unrest among its 'alienated youth', is considering the expansion of its armed forces, despite the problem of making credible the expansion of a non-existent external threat.

Sporadic efforts have been made to promote general recognition of broad national values free of military connotation, but they have been ineffective. For example, to enlist public support of even such modest programmes of social adjustment as 'fighting inflation' or 'maintaining physical fitness' it has been necessary for the Government to utilize a patriotic (i.e. military) incentive. It sells 'defence' bonds and it equates health with military preparedness. This is not surprising; since the concept of 'nationhood' implies readiness for war, a 'national' programme must do likewise.

In general, the war system provides the basic motivation for primary social organization. In so doing, it reflects on the societal level the incentives of individual human behaviour. The most important of these, for social purposes, is the individual psychological rationale for allegiance to a society and its values. Allegiance requires a cause, a cause requires an enemy. This much is obvious; the critical point is that the enemy that defines the cause must seem genuinely formidable. Roughly speaking, the presumed power of the 'enemy' sufficient to warrant an individual sense of allegiance to a society must be proportionate to the size and complexity of the society. Today, of course, that power must be one of unprecedented magnitude and frightfulness.

It follows from the patterns of human behaviour, that the credibility of a social 'enemy' demands similarly a readiness of response in proportion to its menace. In a broad social context, 'an eye for an eye' still characterizes the only acceptable attitude toward a presumed threat of aggression, despite contrary religious and moral precepts governing personal conduct. The remoteness of personal decision from social consequence in a modern society makes it easy for its members to maintain this attitude without being aware of it. A recent example is the war in Vietnam; a less recent one was the bombing of Hiroshima and Nagasaki.[9] In each case, the extent and gratuitousness of the slaughter were abstracted into political formulae by most Americans, once the proposition that the victims were 'enemies' was established. The war system makes such an abstracted response possible in non-military contexts as well. A conventional example of this mechanism is the inability of most people to connect, let us say, the starvation of millions in India with their own past conscious political decision-making. Yet the sequential logic linking a decision to restrict grain production in America with an eventual famine in Asia is obvious, unambiguous' and unconcealed.

What gives the war system its pre-eminent role in social organization, as elsewhere, is its unmatched authority over life and death. It must be emphasized again that the war system is not a mere social extension of the presumed need for individual human violence, but itself in turn serves to rationalize most non-military killing. It also provides the precedent for the collective willingness of members of a society to pay a blood price for institutions far less central to social organization than war. To take a handy example, 'rather than accept speed limits of twenty miles an hour we prefer to let automobiles kill forty thousand people a year'.[10] A Rand analyst puts it in more general terms and less rhetorically: 'I am sure that there is, in effect, a desirable level of automobile accidents – desirable, that is, from a broad point of view; in the sense that it is a necessary concomitant of things of greater value to society.'[11] The point may seem too obvious for iteration, but it is essential to an understanding of the important motivational function of war as a model for collective sacrifice.

A brief look at some defunct pre-modern societies is instructive. One of the most noteworthy features common to the larger, more complex, and more successful of ancient civilizations was their widespread use of the blood sacrifice. If one were to limit consideration to those cultures whose regional hegemony was so complete that the prospect of 'war' had become virtually inconceivable – as was the case with several of the great pre-Columbian societies of the Western Hemisphere – it would be found that some form of ritual killing occupied a position of paramount social importance in each. Invariably, the ritual was invested with mythic or religious significance; as with all religious and totemic practice, however, the ritual masked a broader and more important social function.

In these societies, the blood sacrifice served the purpose of maintaining a vestigial 'earnest' of the society's capability and willingness to make war – i.e. kill and be killed – in the event that some mystical – i.e. unforeseen – circumstance were to give rise to the possibility. That the 'earnest' was not an adequate substitute for genuine military organization when the unthinkable enemy, such as the Spanish conquistadores, actually appeared on the scene in no way negates the function of the ritual. It was primarily, if not exclusively, a symbolic reminder that war had once been the central organizing-force of the society, and that this condition might recur.

It does not follow that a transition to total peace in modern societies would require the use of this model, even in less 'barbaric' guise. But the historical analogy serves as a reminder that a viable substitute for war as a social system cannot be a mere symbolic charade. It must involve real risk of real personal destruction, and on a scale consistent with the size and complexity of modern social systems. Credibility is the key. Whether the substitute is ritual in nature or functionally substantive, unless it provides a believable life-and-death threat it will not serve the socially organizing-function of war.

The existence of an accepted external menace, then, is essential to social cohesiveness as well as to the acceptance of political authority. The menace must be believable, it must be of a magnitude consistent with the complexity of the society threatened, and it must appear, at least to affect the entire society.

Ecological

Man, like all other animals, is subject to the continuing process of adapting to the limitations of his environment. But the principal mechanism he has utilized for this purpose is unique among living creatures. To forestall the inevitable historical cycles of inadequate food supply, post-Neolithic man destroys surplus members of his own species by organized warfare.

Ethologists[12] have often observed that the organized slaughter of members of their own species is virtually unknown among other animals. Man's special propensity to kill his own kind (shared to a limited degree with rats) may be attributed to his inability to adapt anachronistic patterns of survival (like primitive hunting) to his development of 'civilizations' in which these patterns cannot be effectively sublimated. It may be attributed to other causes that have been suggested, such as a maladapted 'territorial instinct', etc. Nevertheless, it exists and its social expression in war constitutes a biological control of his relationship to his natural environment that is peculiar to man alone.

War has served to help assure the *survival* of the human species. But as an evolutionary device to *improve* it, war is almost unbelievably inefficient. With few exceptions, the selective processes of other living creatures promote both specific survival *and* genetic improvement. When a conventionally adaptive animal faces one of its periodic crises of insufficiency, it is the 'inferior' members of the species that normally disappear. An animal's social response to such a crisis may take the form of a mass migration, during which the weak fall by the wayside. Or it may follow the dramatic and more efficient pattern of lemming societies, in which the weaker members voluntarily disperse, leaving available food supplies for the stronger. In either case, the strong survive and the weak fall. In human societies, those who fight and die in wars for survival are in general its biologically stronger members. This is natural selection in reverse.

The regressive genetic effect of war has been often noted[13] and equally often deplored, even when it confuses biological and cultural factors.[14] The disproportionate loss of the *biologically* stronger remains inherent in traditional warfare. It serves to underscore the fact that survival of the species, rather than its improvement, is the fundamental purpose of natural selection, if it can be said to have purpose, just as it is the basic premise of this study.

But as the polemologist Gaston Bouthoul[15] has pointed out, other institutions that were developed to serve this ecological function have proved even less satisfactory. (They include such established forms as these: infanticide, practised chiefly in ancient and primitive societies; sexual mutilation; monasticism; forced emigration; extensive capital punishment, as in old China and eighteenth-century England; and other similar, usually localized, practices.)

Man's ability to increase his productivity of the essentials of physical life suggests that the need for protection against cyclical famine may be nearly obsolete.[16] It has thus tended to reduce the apparent importance of the basic ecological function of war, which is generally disregarded by peace-theorists. Two aspects of it remain especially relevant, however. The first is obvious: current rates of population growth, compounded by environmental threat of chemical and other contaminants, may well bring about a new crisis of insufficiency. If so, it is likely to be one of unprecedented global magnitude, not merely regional or temporary. Conventional methods of warfare would almost surely prove inadequate, in this event, to reduce the consuming population to a level consistent with survival of the species.

The second relevant factor is the efficiency of modern methods of mass destruction. Even if their use is not required to meet a world population crisis, they offer, perhaps paradoxically, the first opportunity in the history of man to halt the regressive genetic effects of natural selection by war. Nuclear weapons are indiscriminate. Their application would bring to an end the disproportionate destruction of the physically stronger members of the species (the 'warriors') in periods of war. Whether this prospect of genetic gain would offset the unfavourable mutations anticipated from post-nuclear radioactivity we have not yet determined. What gives the question a bearing on our study is the possibility that the determination may yet have to be made.

Another secondary ecological trend bearing on projected population growth is the regressive effect of certain medical advances. Pestilence, for example, is no longer an important factor in population control. The problem of increased life expectancy has been aggravated. These advances also pose a potentially more sinister problem, in that undesirable genetic traits that were formerly self-liquidating are now medically maintained. Many diseases that were once fatal at pre-procreational ages are now cured; the effect of this development is to perpetuate undesirable susceptibilities

and mutations. It seems clear that a new quasi-eugenic function of war is now in process of formation that will have to be taken into account in any transition plan. For the time being, the Department of Defense appears to have recognized such factors, as has been demonstrated by the planning under way by the Rand Corporation to cope with the breakdown in the ecological balance anticipated after a thermonuclear war. The Department has also begun to stockpile birds, for example, against the expected proliferation of radiation-resistant insects, etc.

Cultural and scientific
The declared order of values in modern societies gives a high place to the so-called 'creative' activities, and an even higher one to those associated with the advance of scientific knowledge. Widely held social values can be translated into political equivalents, which in turn may bear on the nature of a transition to peace. The attitudes of those who hold these values must be taken into account in the planning of the transition. The dependence, therefore, of cultural and scientific achievement on the war system would be an important consideration in a transition plan even if such achievement had no inherently necessary social function.

Of all the countless dichotomies invented by scholars to account for the major differences in art styles and cycles, only one has been consistently unambiguous in its application to a variety of forms and cultures. However it may be verbalized, the basic distinction is this: Is the work war-oriented or is it not? Among primitive peoples, the war dance is the most important art form. Elsewhere, literature, music, painting, sculpture, and architecture that has won lasting acceptance has invariably dealt with a theme of war, expressly or implicitly, and has expressed the centricity of war to society. The war in question may be national conflict, as in Shakespeare's plays, Beethoven's music, or Goya's paintings, or it may be reflected in the form of religious, social, or moral struggle, as in the work of Dante, Rembrandt, and Bach. Art that cannot be classified as war-oriented is usually described as 'sterile', 'decadent', and so on. Application of the 'war standard' to works of art may often leave room for debate in individual cases, but there is no question of its role as the fundamental determinant of cultural values. Aesthetic and moral standards have common anthropological origin, in the exaltation of bravery, the willingness to kill and risk death in tribal warfare.

It is also instructive to note that the character of a society's culture has borne a close relationship to its war-making potential, in the context of its times. It is no accident that the current 'cultural explosion' in the United States is taking place during an era marked by an unusually rapid advance in weaponry. This relationship is more generally recognized than the literature on the subject would suggest. For example, many artists and writers are now beginning to express concern over the limited creative options they envisage in the warless world they think, or hope, may be soon upon us. They are currently preparing for this possibility by unprecendented experimentation with meaningless forms; their interest in recent years has been increasingly engaged by the abstract pattern, the gratuitous emotion, the random happening, and the unrelated sequence.

The relationship of war to scientific research and discovery is more explicit. War is the principal motivational force for the development of science at every level, from the abstractly conceptual to the narrowly technological. Modern society places a high value on 'pure' science, but it is historically inescapable that all the significant discoveries that have been made about the natural world have been inspired by the real or imaginary military necessities of their epochs. The consequences of the discoveries have indeed gone far afield, but war has always provided the basic incentive.

Beginning with the development of iron and steel, and proceeding through the discoveries of the laws of motion and thermodynamics to the age of the atomic particle, the synthetic polymer, and the space capsule, no important scientific advance has not been at least indirectly initiated by an implicit requirement of weaponry. More prosaic examples include the transistor radio (an outgrowth of military communications requirements), the assembly line (from Civil War firearms needs), the steel-frame building (from the steel battleship), the canal lock, and so on. A typical adaptation can be seen in a device as modest as the common lawn-mower; it developed from the revolving scythe devised by Leonardo da Vinci to precede a horse-powered vehicle into enemy ranks.

The most direct relationship can be found in medical technology. For example, a giant 'walking machine', an amplifier of body motions invented for military use in difficult terrain, is now making it possible for many previously confined to wheelchairs to walk. The Vietnam War alone has led to spectacular improvements in amputation procedures, blood-handling techniques, and surgical logistics. It has stimulated new large-scale research on malaria and other tropical parasite diseases; it is hard to estimate how long this work would otherwise have been delayed, despite its enormous non-military importance to nearly half the world's population.

Other

We have elected to omit from our discussion of the non-military functions of war those we do not consider critical to a transition programme. This is not to say they are unimportant, however, but only that they appear to present no special problems for the organization of a peace-oriented social system. They include the following:

War as a general social release. This is a psychosocial function, serving the same purpose for a society as do the holiday, the celebration, and the orgy for the individual – the release and redistribution of undifferentiated tensions. War provides for the periodic necessary readjustment of standards of social behaviour (the 'moral climate') and for the dissipation of general boredom, one of the most consistently undervalued and unrecognized of social phenomena.

War as a generational stabilizer. This psychological function, served by other behaviour patterns in other animals, enables the physically deteriorating older generation to maintain its control of the younger, destroying it if necessary.

War as an ideological clarifier. The dualism that characterizes the traditional dialectic of all branches of philosophy and of stable political relationships stems from war as the prototype of conflict. Except for secondary considerations, there cannot be, to put it as simply as possible, more than two sides to a question because there cannot be more than two sides to a war.

War as the basis for international understanding. Before the development of modern communications, the strategic requirements of war provided the only substantial incentive for the enrichment of one national culture with the achievements of another. Although this is still the case in many international relationships, the function is obsolescent.

We have also forgone extended characterization of those functions we assume to be widely and explicitly recognized. An obvious example is the role of war as controller of the quality and degree of unemployment. This is more than an economic and political sub-function; its sociological, cultural, and ecological aspects are also important, although often teleconomic. But none affect the general problem of substitution. The same is true of certain other functions; those we have included are sufficient to define the scope of the problem.

6   Substitutes for the functions of war

By now it should be clear that the most detailed and comprehensive master plan for a transition to world peace will remain academic if it fails to deal forthrightly with the problem of the critical non-military functions of war. The social needs they serve are essential; if the war system no longer exists to meet them, substitute institutions will have to be established for the purpose. These surrogates must be 'realistic', which is to say of a scope and nature that can be conceived and implemented in the context of present-day social capabilities. This is not the truism it may appear to be; the requirements of radical social change often reveal the distinction between a most conservative projection and a wildly utopian scheme to be fine indeed.

In this section we will consider some possible substitutes for these functions. Only in rare instances have they been put forth for the purposes which concern us here, but we see no reason to limit ourselves to proposals that address themselves explicitly to the problem as we have outlined it. We will disregard the ostensible, or military, functions of war; it is a premiss of this study that the transition to peace implies absolutely that they will no longer exist in any relevant sense. We will also disregard the non-critical functions exemplified at the end of the preceding section.

Economic
Economic surrogates for war must meet two principal criteria. They must be 'wasteful', in the common sense of the word, and

they must operate outside the normal supply–demand system. A corollary that should be obvious is that the magnitude of the waste must be sufficient to meet the needs of a particular society. An economy as advanced and complex as our own requires the planned average annual destruction of not less than 10 per cent of gross national product[17] if it is effectively to fulfil its stabilizing-function. When the mass of a balance wheel is inadequate to the power it is intended to control, its effect can be self-defeating, as with a runaway locomotive. The analogy, though crude,[18] is especially apt for the American economy, as our record of cyclical depressions shows. All have taken place during periods of grossly inadequate military spending.

Those few economic conversion programmes which by implication acknowledge the non-military economic function of war (at least to some extent) tend to assume that so-called social-welfare expenditures will fill the vacuum created by the disappearance of military spending. When one considers the backlog of unfinished business – proposed but still unexecuted – in this field, the assumption seems plausible. Let us examine briefly the following list, which is more or less typical of general social-welfare programmes.[19]

Health. Drastic expansion of medical research, education, and training-facilities; hospital and clinic construction; the general objective of *complete* government-guaranteed health care for all, at a level consistent with current developments in medical technology.

Education. The equivalent of the foregoing in teacher-training; schools and libraries; the drastic upgrading of standards, with the general objective of making available for all an attainable educational goal equivalent to what is now considered a professional degree.

Housing. Clean, comfortable, safe, and spacious living space for all, at the level now enjoyed by about 15 per cent of the population in this country (less in most others).

Transportation. The establishment of a system of mass public transportation making it possible for all to travel to and from areas of work and recreation quickly, comfortably, and conveniently, and to travel privately for pleasure rather than necessity.

Physical environment. The development and protection of water supplies, forests, parks, and other natural resources; the elimination of chemical and bacterial contaminants from air, water, and soil.

Poverty. The genuine elimination of poverty, defined by a standard consistent with current economic productivity, by means of a guaranteed annual income or whatever system of distribution will best assure its achievement.

This is only a sampler of the more obvious domestic social-welfare items, and we have listed it in a deliberately broad, perhaps extravagant, manner. In the past, such a vague and ambitious-sounding 'programme' would have been dismissed out of hand, without serious consideration; it would clearly have been, *prima facie*, far too costly, quite apart from its political implications.[20] Our objection to it, on the other hand, could hardly be more contradictory. As an economic substitute for war, it is inadequate because it would be far too cheap.

If this seems paradoxical, it must be remembered that up to now all proposed social-welfare expenditures have had to be measured *within* the war economy, not as a replacement for it. The old slogan about a battleship or an ICBM [intercontinental ballistic missile] costing as much as x hospitals or y schools or z homes takes on a very different meaning if there are to be no more battleships or ICBMs.

Since the list is general, we have elected to forestall the tangential controversy that surrounds arbitrary cost projections by offering no individual cost estimates. But the maximum programme that could be physically effected along the lines indicated could approach the established level of military spending only for a limited time – in our opinion, subject to a detailed cost-and-feasibility analysis, less than ten years. In this short period, at this rate, the major goals of the programme would have been achieved. Its capital-investment phase would have been completed, and it would have established a permanent comparatively modest level of annual operating cost – *within the framework of the general economy.*

Here is the basic weakness of the social-welfare surrogate. On the short-term basis, a maximum programme of this sort could replace a normal military-spending programme, provided it was designed, like the military model, to be subject to arbitrary control. Public housing starts, for example, or the development of modern medical centres might be accelerated or halted from time to time, as the requirements of a stable economy might dictate. But on the long-term basis, social-welfare spending, no matter how often redefined, would necessarily become an integral, accepted part of the economy, of no more value as a stabilizer than the automobile industry or old age and survivors' insurance. Apart from whatever merit social-welfare programmes are deemed to have for their own sake, their function as a substitute for war in the economy would thus be self-liquidating. They might serve, however, as expedients pending the development of more durable substitute measures.

Another economic surrogate that has been proposed is a series of giant 'space-research' programmes. These have already demonstrated their utility in more modest scale within the military economy. What has been implied, although not yet expressly put forth, is the development of a long-range sequence of space-research projects with largely unattainable goals. This kind of programme offers several advantages lacking in the social-welfare model. First, it is unlikely to phase itself out, regardless of the predictable 'surprises' science has in store for us: the universe is too big. In the event some individual project unexpectedly succeeds there would be no dearth of substitute problems. For example, if colonization of the moon proceeds on schedule, it could then become 'necessary' to establish a beachhead on Mars or Jupiter, and so on. Second, it need be no more dependent on the general supply-demand economy than its military prototype. Third, it lends itself extraordinarily well to arbitrary control.

Space research can be viewed as the nearest modern equivalent yet devised to the pyramid-building, and similar ritualistic enterprises, of ancient societies. It is true that the scientific value of the space programme, even of what has already been accomplished, is substantial on its own terms. But current programmes are absurdly and obviously disproportionate, in the relationship of the knowledge sought to the expenditures committed. All but a small fraction of the space budget, measured by the standards of comparable scientific objectives, must be charged *de facto* to the military economy. Future space research, projected as a war surrogate, would further reduce the 'scientific' rationale of its budget to a minuscule percentage indeed. As a purely economic substitute for war, therefore, extension of the space programme warrants serious consideration.

In Section 3 [not reprinted here] we pointed out that certain disarmament models, which we called conservative, postulated extremely expensive and elaborate inspection systems. Would it be possible to extend and institutionalize such systems to the point where they might serve as economic surrogates for war spending? The organization of fail-safe inspection machinery could well be ritualized in a manner similar to that of established military processes. 'Inspection teams' might be very like armies, and their technical equipment might be very like weapons. Inflating the inspection budget to military scale presents no difficulty. The appeal of this kind of scheme lies in the comparative ease of transition between two parallel systems.

The 'elaborate inspection' surrogate is fundamentally fallacious, however. Although it might be economically useful, as well as politically necessary, during the disarmament transition, it would fail as a substitute for the economic function of war for one simple reason. Peace-keeping inspection is part of a war system, not of a peace system. It implies the possibility of weapons maintenance or manufacture, which could not exist in a world at peace as here defined. Massive inspection also implies sanctions, and thus war-readiness.

The same fallacy is more obvious in plans to create a patently useless 'defence conversion' apparatus. The long-discredited proposal to build 'total' civil-defence facilities is one example; another is the plan to establish a giant anti-missile complex (Nike-X, and other defensive guided missiles). These programmes, of course, are economic rather than strategic. Nevertheless, they are not substitutes for military spending but merely different forms of it.

A more sophisticated variant is the proposal to establish the 'Unarmed Forces' of the United States.[21] This would conveniently maintain the entire institutional military structure, redirecting it essentially toward social-welfare activities on a global scale. It would be, in effect, a giant military Peace Corps. There is nothing inherently unworkable about this plan, and using the existing military system to effectuate its own demise is both ingenious and convenient. But even on a greatly magnified world basis, social-welfare expenditures must sooner or later re-enter the atmosphere of the normal economy. The practical transitional virtues of such a scheme would thus be eventually negated by its inadequacy as a permanent economic stabilizer.

Political

The war system makes the stable government of societies possible. It does this essentially by providing an external necessity for a society to accept political rule. In so doing, it establishes the basis for nationhood and the authority of government to control its constituents. What other institution or combination of programmes might serve these functions in its place?

. . . The end of war means the end of national sovereignty, and thus the end of nationhood as we know it today. But this does not necessarily mean the end of nations in the administrative sense, and internal political power will remain essential to a stable society. The emerging 'nations' of the peace epoch must continue to draw political authority from some source.

A number of proposals have been made governing the relations between nations after total disarmament; all are basically juridical in nature. They contemplate institutions more or less like a World Court, or a United Nations, but vested with real authority. They may or may not serve their ostensible post-military purpose of settling international disputes, but we need not discuss that here. None would offer effective external pressure on a peace-world nation to organize itself politically.

It might be argued that a well-armed international police force, operating under the authority of such a supranational 'court', could well serve the function of external enemy. This, however, would constitute a military operation, like the inspection schemes mentioned, and, like them, would be inconsistent with the premiss of an end to the war system. It is possible that a variant of the 'Unarmed Forces' idea might be developed in such a way that its 'constructive' (i.e. social-welfare) activities could be combined with an economic 'threat' of sufficient size and credibility to warrant political organization. Would this kind of threat also be contradictory to our basic premiss? – that is, would it be inevitably military? Not necessarily, in our view, but we are sceptical of its capacity to evoke credibility. Also, the obvious destabilizing effect of any global social-welfare surrogate on politically necessary class relationships would create an entirely new set of transition problems at least equal in magnitude.

Credibility, in fact, lies at the heart of the problem of developing a political substitute for war. This is where the space-race proposals, in many ways so well suited as economic substitutes for war, fall short. The most ambitious and unrealistic space project cannot of itself generate a believable external menace. It has been hotly argued[22] that such a menace would offer the 'last, best hope of peace', etc., by uniting mankind against the danger of destruction by 'creatures' from other planets or from outer space. Experiments have been proposed to test the credibility of an out-of-our-world invasion threat; it is possible that a few of the more difficult-to-explain 'flying-saucer' incidents of recent years were in fact early experiments of this kind. If so, they could hardly have been judged encouraging. We anticipate no difficulties in making a 'need' for a giant super space programme credible for economic purposes, even were there not ample precedent; extending it, for political purposes, to include features unfortunately associated with science fiction would obviously be a more dubious undertaking.

Nevertheless, an effective political substitute for war would require 'alternate enemies', some of which might seem equally far-fetched in the context of the current war system. It may be, for instance, that gross pollution of the environment can eventually replace the possibility of mass destruction by nuclear weapons as the principal apparent threat to the survival of the species. Poisoning of the air, and of the principal sources of food and water supply, is already well advanced, and at first glance would seem promising in this respect; it constitutes a threat that can be dealt with only through social organization and political power. But from present indications it will be a generation to a generation and a half before environmental pollution, however severe, will be sufficiently menacing, on a global scale, to offer a possible basis for a solution.

It is true that the rate of pollution could be increased selectively for this purpose; in fact, the mere modifying of existing programmes for the deterrence of pollution could speed up the process enough to make the threat credible much sooner. But the pollution problem has been so widely publicized in recent years that it seems highly improbable that a programme of deliberate environmental poisoning could be implemented in a politically acceptable manner.

However unlikely some of the possible alternate enemies we have mentioned may seem, we must emphasize that one *must* be found, of credible quality and magnitude, if a transition to peace is ever to come about without social disintegration. It is more probable, in our judgement, that such a threat will have to be invented, rather than developed from unknown conditions. For this reason, we believe further speculation about its putative nature ill-advised in this context. Since there is considerable doubt, in our minds, that *any* viable political surrogate can be devised, we are reluctant to compromise, by premature discussion, any possible option that may eventually lie open to our government.

Sociological

Of the many functions of war we have found convenient to group together in this classification, two are critical. In a world of peace, the continuing stability of society will require: (1) an effective substitute for military institutions that can neutralize destabilizing social elements and (2) a credible motivational surrogate for war that can ensure social cohesiveness. The first is an essential element of social control; the second is the basic mechanism for adapting individual human drives to the needs of society.

Most proposals that address themselves, explicitly or otherwise, to the post-war problem of controlling the socially alienated turn to some variant of the Peace Corps or the so-called Job Corps for a solution. The socially disaffected, the economically unprepared, the psychologically unconformable, the hard-core 'delinquents', the incorrigible 'subversives', and the rest of the unemployable are seen as somehow transformed by the disciplines of a service modelled on military precedent into more or less dedicated social-service workers. This presumption also informs the otherwise hard-headed ratiocination of the 'Unarmed Forces' plan.

The problem has been addressed, in the language of popular sociology, by Secretary McNamara. 'Even in our abundant societies, we have reason enough to worry over the tensions that coil and tighten among underprivileged young people, and finally flail out in delinquency and crime. What are we to expect . . . where mounting frustrations are likely to fester into eruptions of violence and extremism?' In a seemingly unrelated passage, he continues:

It seems to me that we could move toward remedying that inequity [of the Selective Service System] by asking every young person in the United States to give two years of service to his country – whether in one of the military services, in the Peace Corps, or in some other volunteer developmental work at home or abroad. We could encourage other countries to do the same.[23]

Here, as elsewhere throughout this significant speech, Mr McNamara has focused, indirectly but unmistakably, on one of the key issues bearing on a possible transition to peace, and has later indicated, also indirectly, a rough approach to its resolution, again phrased in the language of the current war system.

It seems clear that Mr McNamara and other proponents of the Peace Corps surrogate for this war function lean heavily on the success of the paramilitary Depression programmes mentioned in the last section. We find the precedent wholly inadequate in degree. Neither the lack of relevant precedent, however, nor the dubious social-welfare sentimentality characterizing this approach warrant its rejection without careful study. It may be viable – provided, first, that the military origin of the Corps format be effectively rendered out of its operational activity, and second, that the transition from paramilitary activities to 'developmental work' can be effected without regard to the attitudes of the Corps personnel or to the 'value of the work it is expected to perform.

Another possible surrogate for the control of potential enemies of society is the reintroduction, in some form consistent with modern technology and political processes, of slavery. Up to now, this has been suggested only in fiction, notably in the works of Wells, Huxley, Orwell, and others engaged in the imaginative anticipation of the sociology of the future. But the fantasies projected in *Brave New World* and *1984* have seemed less and less implausible over the years since their publication. The traditional association of slavery with ancient pre-industrial cultures should not blind us to its adaptability to advanced forms of social organization, nor should its equally traditional incompatibility with Western moral and economic values. It is entirely possible that the development of a sophisticated form of slavery may be an absolute prerequisite for social control in a world at peace. As a practical matter, conversion of the code of military discipline to a euphemized form of enslavement would entail surprisingly little revision; the logical first step would be the adoption of some form of 'universal' military service.

When it comes to postulating a credible substitute for war capable of directing human behaviour patterns in behalf of social organization, few options suggest themselves. Like its political function, the motivational function of war requires the existence of a genuinely menacing social enemy. The principal difference is that for purposes of motivating basic allegiance, as distinct from accepting political authority, the 'alternate enemy' must imply a more immediate, tangible, and directly felt threat of destruction. It must justify the need for taking and paying a 'blood price' in wide areas of human concern.

In this respect, the possible substitute enemies noted earlier would be insufficient. One exception might be the environmental-pollution model, if the danger to society it posed was genuinely imminent. The fictive models would have to carry the weight of extraordinary conviction, underscored with a not-inconsiderable actual sacrifice of life; the construction of an up-to-date mythological or religious structure for this purpose would present difficulties in our era, but must certainly be considered.

Games theorists have suggested, in other contexts, the development of 'blood games' for the effective control of individual aggressive impulses. It is an ironic commentary on the current state of war and peace studies that it was left not to scientists but to the makers of a commercial film[24] to develop a model for this notion, on the implausible level of popular melodrama, as a ritualized man-hunt. More realistically, such a ritual might be socialized, in the manner of the Spanish Inquisition and the less formal witch trials of other periods, for purposes of 'social purification', 'state security', or other rationale both acceptable and credible to post-war societies. The feasibility of such an updated version of still another ancient institution, though doubtful, is considerably less fanciful than the wishful notion of many peace-planners that a lasting condition of peace can be brought about without the most painstaking examination of every possible surrogate for the essential functions of war. What is involved here, in a sense, is the quest for William James's 'moral equivalent of war'.

It is also possible that the two functions considered under this heading may be jointly served, in the sense of establishing the anti-social, for whom a control institution is needed, as the 'alternate enemy' needed to hold society together. The relentless and irreversible advance of unemployability at all levels of society, and the similar extension of generalized alienation from accepted values[25] may make some such programme necessary even as an adjunct to the war system. As before, we will not speculate on the specific forms this kind of programme might take, except to note that there is again ample precedent, in the treament meted out to disfavoured, allegedly menacing, ethnic groups in certain societies during certain historical periods.[26]

Ecological

Considering the shortcomings of war as a mechanism of selective population control, it might appear that devising substitutes for this function should be comparatively simple. Schematically this is so, but the problem of timing the transition to a new ecological balancing device makes the feasibility of substitution less certain.

It must be remembered that the limitation of war in this function is entirely eugenic. War has not been genetically progressive. But as a system of gross population control to preserve the species it cannot fairly be faulted. And, as has been pointed out, the nature of war is itself in transition. Current trends in warfare – the increased strategic bombing of civilians and the greater military importance now attached to the destruction of sources of supply (as opposed to purely 'military' bases and personnel) – strongly suggest that a truly qualitative improvement is in the making. Assuming the war system is to continue, it is more than probable that the regressively selective quality of war will have been reversed, as its victims become more genetically representative of their societies.

There is no question but that a universal requirement that procreation be limited to the products of artificial insemination would provide a fully adequate substitute control for population levels. Such a reproductive system would, of course, have the added advantage of being susceptible of direct eugenic management. Its predictable further development – conception and embryonic growth taking place wholly under laboratory conditions – would extend these controls to their logical conclusion. The ecological function of war under these circumstances would not only be superseded but surpassed in effectiveness.

The indicated intermediate step – total control of conception with a variant of the ubiquitous 'pill', via water supplies or certain essential foodstuffs, offset by a controlled 'antidote' – is already under development.[27] There would appear to be no foreseeable need to revert to any of the outmoded practices referred to in the previous section (infanticide, etc.) as there might have been if the possibility of transition to peace had arisen two generations ago.

The real question here, therefore, does not concern the viability of this war substitute, but the political problems involved in bringing it about. It cannot be established while the war system is still in effect. The reason for this is simple: excess population is war material. As long as any society must contemplate even a remote possibility of war, it must maintain a maximum supportable population, even when so doing critically aggravates an economic liability. This is paradoxical, in view of war's role in reducing excess population, but it is readily understood. War controls the *general* population level, but the ecological interest of any single society lies in maintaining its hegemony *vis-à-vis* other societies. The obvious analogy can be seen in any free-enterprise economy. Practices damaging to the society as a whole – both competitive and monopolistic – are abetted by the conflicting economic motives of individual capital interests. The obvious precedent can be found in the seemingly irrational political difficulties which have blocked universal adoption of simple birth-control methods. Nations desperately in need of increasing unfavourable production–consumption ratios are nevertheless unwilling to gamble their possible military requirements of twenty years hence for this purpose. Unilateral population control, as practised in ancient Japan and in other isolated societies, is out of the question in today's world.

Since the eugenic solution cannot be achieved until the transition to the peace system takes place, why not wait? One must qualify the inclination to agree. As we noted earlier, a real possibility of an unprecedented global crisis of insufficiency exists today, which the war system may not be able to forestall. If this should come to pass before an agreed-upon transition to peace were completed, the result might be irrevocably disastrous. There is clearly no solution to this dilemma; it is a risk which must be taken. But it tends to support the view that if a decision is made to eliminate the war system, it were better done sooner than later.

Cultural and scientific

Strictly speaking, the function of war as the determinant of cultural values and as the prime mover of scientific progress may not be critical in a world without war. Our criterion for the basic non-military functions of war has been: are they necessary to the survival and stability of society? The absolute need for substitute cultural value determinants and for the continued advance of scientific knowledge is not established. We believe it important, however, in behalf of those for whom these functions hold subjective significance, that it be known what they can reasonably expect in culture and science after a transition to peace.

So far as the creative arts are concerned, there is no reason to believe they would disappear, but only that they would change in character and relative social importance. The elimination of war would in due course deprive them of their principal conative force, but it would necessarily take some time for the effect of this withdrawal to be felt. During the transition, and perhaps for a generation thereafter, themes of socio-moral conflict inspired by the war system would be increasingly transferred to the idiom of purely personal sensibility. At the same time, a new aesthetic would have to develop. Whatever its name, form, or rationale, its function would be to express, in language appropriate to the new period, the once-discredited philosophy that art exists for its own sake. This aesthetic would reject unequivocally the classic requirement of paramilitary conflict as the substantive content of great art. The eventual effect of the peace-world philosophy of art would be democratizing in the extreme, in the sense that a generally acknowledged subjectivity of artistic standards would equalize their new, content-free 'values'.

What may be expected to happen is that art would be reassigned the role it once played in a few primitive peace-oriented social systems. This was the function of pure decoration, entertainment, or play, entirely free of the burden of expressing the socio-moral values and conflicts of a war-oriented society. It is interesting that the groundwork for such value-free aesthetic is already being laid today, in growing experimentation in art without content, perhaps in anticipation of a world without conflict. A cult has developed around a new kind of cultural determinism,[28] which proposes that the technological form of a cultural expression determines its values rather than does its ostensibly meaningful content. Its clear implication is that there is no 'good' or 'bad' art, only that which is appropriate to its (technological) times and that which is not. Its cultural effect has been to promote circumstantial constructions and unplanned expressions; it denies to art the relevance of sequential logic. Its significance in this context is that it provides a working model of one kind of value-free culture we might reasonably anticipate in a world at peace.

So far as science is concerned, it might appear at first glance that a giant space-research programme, the most promising among the proposed economic surrogates for war, might also serve as the basic stimulator of scientific research. The lack of fundamental organized social conflict inherent in space work, however, would rule it out as an adequate motivational substitute for war when applied to 'pure' science. But it could no doubt sustain the broad range of *technological* activity that a space budget of military dimensions would require. A similarly scaled social-welfare programme could provide a comparable impetus to low-keyed technological advances, especially in medicine, rationalized construction methods, educational psychology, etc. The eugenic substitute for the ecological function of war would also require continuing research in certain areas of the life sciences.

Apart from these partial substitutes for war, it must be kept in mind that the momentum given to scientific progress by the great wars of the past century, and even more by the anticipation of World War III, is intellectually and materially enormous. It is our finding that if the war system were to end tomorrow this momentum is so great that the pursuit of scientific knowledge could reasonably be expected to go forward without noticeable diminution for perhaps two decades.[29] It would then continue, at a progressively decreasing tempo, for at least another two decades before the 'bank account' of today's unresolved problems would become exhausted. By the standards of the questions we have learned to ask today, there would no longer be anything worth knowing still unknown; we cannot conceive, by definition, of the scientific questions to ask once those we can now comprehend are answered.

This leads unavoidably to another matter: the intrinsic value of the unlimited search for knowledge. We of course offer no independent value judgements here, but it is germane to point out that a substantial minority of scientific opinion feels that search to be circumscribed in any case. This opinion is itself a factor in considering the need for a substitute for the scientific function of war. For the record, we must also take note of the precedent that during long periods of human history, often covering thousands of years, in which no intrinsic social value was assigned to scientific progress, stable societies did survive and flourish. Although this could not have been possible in the modern industrial world, we cannot be certain it may not again be true in a future world at peace.

7   Summary and conclusions

The nature of war

War is not, as is widely assumed, primarily an instrument of policy utilized by nations to extend or defend their expressed political values or their economic interests. On the contrary, it is itself the principal basis of organization on which all modern societies are constructed. The common proximate cause of war is the apparent interference of one nation with the aspirations of another. But at the root of all ostensible differences of national interest lie the dynamic requirements of the war system itself for periodic armed conflict. Readiness for war characterizes contemporary social systems more broadly than their economic and political structures, which it subsumes.

Economic analyses of the anticipated problems of transition to peace have not recognized the broad pre-eminence of war in the definition of social systems. The same is true, with rare and only partial exceptions, of model disarmament 'scenarios'. For this reason, the value of this previous work is limited to the mechanical aspects of transition. Certain features of these models may perhaps be applicable to a real situation of conversion to peace; this will depend on their compatibility with a substantive, rather than a procedural, peace plan. Such a plan can be developed only from the premiss of full understanding of the nature of the war system it proposes to abolish, which in turn presupposes detailed comprehension of the functions the war system performs for society. It will require the construction of a detailed and feasible system of substitutes for those functions that are necessary to the stability and survival of human societies.

The functions of war

The visible, military function of war requires no elucidation; it is not only obvious but also irrelevant to a transition to the condition of peace, in which it will by definition be superfluous. It is also subsidiary in social significance to the implied, non-military functions of war; those critical to transition can be summarized in five principal groupings.

(1)   *Economic.* War has provided both ancient and modern societies with a dependable system for stabilizing and controlling na-

tional economies. No alternate method of control has yet been tested in a complex modern economy that has shown itself remotely comparable in scope or effectiveness.

(2) *Political.* The permanent possibility of war is the foundation for stable government; it supplies the basis for general acceptance of political authority. It has enabled societies to maintain necessary class distinctions, and it has ensured the subordination of the citizen to the state, by virtue of the residual war powers inherent in the concept of nationhood. No modern political ruling group has successfully controlled its constituency after failing to sustain the continuing credibility of an external threat of war.

(3) *Sociological.* War, through the medium of military institutions, has uniquely served societies, throughout the course of known history, as an indispensable controller of dangerous social dissidence and destructive anti-social tendencies. As the most formidable of threats to life itself, and as the only one susceptible to mitigation by social organization alone, it has played another equally fundamental role: the war system has provided the machinery through which the motivational forces governing human behaviour have been translated into binding social allegiance. It has thus ensured the degree of social cohesion necessary to the viability of nations. No other institution, or groups of institutions, in modern societies, has successfully served these functions.

(4) *Ecological.* War has been the principal evolutionary device for maintaining a satisfactory ecological balance between gross human population and supplies available for its survival. It is unique to the human species.

(5) *Cultural and scientific.* War-orientation has determined the basic standards of value in the creative arts, and has provided the fundamental motivational source of scientific and technological progress. The concepts that the arts express values independent of their own forms and that the successful pursuit of knowledge has intrinsic social value have long been accepted in modern societies; the development of the arts and sciences during this period has been corollary to the parallel development of weaponry.

Substitutes for the functions of war: criteria

The foregoing functions of war are essential to the survival of the social systems we know today. With two possible exceptions they are also essential to any kind of stable social organization that might survive in a warless world. Discussion of the ways and means of transition to such a world are meaningless unless (a) substitute institutions can be devised to fill these functions, or (b) it can reasonably be hypothecated that the loss or partial loss of any one function need not destroy the viability of future societies.

Such substitute institutions and hypotheses must meet varying criteria. In general, they must be technically feasible, politically acceptable, and potentially credible to the members of the societies that adopt them. Specifically, they must be characterized as follows:

(1) *Economic.* An acceptable economic surrogate for the war system will require the expenditure of resources for completely non-productive purposes at a level comparable to that of the military expenditures otherwise demanded by the size and complexity of each society. Such a substitute system of apparent 'waste' must be of a nature that will permit it to remain independent of the normal supply–demand economy; it must be subject to arbitrary political control.

(2) *Political.* A viable political substitute for war must posit a generalized external menace to each society of a nature and degree sufficient to require the organization and acceptance of political authority.

(3) *Sociological.* First, in the permanent absence of war, new institutions must be developed that will effectively control the socially destructive segments of societies. Second, for purposes of adapting the physical and psychological dynamics of human behaviour to the needs of social organization, a credible substitute for war must generate an omnipresent and readily understood fear of personal destruction. This fear must be of a nature and degree sufficient to ensure adherence to societal values to the full extent that they are acknowledged to transcend the value of individual human life.

(4) *Ecological.* A substitute for war in its function as the uniquely human system of population control must ensure the survival, if

not necessarily the improvement, of the species, in terms of its relation to environmental supply.

(5) *Cultural and scientific.* A surrogate for the function of war as the determinant of cultural values must establish a basis of socio-moral conflict of equally compelling force and scope. A substitute motivational basis for the quest for scientific knowledge must be similarly informed by a comparable sense of internal necessity.

Substitutes for the functions of war: models
    The following substitute institutions, among others, have been proposed for consideration as replacements for the non-military functions of war. That they may not have been originally set forth for that purpose does not preclude or invalidate their possible application here.

(1) *Economic.* (a) A comprehensive social-welfare programme, directed toward maximum improvement of general conditions of human life. (b) A giant open-end space-research programme, aimed at unreachable targets. (c) A permanent, ritualized, ultra-elaborate disarmament inspection system, and variants of such a system.

(2) *Political.* (a) An omnipresent, virtually omnipotent international police force. (b) An established and recognized extraterrestrial menace. (c) Massive global environmental pollution. (d) Fictitious alternate enemies.

(3) *Sociological. Control function.* (a) Programmes generally de-rived from the Peace Corps model. (b) A modern, sophisticated form of slavery. *Motivational function.* (a) Intensified environmen-tal pollution. (b) New religions or other mythologies. (c) Socially oriented blood games. (d) Combination forms.

(4) *Ecological.* A comprehensive programme of applied eugenics.

(5) *Cultural.* No replacement institution offered. *Scientific.* The secondary requirements of the space-research, social-welfare, and/or eugenics programmes.

Substitutes for the functions of war: evaluation
    The models listed above reflect only the beginning of the quest

for substitute institutions for the functions of war, rather than a recapitulation of alternatives. It would be both premature and inapproapriate, therefore, to offer final judgements on their applicability to a transition to peace and after. Furthermore, since the necessary but complex project of correlating the compatibility of proposed surrogates for different functions could be treated only in exemplary fashion at this time, we have elected to withhold such hypothetical correlations as were tested as statistically inadequate.[30]

Nevertheless, some tentative and cursory comments on these proposed functional 'solutions' will indicate the scope of the difficulties involved in this area of peace planning.

Economic. The social-welfare model cannot be expected to remain outside the normal economy after the conclusion of its predominantly capital-investment phase; its value in this function can therefore be only temporary. The space-research substitute appears to meet both major criteria, and should be examined in greater detail, especially in respect to its probable effects on other war functions. 'Elaborate inspection' schemes, although superficially attractive, are inconsistent with the basic premiss of transition to peace. The 'Unarmed Forces' variant, logistically similar, is subject to the same functional criticism as the general social-welfare model.

Political. Like the inspection-scheme surrogates, proposals for plenipotentiary international police are inherently incompatible with the ending of the war system. The 'Unarmed Forces' variant, amended to include unlimited powers of economic sanction, might conceivably be expanded to constitute a credible external menace. Development of an acceptable threat from 'outer space', presumably in conjunction with a space-research surrogate for economic control, appears unpromising in terms of credibility. The environmental-pollution model does not seem sufficiently responsive to immediate social control, except through arbitrary acceleration of current pollution trends; this in turn raises questions of political acceptability. New, less regressive, approaches to the creation of fictitious global 'enemies' invite further investigation.

Sociological. Control function. Although the various substitutes proposed for this function that are modelled roughly on the Peace Corps appear grossly inadequate in potential scope, they should not be ruled out without further study. Slavery, in a technologically modern and conceptually euphemized form, may prove a more efficient and flexible institution in this area. *Motivational function.* Although none of the proposed substitutes for war as the guarantor of social allegiance can be dismissed out of hand, each presents serious and special difficulties. Intensified environmental threats may raise ecological dangers; myth-making dissociated from war may no longer be politically feasible; purposeful blood games and rituals can far more readily be devised than implemented. An institution combining this function with the preceding one, based on, but not necessarily imitative of, the precedent of organized ethnic repression, warrants careful consideration.

Ecological. The only apparent problem in the application of an adequate eugenic substitute for war is that of timing; it cannot be effectuated until the transition to peace has been completed, which involves a serious temporary risk of ecological failure.

Cultural. No plausible substitute for this function of war has yet been proposed. It may be, however, that a basic cultural value determinant is not necessary to the survival of a stable society. *Scientific.* The same might be said for the function of war as the prime mover of the search for knowledge. However, adoption of either a giant space-research programme, a comprehensive social-welfare programme, or a master programme of eugenic control would provide motivation for limited technologies.

General conclusions

It is apparent, from the foregoing, that no programme or combination of programmes yet proposed for a transition to peace has remotely approached meeting the comprehensive functional requirements of a world without war. Although one projected system for filling the economic function of war seems promising, similar optimism cannot be expressed in the equally essential political and sociological areas. The other major non-military functions of war – ecological, cultural, scientific – raise very different problems, but it is at least possible that detailed programming of substitutes in these areas is not prerequisite to transition. More important, it is not enough to develop adequate but separate surrogates for the major war functions; they must be fully compatible and in no degree self-cancelling.

Until such a unified programme is developed, at least hypothetically, it is impossible for this or any other group to furnish meaningful answers to the questions originally presented to us. When asked how best to prepare for the advent of peace, we must first reply, as strongly as we can, that the war system cannot responsibly be allowed to disappear until (1) we know exactly what it is we plan to put in its place, and (2) we are certain, beyond reasonable doubt, that these substitute institutions will serve their purposes in terms of the survival and stability of society. It will then be time enough to develop methods for effectuating the transition; procedural programming must follow, not precede, substantive solutions.

Such solutions, if indeed they exist, will not be arrived at without a revolutionary revision of the modes of thought heretofore considered appropriate to peace research. That we have examined the fundamental questions involved from a dispassionate, value-free point of view should not imply that we do not appreciate the intellectual and emotional difficulties that must be overcome on all decision-making levels before these questions are generally acknowledged by others for what they are. They reflect, on an intellectual level, traditional emotional resistance to new (more lethal and thus more 'shocking') forms of weaponry. The understated comment of then-Senator Hubert Humphrey on the publication of *On Thermonuclear War* is still very much to the point: 'New thoughts, particularly those which appear to contradict current assumptions, are always painful for the mind to contemplate.'

Nor, simply because we have not discussed them, do we minimize the massive reconciliation of conflicting interests which domestic as well as international agreement on proceeding toward genuine peace presupposes. This factor was excluded from the purview of our assignment, but we would be remiss if we failed to take it into account. Although no insuperable obstacle lies in the path of reaching such general agreements, formidable short-term private-group and general-class interest in maintaining the war system is well established and widely recognized. The resistance to peace stemming from such interest is only tangential, in the long run, to the basic functions of war, but it will not be easily overcome, in this country or elsewhere. Some observers, in fact, believe that it cannot be overcome at all in our time, that the price of peace is, simply, too high. This bears on our overall conclusions to the extent that timing in the transference to substitute institutions may often be the critical factor in their political feasibility.

It is uncertain, at this time, whether peace will ever be possible. It is far more questionable, by the objective standard of continued social survival rather than that of emotional pacifism, that it would be desirable even if it were demonstrably attainable. The war system, for all its subjective repugnance to important sections of 'public opinion', has demonstrated its effectiveness since the beginning of recorded history; it has provided the basis for the development of many impressively durable civilizations, including that which is dominant today. It has consistently provided unambiguous social priorities. It is, on the whole, a known quantity. A viable system of peace, assuming that the great and complex questions of substitute institutions raised in this Report are both soluble and solved, would still constitute a venture into the unknown, with the inevitable risks attendant on the unforeseen, however small and however well hedged.

Government decision-makers tend to choose peace over war whenever a real option exists, because it usually appears to be the 'safer' choice. Under most immediate circumstances they are likely to be right. But in terms of long-range social stability, the opposite is true. At our present state of knowledge and reasonable inference, it is the war system that must be identified with stability, the peace system with social speculation, however justifiable the speculation may appear, in terms of subjective moral or emotional values. A nuclear physicist once remarked, in respect to a possible disarmament agreement: 'If we could change the world into a world in which no weapons could be made, that would be stabilizing. But agreements we can expect with the Soviets would be destabilizing.'[31] The qualification and the bias are equally irrelevant; *any* condition of genuine total peace, however achieved, would be destabilizing until proved otherwise.

If it were necessary at this moment to opt irrevocably for the retention or for the dissolution of the war system, common prudence would dictate the former course. But it is not yet necessary, late as the hour appears. And more factors must eventually enter the war–peace equation than even the most determined search for alternative institutions for the functions of war can be expected to reveal. One group of such factors has been given only passing mention in this Report; it centres around the possible obsolescence of the war system itself. We have noted, for instance, the limitations of the war system in filling its ecological function and the declining importance of this aspect of war. It by no means stretches the imagination to visualize comparable developments which may compromise the efficacy of war as, for example, an economic controller or as an organizer of social allegiance. This kind of possibility, however remote, serves as a reminder that all calculations of contingency not only involve the weighing of one group of risks against another, but require a respectful allowance for error on both sides of the scale.

A more expedient reason for pursuing the investigation of alternate ways and means to serve the current functions of war is narrowly political. It is possible that one or more major sovereign nations may arrive, through ambiguous leadership, at a position in which a ruling administrative class may lose control of basic public opinion or of its ability to rationalize a desired war. It is not hard to imagine, in such a circumstance, a situation in which such governments may feel forced to initiate serious full-scale disarmament proceedings (perhaps provoked by 'accidental' nuclear explosions), and that such negotiations may lead to the actual disestablishment of military institutions. As our Report has made clear, this could be catastrophic. It seems evident that, in the event an important part of the world is suddenly plunged without sufficient warning into an inadvertent peace, even partial and inadequate preparation for the possibility may be better than none. The difference could even be critical. The models considered in the preceding chapter, both those that seem promising and those that do not, have one positive feature in common – an inherent flexibility of phasing. And despite our strictures against knowingly proceeding into peace-transition procedures without thorough substantive preparation, our government must nevertheless be ready to move in this direction with whatever limited resources of planning are on hand at the time – if circumstances so require. An arbitrary all-or-nothing approach is no more realistic in the development of contingency peace-programming than it is anywhere else.

But the principal cause for concern over the continuing effectiveness of the war system, and the more important reason for hedging with peace-planning, lies in the backwardness of current war-system programming. Its controls have not kept pace with the technological advances it has made possible. Despite its unarguable success to date, even in this era of unprecedented potential in mass destruction, it continues to operate largely on a *laissez-faire* basis. To the best of our knowledge, no serious quantified studies have ever been conducted to determine, for example:

- optimum levels of armament production, for purposes of economic control, at any given series of chronological points and under any given relationship between civilian production and consumption patterns;
- correlation factors between draft-recruitment policies and mensurable social dissidence;
- minimum levels of population destruction necessary to maintain war-threat credibility under varying political conditions;
- optimum cyclical frequency of 'shooting' wars under varying circumstances of historical relationship.

These and other war-function factors are fully susceptible to analysis by today's computer-based systems,[32] but they have not been so treated; modern analytical techniques have up to now been relegated to such aspects of the ostensible functions of war as procurement, personnel deployment, weapons analysis, and the like. We do not disparage these types of application, but only deplore their lack of utilization to greater capacity in attacking problems of broader scope. Our concern for efficiency in this context is not aesthetic, economic, or humanistic. It stems from the axiom that no system can long survive at either input or output levels that consistently or substantially deviate from an optimum range. As their data grow increasingly sophisticated, the war system and its functions are increasingly endangered by such deviations.

Our final conclusion, therefore, is that it will be necessary for our government to plan in depth for two general contingencies. The first, and lesser, is the possibility of a viable general peace; the second is the successful continuation of the war system. In our view, careful preparation for the possibility of peace should be extended, not because we take the position that the end of war would necessarily be desirable, if it is in fact possible, but because it may be thrust upon us in some form whether we are ready for it or not. Planning for rationalizing and quantifying the war system, on the other hand, to ensure the effectiveness of its major stabilizing-functions, is not only more promising in respect to anticipated results, but is essential; we can no longer take for granted that it will continue to serve our purposes well merely because it always has. The objective of government policy in regard to war and peace, in this period of uncertainty, must be to preserve maximum options. The recommendations which follow are directed to this end.

8 Recommendations

(1) We propose the establishment, under executive order of the President, of a permanent War/Peace Research Agency, empowered and mandated to execute the programmes described in (2) and (3) below. This agency (a) will be provided with non-accountable funds sufficient to implement its responsibilities and decisions at its own discretion, and (b) will have authority to preempt and utilize, without restriction, any and all facilities of the executive branch of the government in pursuit of its objectives. It will be organized along the lines of the National Security Council, except that none of its governing, executive, or operating personnel will hold other public office or governmental responsibility. Its directorate will be drawn from the broadest practicable spectrum of scientific disciplines, humanistic studies, applied creative arts, operating-technologies, and otherwise unclassified professional occupations. It will be responsible solely to the President, or to other officers of government temporarily deputized by him. Its operations will be governed entirely by its own rules of procedure. Its authority will expressly include the unlimited right to withhold information on its activities and its decisions, from anyone except the President, whenever it deems such secrecy to be in the public interest.

(2) The first of the War/Peace Research Agency's two principal responsibilities will be to determine all that can be known, including what can reasonably be inferred in terms of relevant statistical probabilities, that may bear on an eventual transition to a general condition of peace. The findings in this Report may be considered to constitute the beginning of this study and to indicate its orientation; detailed records of the investigations and findings of the Special Study Group on which this Report is based, will be furnished the Agency, along with whatever clarifying-data the Agency deems necessary. This aspect of the Agency's work will hereinafter be referred to as 'Peace Research'.

The Agency's Peace Research activities will necessarily include, but not be limited to, the following:

(a) The creative development of possible substitute institutions for the principal non-military functions of war.

(b) The careful matching of such institutions against the criteria summarized in this Report, as refined, revised, and extended by the Agency.

(c) The testing and evaluation of substitute institutions, for acceptability, feasibility, and credibility, against hypothecated transitional and post-war conditions; the testing and evaluation of the effects of the anticipated atrophy of certain unsubstituted functions.

(d) The development and testing of the correlativity of multiple substitute institutions, with the eventual objective of establishing a comprehensive programme of compatible war substitutes suitable for a planned transition to peace, if and when this is found to be possible and subsequently judged desirable by appropriate political authorities.

(e) The preparation of a wide-ranging schedule of partial, uncorrelated, crash programmes of adjustment suitable for reducing the dangers of an unplanned transition to peace effected by *force majeure*.

Peace Research methods will include but not be limited to, the following:

(a) The comprehensive interdisciplinary application of historical, scientific, technological, and cultural data.

(b) The full utilization of modern methods of mathematical modelling, analogical analysis, and other, more sophisticated, quantitative techniques in process of development that are compatible with computer-programming.

(c) The heuristic 'peace games' procedures developed during the course of its assignment by the Special Study Group, and further extensions of this basic approach to the testing of institutional functions.

(3) The War/Peace Research Agency's other principal responsibility will be 'War Research'. Its fundamental objective will be to ensure the continuing viability of the war system to fulfil its essential non-military functions for as long as the war system is judged

necessary to or desirable for the survival of society. To achieve this end, the War Research groups within the agency will engage in the following activities:

(a) *Quantification of existing applications of the non-military functions of war.* Specific determinations will include, but not be limited to: (i) the gross amount and the net proportion of non-productive military expenditures since World War II assignable to the need for war as an economic stabilizer; (ii) the amount and proportion of military expenditures and destruction of life, property, and natural resources during this period assignable to the need for war as an instrument for political control; (iii) similar figures, to the extent that they can be separately arrived at, assignable to the need for war to maintain social cohesiveness; (iv) levels of recruitment and expenditures on the draft and other forms of personnel deployment attributable to the need for military institutions to control social disaffection; (v) the statistical relationship of war casualties to world food supplies; (vi) the correlation of military actions and expenditures with cultural activities and scientific advances (including necessarily, the development of mensurable standards in these areas).

(b) *Establishment of a* priori *modern criteria for the execution of the non-military functions of war.* These will include, but not be limited to: (i) calculation of minimum and optimum ranges of military expenditure required, under varying hypothetical conditions, to fulfil these several functions, separately and collectively; (ii) determination of minimum and optimum levels of destruction of life, property, and natural resources prerequisite to the credibility of external threat essential to the political and motivational functions; (iii) development of a negotiable formula governing the relationship between military recruitment and training policies and the exigencies of social control.

(c) *Reconciliation of these criteria with prevailing economic, political, sociological, and ecological limitations.* The ultimate object of this phase of War Research is to rationalize the heretofore informal operations of the war system. It should provide practical working-procedures through which responsible governmental authority may resolve the following war-function problems, among others, under any given circumstances: (i) how to determine the optimum quantity, nature, and timing of military expenditures to ensure a desired degree of economic control; (ii) how to organize the recruitment, deployment, and ostensible use of military personnel to ensure a desired degree of acceptance of authorized social values; (iii) how to compute on a short-term basis, the nature and extent of the loss of life and other resources which should be suffered and/or inflicted during any single outbreak of hostilities to achieve a desired degree of internal political authority and social allegiance; (iv) how to project, over extended periods, the nature and quality of overt warfare which must be planned and budgeted to achieve a desired degree of contextual stability for the same purpose; factors to be determined must include frequency of occurrence, length of phase, intensity of physical destruction, extensiveness of geographical involvement, and optimum mean loss of life; (v) how to extrapolate accurately from the foregoing, for ecological purposes, the continuing effect of the war system, over such extended cycles, on population pressures, and to adjust the planning of casualty rates accordingly.

War Research procedures will necessarily include, but not be limited to, the following:

(a) The collation of economic, military, and other relevant data into uniform terms, permitting the reversible translation of heretofore discrete categories of information.[33]
(b) The development and application of appropriate forms of cost-effectiveness analysis suitable for adapting such new constructs to computer terminology, programming, and projection.[34]
(c) Extension of the 'war games' methods of systems testing to apply, as a quasi-adversary proceeding to the non-military functions of war.[35]

(4) Since both programmes of the War/Peace Research Agency will share the same purpose – to maintain governmental freedom of choice in respect to war and peace until the direction of social survival is no longer in doubt – it is of the essence of this proposal that the Agency be constituted without limitation of time. Its examination of existing and proposed institutions will be self-liquidating when its own function shall have been superseded by the historical developments it will have, at least in part, initiated.

AUTHOR'S NOTES

1. Arthur I. Waskow, *Toward the Unarmed Forces of the United States* (Washington, DC: Institute for Policy Studies, 1966) p. 9. (This is the unabridged edition of the text of a report and proposal prepared for a seminar of strategists and Congressmen in 1965; it was later given limited distribution among other persons engaged in related projects.)
2. David T. Bazelon, 'The Politics of the Paper Economy', *Commentary*, Nov 1962, p. 409.
3. *The Economic Impact of Disarmament* (Washington, DC: US Government Printing Office, Jan 1962).
4. David T. Bazelon, 'The Scarcity Makers', *Commentary*, Oct 1962, p. 298.
5. Frank Pace, Jr, in an address before the American Bankers' Association, Sep 1957.
6. A random example, taken in this case from a story by David Deitch in the *New York Herald Tribune* (9 Feb 1966).
7. See L. Gumplowicz, in *Geschichte der Staatstheorien* (Innsbruck: Wagner, 1905) and earlier writings.
8. K. Fischer, *Das Militär* (Zurich: Steinmetz Verlag, 1932) pp. 42–3.
9. The obverse of this phenomenon is responsible for the principal combat problem of present-day infantry officers: the unwillingness of otherwise 'trained' troops to fire at an enemy close enough to be recognizable as an individual rather than simply as a target.
10. Herman Kahn, *On Thermonuclear War* (Princeton, NJ: Princeton University Press, 1960) p. 42.
11. John D. Williams, 'The Nonsense about Safe Driving', *Fortune*, Sep 1958.
12. See most recently K. Lorenz, in *Das Sogenannte Böse: zur Naturgeschichte der Aggression* (Vienna: G. Borotha-Schoeler Verlag, 1964).
13. Beginning with Herbert Spencer and his contemporaries, but largely ignored for nearly a century.
14. As in recent draft-law controversy, in which the issue of selective deferment of the culturally privileged is often carelessly equated with the preservation of the biologically 'fittest'.
15. G. Bouthoul, in *La Guerre* (Paris: Presses Universitaires de France, 1953) and many other more detailed studies. The useful concept of 'polemology', for the study of war as an independent discipline, is his, as is the notion of 'demographic relaxation', the sudden temporary decline in the rate of population increase after major wars.
16. This seemingly premature statement is supported by one of our own test studies. But it hypothecates both the stabilizing of world population growth and the institution of fully adequate environmental controls. Under these two conditions, the probability of the permanent elimination of involuntary global famine is 68 per cent by 1976 and 95 per cent by 1981.
17. This round figure is the median taken from our computations, which cover varying contingencies, but it is sufficient for the purpose of general discussion.

18. But less misleading than the more elegant traditional metaphor, in which war expenditures are referred to as the 'ballast' of the economy but which suggests incorrect quantitative relationships.

19. Typical in generality, scope, and rhetoric. We have not used any published programme as a model; similarities are unavoidably coincidental rather than tendentious.

20. See the reception of a 'Freedom Budget for all Americans', proposed by A. Philip Randolph *et al.*; it is a ten-year plan, estimated by its sponsors to cost $185 billion [thousand million].

21. Waskow, *Toward the Unarmed Forces*.

22. By several current theorists, most extensively and effectively by Robert R. Harris in *The Real Enemy*, an unpublished doctoral dissertation made available to this study.

23. American Society of Newspaper Editors, Montreal, P.Q., Canada, 18 May 1966.

24. *The Tenth Victim*.

25. For an examination of some of its social implications, see Seymour Rubenfeld, *Family of Outcasts: A New Theory of Delinquency* (New York: Free Press, 1965).

26. As in Nazi Germany; this type of 'ideological' ethnic repression, directed to specific sociological ends, should not be confused with traditional economic exploitation, as of Negroes in the United States, South Africa, etc.

27. By teams of experimental biologists in Massachusetts, Michigan, and California, as well as in Mexico and the USSR. Preliminary test applications are scheduled in South-east Asia, in countries not yet announced.

28. Expressed in the writings of H. Marshall McLuhan, in *Understanding Media: The Extensions of Man* (New York: McGraw-Hill, 1964) and elsewhere.

29. This rather optimistic estimate was derived by plotting a three-dimensional distribution of three arbitrarily defined variables; the macro-structural, relating to the extension of knowledge beyond the capacity of conscious experience; the organic, dealing with the manifestations of terrestrial life as inherently comprehensible; and the infra-particular, covering the sub-conceptual requirements of natural phenomena. Values were assigned to the known and unknown in each parameter, tested against data from earlier chronologies, and modified heuristically until predictable correlations reached a useful level of accuracy. 'Two decades' means, in this case, 20.6 years, with a standard deviation of only 1.8 years. (An incidental finding, not pursued to the same degree of accuracy, suggests a greatly accelerated resolution of issues in the biological sciences after 1972.)

30. Since they represent an examination of too small a percentage of the eventual options, in terms of 'multiple mating', the sub-system we developed for this application. But an example will indicate how one of the most frequently recurring correlation problems – chronological phasing – was brought to light in this way. One of the first combinations tested showed remarkably high coefficients of compatibility, on a *post hoc* static basis, but no variations of timing, using a thirty-year

transition module, permitted even marginal synchronization. The combination was thus disqualified. This would not rule out the possible adequacy of combinations using modifications of the same factors, however, since minor variations in a proposed final condition may have disproportionate effects on phasing.

31. Edward Teller, quoted in *War/Peace Report*, Dec 1964.
32. E.g., the highly publicized 'Delphi technique' and other, more sophisticated procedures. A new system, especially suitable for institutional analysis, was developed during the course of this study in order to hypothecate mensurable 'peace games'; a manual of this system is being prepared and will be submitted for general distribution among appropriate agencies. For older, but still useful, techniques, see Norman C. Dalkey's *Games and Simulations* (Santa Monica, Calif.: Rand, 1964).
33. A primer-level example of the obvious and long overdue need for such translation is furnished by H. Kahn in *Thinking about the Unthinkable* (New York: Avon, 1964) p. 102. Under the heading 'Some Awkward Choices' he compares four hypothetical policies: a certain loss of $3000; a .1 chance of loss of $300 000; a .01 chance of loss of $30 000 000; and a .001 chance of loss of $3 000 000 000. A government decision-maker would 'very likely' choose in that order. But what if 'lives are at stake rather than dollars'? Kahn suggests that the order of choice would be reversed, although current experience does not support this opinion. Rational war research can and must make it possible to express, without ambiguity, lives in terms of dollars and *vice versa*; the choices need not be, and cannot be, 'awkward'.
34. Again, an overdue extension of an obvious application of techniques up to now limited to such circumscribed purposes as improving kill–ammunition ratios determining local choice between precision and saturation bombing, and other minor tactical, and occasionally strategic, ends. The slowness of Rand, Institute for Defense Analyses, and other responsible analytic organizations to extend cost-effectiveness and related concepts beyond early-phase applications has already been widely remarked on and criticized elsewhere.
35. The inclusion of institutional factors in war-game techniques has been given some rudimentary consideration in the Hudson Institute's *Study for Hypothetical Narratives for Use in Command and Control Systems Planning* (by William Pfaff and Edmund Stillman; final report published 1963). But here, as with other war and peace studies to date, what has blocked the logical extension of new analytic techniques has been a general failure to understand and properly evaluate the non-military functions of war.

III   JONATHAN SCHELL, 'THE CHOICE' (*extract*)

Jonathan Schell in the following passages brings out the strange situation today's nuclear powers, especially the United States and the Soviet Union, find themselves in, as a result of the doctrine of 'mutually assured destruction' (MAD). They must develop an arsenal capable of destroying the inhabitable earth many times over, threaten to use it in order to avoid using it, appear to want to use it in order to give credibility to their threats, possibly even intend to use it, so that the 'other side' may never pick up any psychological signals of weakness of resolve: and presumably, in case of an actual attack, in order to avoid defending themselves against the indefensible, launch an offensive strike which would destroy billions of people for whom no hostility is felt. Although such developments can be called 'paradoxical', at least in one sense of the word, Schell believes 'paradox' is too soft a term for what he considers to be blatant contradictions in thinking and behaviour. Paradoxes, after all, may simply provide us with speculative insights about 'the human condition'; but the realization that we are caught up in a contradiction may impel us to search for a practical solution.

The text below is reprinted from Jonathan Schell, *The Fate of the Earth* (New York: Random House; London: Jonathan Cape, 1982) pp. 196–204.

The central proposition of the deterrence doctrine – the piece of logic on which the world theoretically depends to see the sun rise tomorrow – is that a nuclear holocaust can best be prevented if each nuclear power, or bloc of powers, holds in readiness a nuclear force with which it 'credibly' threatens to destroy the entire society of any attacker, even after suffering the worst possible 'first strike' that the attacker can launch. Robert McNamara, who served as Secretary of Defense for seven years under Presidents Kennedy and Johnson, defined the policy, in his book *The Essence of Security*, published in 1968, in the following terms: 'Assured destruction is the very essence of the whole deterrence concept. We must possess an actual assured-destruction capability, and that capability also must be credible. The point is that a potential aggressor must believe that our assured-destruction capability is in fact actual, and that our will to use it in retaliation to an attack is in fact unwavering.' Thus, deterrence 'means the certainty of suicide to the aggressor, not merely to his military forces, but to his society as a whole.' Let us picture what is going on here. There are two possible eventualities: success of the strategy or its failure. If it succeeds, both sides are frozen into inaction by fear of retaliation by the other side. If it fails, one side annihilates the other, and then the leaders of the second side annihilate the 'society as a whole' of the attacker, and the earth as a whole suffers the consequences of a full-scale holocaust, which might include the extinction of man. In point of fact, neither the United States nor the Soviet Union has ever adopted the 'mutual-assured-destruction' doctrine in pure form; other aims, such as attempting to reduce the damage of the adversary's nuclear attack and increasing the capacity for destroying the nuclear forces of the adversary, have been mixed in. Nevertheless, underlying these deviations the concept of deterring a first strike by preserving the capacity for a devastating second strike has remained constant. The strategists of deterrence have addressed the chief issue in any sane policy in a nuclear-armed world – the issue of survival – and have come up with this answer: salvation from extinction by nuclear weapons is to be found in the nuclear weapons themselves. The possession of nuclear weapons by the great powers, it is believed, will prevent the use of nuclear weapons by those same powers. Or, to put it more accurately, the threat of their use by those powers will prevent their use. Or, in the words of Bernard Brodie, a pioneer in nuclear strategy, in *The Absolute Weapon: Atomic Power and World Order*, a book published in 1946: 'Thus far, the chief purpose of our military establishment has been to win wars. From now on its chief purpose must be to avert them. It can have almost no other useful purpose.' Or, in the classic, broad formulation of Winston Churchill, in a speech to the House of Commons in 1955: 'Safety will be the sturdy child of terror, and survival the twin brother of annihilation.'

This doctrine, in its detailed as well as its more general formulations, is diagrammatic of the world's failure to come to terms with the nuclear predicament. In it, two irreconcilable purposes clash. The first purpose is to permit the survival of the species, and this is expressed in the doctrine's aim of frightening everybody into holding back from using nuclear weapons at all; the second purpose is to serve national ends, and this is expressed in the doctrine's permitting the defence of one's nation and its interests by threatening to use nuclear weapons. The strategists are pleased to call this clash of two opposing purposes in one doctrine a paradox, but in actuality it is a contradiction. We cannot both threaten ourselves with something and hope to avoid that same thing by making the threat – both intend to do something and intend not to do it. The head-on contradiction between these aims has set up a cross-current of tension within the policies of each super-power. The 'safety' that Churchill mentions may be emphasized at one moment, and at the next moment it is the 'terror' that comes to the fore. And since the deterrence doctrine pairs the safety and the terror, and makes the former depend on the latter, the world is never quite sure from day to day which one is in the ascendant – if, indeed, the distinction can be maintained in the first place. All that the world can know for certain is that at any moment the fireballs may arrive. I have said that we do not have two earths, one to blow up experimentally and the other to live on; nor do we have two souls, one for reacting to daily life and the other for reacting to the peril to all life. But neither do we have two wills, one with which we can intend to destroy our species and the other with which we can intend to save ourselves. Ultimately, we must all live together with one soul and one will on our one earth.

For all that, the adoption of the deterrence doctrine represented a partial recognition that the traditional military doctrine had become an anachronism – a doctrine that was suited well enough to the pre-nuclear world but lost all application and relevance when the first nuclear bomb flashed over the New Mexico desert. In assessing the advance made by deterrence, we must acknowledge how radically it departed from traditional military doctrine. Traditional military doctrine and nuclear doctrine are based on wholly different factual circumstances, each set of which corresponds to the technical realities of its period. Traditional military doctrine began, as I have suggested, with the premise that the amounts of force available to the belligerents were small enough to permit one side or the other to exhaust itself before both sides were annihilated. Nuclear doctrine, on the other hand, begins with the premise that the amounts of force are so great that both sides, and perhaps all mankind, will be annihilated before either side exhausts its forces. Like postulates in geometry, these two premisses determine the entire systems of thought that follow, and no discussion of military strategy can make any sense unless one clearly specifies which premise one is starting from. But, as I pointed out at some length at the outset of these observations, there is no longer room for doubt that in our time the second premiss is the correct one.

The chief virtue of the doctrine of nuclear deterrence is that it begins by accepting this basic fact of life in the nuclear world, and does so not only on the rhetorical plane but on the practical plane of strategic planning. Hence, it acknowledges that victory can no longer be obtained in a contest between two well-armed nuclear powers, such as the United States and the Soviet Union. Senator Barry Goldwater wrote a book, published in 1962, whose title was *Why Not Victory?* To this question the strategists of deterrence have a decisive answer: because in the present-day, nuclear world 'victory' is oblivion. From this recognition flows the conclusion, arrived at by Brodie in 1946, that the sole purpose of possessing nuclear strategic arms is not to win war but to prevent it. The adoption of the aim of preventing rather than winning war requires the adoption of other policies that fly in the face of military tradition. One is abandonment of the military defence of one's nation – of what used to be at the centre of all military planning and was the most hallowed justification of the military calling. The policy of deterrence does not contemplate doing anything in defence of the homeland; it only promises that if the homeland is annihilated the aggressor's homeland will be annihilated, too. In fact, the policy goes further than this: it positively requires that each side leave its population open to attack, and make no serious effort to protect it. This requirement follows from the basic logic of deterrence, which is that safety is 'the sturdy child of terror'. According to this logic, the safety can be only as great as the terror is, and the terror therefore has to be kept relentless. If it were to be diminished – by, for example, building bomb shelters that protected some significant part of the population – then safety would be diminished, too, because the protected side might be tempted to launch a holocaust, in the belief that it could 'win' the hostilities. That is why in nuclear strategy 'destruction' must, perversely, be 'assured', as though our aim were to destroy, and not to save, mankind.

In strategic terms, the requirement that the terror be perfected, and never allowed to deteriorate toward safety, translates into the requirement that the retaliatory force of both sides be guaranteed – first, by making sure that the retaliatory weapons cannot be destroyed in a first strike, and, second, by making sure that the society of the attacking power *can* be destroyed in the second strike. And since in this upside-down scheme of things the two sides will suffer equally no matter which one opens the hostilities, each side actually has an interest in maintaining its adversary's retaliatory forces as well as its own. For the most dangerous of all the configurations of forces is that in which one side appears to have the ability to destroy the nuclear forces of the other in a first strike. Then not only is the stronger side theoretically tempted to launch hostilities but – what is probably far more dangerous – the other side, fearful of completely losing its forces, might, in a crisis, feel compelled to launch the first strike itself. If on either side the population becomes relatively safe from attack or the retaliatory strike becomes vulnerable to attack, a temptation to launch a first strike is created, and 'stability' – the leading virtue of any nuclear balance of power – is lost. As Thomas Schelling, the economist and noted nuclear theorist, has put it, in *The Strategy of Conflict*, a book published in 1960, once instability is introduced on either side, both sides may reason as follows: 'He, thinking I was about to kill him in self-defense, was about to kill me in self-defense, so I had to kill him in self-defense.' Under deterrence, military 'superiority' is therefore as dangerous to the side that possesses it as it is to the side that is supposedly threatened by it. (According to this logic, the United States should have heaved a sigh of relief when the Soviet Union reached nuclear parity with it, for then stability was achieved.) All these conclusions follow from the deterrence doctrine, yet they run so consistently counter to the far simpler, more familiar, and emotionally more comprehensible logic of traditional military thinking – not to mention instinct and plain common sense, which rebel against any such notion as 'assuring' our own annihilation – that we should not be surprised when we find that the deterrence doctrine is constantly under challenge from traditional doctrine, no matter how glaringly at odds with the facts traditional doctrine may be. The hard-won gains of deterrence, such as they are, are repeatedly threatened by a recrudescence of the old desire for victory, for national defence in the old sense, and for military superiority, even though every one of these goals not only would add nothing to our security but, if it should be pursued far enough, would undermine the precarious safety that the deterrence doctrine tries to provide.

If the virtue of the deterrence policy lies in its acceptance of the basic fact of life in the nuclear world – that a holocaust will bring annihilation to both sides, and possibly the extinction of man as well – its defect lies in the strategic construct that it erects on the foundation of that fact. For if we try to guarantee our safety by threatening ourselves with doom, then we have to mean the threat; but if we mean it, then we are actually planning to do, in some circumstance or other, that which we categorically must never do and are supposedly trying to prevent – namely, extinguish ourselves. This is the circularity at the core of the nuclear-deterrence doctrine; we seek to avoid our self-extinction by threatening to perform the act. According to this logic, it is almost as though if we stopped threatening ourselves with extinction, then extinction would occur. Brodie's formula can be reversed: if the aim of having nuclear forces is to avert annihilation (misnamed 'war' by him), then we must cling for our lives to those same forces. Churchill's dictum can be reversed, too: if safety is the sturdy child of terror, then terror is equally the sturdy child of safety. But who is to guarantee which of the children will be born? And if survival is the twin brother of annihilation, then we must cultivate annihilation. But then we may *get* annihilation. By growing to actually rely on terror, we do more than tolerate its presence in our world: we place our trust in it. And while this is not quite to 'love the bomb', as the saying goes, it decidedly is to place our faith in it, and to give it an all-important position in the very heart of our affairs. Under this doctrine, instead of getting rid of the bomb we build it ever more deeply into our lives.

The logical fault line in the doctrine runs straight through the centre of its main strategic tenet – the proposition that safety is achieved by assuring that any nuclear aggressor will be annihilated in a retaliatory strike. For while the doctrine relies for its success on a nuclear-armed victim's resolve to launch the annihilating second strike, it can offer no sensible or sane justification for launching it in the event. In pre-nuclear military strategy, the deterrent effect of force was a useful by-product of the ability and willingness to wage and win wars. Deterrence was the shadow cast by force, or, in Clausewitz's metaphor, the credit that flowed from the ability to make the cash payment of the favorable decision by arms. The logic of pre-nuclear deterrence escaped circularity by each side's being frankly ready to wage war and try for victory if deterrence failed. Nuclear deterrence, however, supposedly aims solely at forestalling any use of force by either side, and has given up at the outset on a favourable decision by arms. The question, then, is: of what object is nuclear deterrence the shadow? Of what cash payment is it the credit? The theoretical answer, of course, is: the retaliatory strike. Yet since in nuclear-deterrence theory the whole purpose of having a retaliatory capacity is to deter a first strike, one must ask what reason would remain to launch the retaliation once the first strike had actually arrived. Nuclear deterrence requires one to prepare for armed conflict not in order to 'win' it if it breaks out but in order to prevent it from breaking out in the first place. But if armed conflict breaks out anyway, what does one do with one's forces then? In pre-nuclear times, the answer would have required no second thought: it would have been to strive for the decision by arms – for victory. Yet nuclear deterrence begins by assuming, correctly, that victory is impossible. Thus, the logic of the deterrence strategy is dissolved by the very event – the first strike – that it is meant to prevent. Once the action begins, the whole doctrine is self-cancelling. In sum, the doctrine is based on a monumental logical mistake: one cannot credibly deter a first strike with a second strike whose *raison d' être* dissolves the moment the first strike arrives. It follows that, as far as deterrence theory is concerned, there is no reason for either side not to launch a first strike.

What seems to be needed to repair the doctrine is a motive for retaliation – one that is not supplied by the doctrine itself and that lies outside its premises – but the only candidates are those belonging to traditional military doctrine; namely, some variation of victory. The adherents of nuclear victory – whatever that would be – have on occasion noted the logical fallacy on which deterrence is based, and stepped forward to propose their solution: a 'nuclear-war-fighting' capacity. Thus, the answer they give to the question of what to do after the first strike arrives is: fight and 'win' a 'nuclear war'. But victory does not suddenly become possible simply because it offers a solution to the logical contradiction on which the mutual-assured-destruction doctrine rests. The facts remain obdurately what they are: an attack of several thousand megatons will annihilate any country on earth many times over, no matter what line of argument the strategists pursue; and a 'nuclear exchange' will, if it is on a large scale, threaten the life of man. Indeed, if victory were really possible there would have been no need for a deterrence strategy to begin with, and traditional military strategy would have needed no revision. This 'solution' is therefore worse than the error it sets out to remedy. It resolves the contradiction in the deterrence doctrine by denying the tremendous new reality that the doctrine was framed to deal with, and that all of us now have to deal with on virutally every level of our existence. Consequently, this 'solution' could lead us to commit the ultimate folly of exterminating ourselves without even knowing what we were doing. Aiming at 'victory', we would wind up extinct.

In the last analysis, there can be no credible threat without credible use – no shadow without an object, no credit without cash payment. But since use is the thing above all else that we don't want, because it means the end of all of us, we are naturally at a loss to find any rationale for it. To grasp the reality of the contradiction, we have only to picture the circumstances of leaders whose country has just been annihilated in a first strike. Now their country is on its way to becoming a radioactive desert, but the retaliatory nuclear force survives in its silos, bombers, and submarines. These leaders of nobody, living in underground shelters or in 'doomsday' planes that could not land, would possess the means of national defence but no nation to defend. What rational purpose could they have in launching the retaliatory strike? Since there was no longer a nation, 'national security' could not be the purpose. Nor could defence of other peoples be the purpose, since the retaliatory strike might be the action that would finally break the back of the ecosphere and extinguish the species. In these circumstances, it seems to me, it is really an open question whether the leaders would decide to retaliate or not.

Index

Papacy, 23n
Paradoxes of modern warfare,
  247–308
Paramilitary, 261
Parousia, 210
Patriotism, 217
Patten, Simon, 220
Paul, 10, 23, 154–5, 169–70, 174,
  203, 229
Pax Romana, 5
Peace
  and: Christian gospel, 149;
    distributive justice, 128–47;
    human aggression, 213–46;
    international federation,
    39–127; military
    preparedness, 247–308;
    religious or moral
    revitalization, 148–212;
    world government, 1–38
  Corps, 214, 274, 277, 278
  eternal, 66ff.
  through sublimation of
    aggression, 213–46
Peaceful coexistence, 122
Pendergast, 113
Perón, 111
Peter, St, 199
Pfaff, William, 300n
Philosopher, the, *see* Aristotle
Philosophical anthropology, 245
Philosophy as poetry, 238
Pilate, 188
Plautus, 230n
Plato, 66, 164
Poetry, philosophy as, 238
Political
  cause of war, 138
  functions of war, 259f.:
    substitute, 275f.; summary
    and conclusions, 285f.
Pollution, 276
Pope, Alexander, 85n
Population
  growth, 266
  need for stability, 30
  race, and creed, 29
Possible intellect, 8

Power, desire for, as cause of war,
  161
Powers of European Republic, 52
Pride, 243
Prince Charles, 176
Propagandist tendency, 237
'Property is Theft', 136
Protestants, 130
Proudhon, Pierre-Joseph, 136
Psalms
  1:3, 6
  49:16, 19
  69, 138
  132:1, 23
Public
  law, 74
  opinion, Christian, and
    violence, 177–88ff.
Publius II, 39, 87–121
Pythagoras, 21

Quakers, 198

Race, creed, and population, 29
Randolph, A. Philip, 299n
Rawls, John, 140–7
Reason and speech, 151
Red Cross, 238
Reiss, Hans, 146n
Religion
  and: peace, 148–212 var.;
    transcendence, 195
  difference of, 77
  as bond, 43
  revolutionary, 196
Religious
  revitalization and peace, 148–212
  war, 236
Rembrandt, 267
Republican (form of government),
  72
Retaliation, 306–8
Revolutionary religion, 196
Right and law, 73
Rights and duties, 144
Roberts, Owen J., 87
Roman Empire, 5